REEL TERROR

EDITED BY
SEBASTIAN WOLFE

Carroll & Graf Publishers, Inc.
New York

First published in Great Britain by Xanadu Publications. Limited 1992.
First published in the United States of America by Carroll & Graf
Publishers, Inc. 1992, by arrangement with Xanadu Publications Limited.

Carroll & Graf Publishers, Inc.,
260 Fifth Avenue,
New York, NY 10001.

Library of Congress Cataloging-in Publication-Data is available.

ISBN 0-88184-821-2

Manufactured in Great Britain.

Contents

Introduction

S ince moving pictures first started flickering in darkened rooms, movie-makers have been trying to scare the pants off their audiences – and they have very often turned to the horrors of the printed page for ideas about how to do it. This book is a collection of some of the best short stories that have inspired some notably frightening films.

It could have started with an extract from *Frankenstein, Dracula, Notre Dame de Paris* or *Doctor Jekyll and Mr Hyde*, all of which were adapted in the early days of silent movies, but extracts are always rather unsatisfactory, and these works are already very familiar as well as being readily available (stories by Edgar Allan Poe and Stephen King are also excluded for this reason). Instead I have included as the earliest item a version of the Golem legend, by I. L. Peretz. This story was filmed several times in Germany in the early years of the century, but the classic version was made at the influential UFA Studios by Paul Wegener and Carl Boese in 1920. Wegener co-wrote it, and also starred as the man-made creature that came to the rescue of the oppressed citizens of sixteenth-century Prague. With its weird subject-matter and dramatic Expessionist sets, this was the film that set the style for the classic horror movies of the next two decades. In Hollywood, James Whale studied it closely before making his famous *Frankenstein*.

By 1932 the style was well established, and the problem for movie-makers in search of greater thrills was to find new ideas – which in some cases meant even more extreme material. Tod Browning had been a circus man before finding success in Hollywood, so it was perhaps no surprise that he turned his attention to a circus story when he wanted a new subject. The story was 'Spurs' by another Tod – Tod Robbins – and it was about circus freaks. Browning's nifty new idea was to eschew the elaborate horror make-up of actors like Boris Karloff and Lon Chaney, and to cast his film with *real* freaks.

He succeeded in providing new thrills, but they were sickening as well as terrifying, and most authorities felt that he had gone much too far; the film was cut extensively in the USA, while in Britain it was banned outright for the best part of thirty years. Then as now, it remains highly disturbing viewing, and it is fascinating to compare the original story (now rare) with the all-too-realistic filmed version that virtually ended Tod Browning's career.

Horror in the 1940s had become something of a production-line, and one of its staples was of course zombies. *The Revenge of the Zombies*, directed by Steve Sekely for Monogram in 1943, starred that stalwart of the horror film, John Carradine, and broke new ground in that the Living Dead were no longer confined to Haiti but let loose on the American mainland: illegal immigrants of a particularly unwelcome nature who, in movies anyway, ran riot over the USA in the ensuing years. I am grateful to Peter Haining for pointing out the similarity between the movie (ostensibly based on an original screenplay) and the story reprinted here, 'While Zombies Walked', which originally appeared in *Weird Tales* magazine. Another film of the '40s offered a further twist on on the 'Walking Dead' theme, this time not a whole walking corpse but just a walking hand: it was *The Beast With Five Fingers*, directed by Robert Florey in 1946, starring the great Peter Lorre and following quite literally W. F. Harvey's classic story. One might doubt the potential of walking hands as a subject to flog to death, but the film was remade in 1960 in Britain as *The Hand*, and there was yet another movie called *The Hand* in 1981, directed by Oliver Stone (of all people) and starring Michael Caine. This one was supposedly based on a novel by Marc Brandel called *The Lizard's Tail*, which featured a severed but still very-much-alive reptilian appendage, but in the movie it's not a tail but – oh, you guessed. There's one in *The Addams Family* too.

Another good idea that has been vamped and revamped, and probably by now vamped to death, is the one embodied (or disembodied) in 'The Fly'. The story by George Langelean is a recognized classic, the sort of one-off idea that writers and film-makers ache for. Ray Russell described it as 'one of the most suspenseful pieces of horror science fiction I have ever read'. It was originally filmed by Kurt Neumann for Twentieth Century Fox in 1958, with a script by James Clavell (now making movies on his own account), and it alternated between moments of real horror and sheer absurdity. Stars Vincent Price and Herbert Marshall had to play one scene – the spider's web episode – back to back to avoid bursting out laughing. There were two sequels, though, *Return of The Fly* (1955) and *Curse of The Fly* (1965), and in 1986 a slick remake by David Cronenberg which spawned its own lamentable sequel, *The Fly II*. Ever get the feeling that movie-makers might be short of ideas (perhaps they should *read* more?)

Die, Monster, Die (1965) was a fair adaptation of a prescient story by the highly influential H. P. Lovecraft, called 'The Color Out Of Space'. In it, a fallen meteorite causes the surrounding flora and fauna to wither and die – or to *change*, as does the scientist-hero played in the film by Boris Karloff. Some have seen Lovecraft's story as prophetic of nuclear radiation and all its horrors, but here it's handled more like Jekyll and Hyde. The movie is also known as *The House at the End of the World* and *The Monster of Terror*, and it was remade, heaven help us, by David Keith in 1987 as *The Curse*.

In the late '60s things changed in all kinds of ways, and the terror film underwent a transformation as a new generation of film-makers armed with a whole new bag of ideas and techniques arrived on the scene. Standing curiously between the old and the new, though, is a strange movie called *The Swimmer*. It was made in 1969 by Frank Perry and Sidney Pollack from a script by Eleanor Perry, who also wrote a 'novelization' of the film: a somewhat bizarre move, since the film was based on the story which is reprinted here which is by John Cheever, no less. It tells of a middle-aged Californian, played in the movie by Burt Lancaster, who travels home swimming the pools of various friends and acquaintances on the way . . . To say more would be to give it away. There are no explicit shocks here, though. The horror is of a more spiritual kind, and none the less disturbing for that. An underrated movie, and a story that will perhaps be outside the normal reading of most horror fans.

Steven Spielberg is a name known to just about everyone, but it was not so in 1971 when he made his directorial debut with *Duel*, made originally as a TV movie and getting a general release only in Britain. Based on a story from *Playboy* by Richard Matheson, and scripted by Matheson following his own story very closely, it is a superb movie based on a very simple idea – one that might have occurred to any put-upon motorist. Richard Matheson, was, of course, one of the major talents in the sf/horror field, with *I Am Legend* and *The Incredible Shrinking Man* among his credits. His original version of 'Duel' is not easy to find, and it is a pleasure to be able to include it here – indeed, one could not wish for a more compelling opening for the book. Another key name in the horror field is that of Robert Bloch, and I am delighted to include his story 'Lucy Comes to Stay', which was not only filmed in its own right as a section of the portmanteau movie *Asylum* (also known as *House of Crazies*, and directed by Roy Ward Baker in 1972), but which also provided the original germ of that most innovative and influential of all shockers, *Psycho*. Much has recently been made of the role of real-life cannibal killer Ed Gein as the prototype of Norman Bates in *Psycho* (and, for that matter, of Buffalo Bill in *The Silence of the Lambs* and a bunch of other slashers) so it's interesting to note that 'Lucy' is just as seminal a source. It was Bloch's last story for *Weird Tales* and, he says, one of his own favourites.

Speilberg – by now a very big name indeed with *Jaws*, *E.T.* and so on under his belt – was involved in 1983's *The Twilight Zone* as co-producer and director of one of the segments. An affecionate tribute to the classic '50s TV series created by Rod Sterling, *The Twilight Zone* featured four stories, each with a different cast and director. Speilberg directed 'Kick the Can', a rather sentimental story about old-age, while George Miller directed 'Nightmare at 20,000 Feet', also scripted from his own story by Richard Matheson. The tale I've chosen is 'It's a *Good* Life' by Jerome Bixby, memorably filmed here by Joe Dante (*Gremlins*, etc.) and starring Jeremy Light as the all-powerful child. This story is regularly voted high in the top ten of all-time best sf/horror tales whenever such polls are held; one of the undisputed classics of the genre, and just about the only thing for which Jerome Bixby is known, although he was a prolific writer.

It was in movies like *The Twilight Zone* that special effects really began to come into their own, and they loom large on the two most recent movies to feature in this collection. *The Company of Wolves*, directed by Neil Jordan in 1984, is a fantastic version of Angela Carter's modern and very sexy reworking of old legends and fairy tales, which were collected in *The Bloody Chamber*.* *Total Recall* (1990), with effects by the *Robocop* people, is a spectacular expansion of a story ('We Can Remember If For You Wholesale') by the wonderful Philip K. Dick, and it has one of the best opening-sentence hooks of any story, ever. Read and enjoy.

It may be instructive for film-buffs to compare the original versions of these stories with the movies that were made for them, but my primary object has been to choose good stories relating to this theme, which I hope will make for good reading, and in doing so to pay a modest tribute to their writers, the dreamers who – let us not forget it – created these strange dreams that in cinemas, on TV and now in videos, have enthralled, delighted and terrified us. Thank you.

SEBASTIAN WOLFE
London, 1992

---

* Sadly, Angela Carter died just before this book went to press. I did not know her well, but liked and admired her enormously, and so have taken the liberty of dedicating this book to her memory.

THE AUTHOR
Richard Matheson

THE STORY
Duel

THE MOVIE
Duel

THE DIRECTOR
Steven Spielberg

At 11.32 a.m., Mann passed the truck.

He was heading west, en route to San Francisco. It was Thursday and unseasonably hot for April. He had his suit coat off, his tie removed and shirt collar opened, his sleeve cuffs folded back. There was sunlight on his left arm and on part of his lap. He could feel the heat of it through his dark trousers as he drove along the two-lane highway. For the past 20 minutes, he had not seen another vehicle going in either direction.

Then he saw the truck ahead, moving up a curving grade between two high green hills. He heard the grinding strain of its motor and saw a double shadow on the road. The truck was pulling a trailer.

He paid no attention to the details of the truck. As he drew behind it on the grade, he edged his car towards the opposite lane. The road ahead had blind curves and he didn't try to pass until the truck had crossed the ridge. He waited until it started around a left curve on the downgrade, then, seeing that the way was clear, pressed down on the accelerator pedal and steered his car into the eastbound lane. He waited until he could see the truck front in his rearview mirror before he turned back into the proper lane.

Mann looked across the countryside ahead. There were ranges of mountains as far as he could see and, all around him, rolling green hills. He whistled softly as the car sped down the winding grade, its tyres making crisp sounds on the pavement.

At the bottom of the hill, he crossed a concrete bridge and, glancing to the right, saw a dry stream bed strewn with rocks and gravel. As the car moved off the bridge, he saw a trailer park set back from the highway to his right. How can anyone live out here? he thought. His shifting gaze caught sight of a pet cemetery ahead and he smiled. Maybe those people in the trailers wanted to be close to the graves of their dogs and cats.

The highway ahead was straight now. Mann drifted into a reverie, the sunlight on his arm and lap. He wondered what Ruth was doing. The kids, of course, were in school and would be for hours yet. Maybe Ruth was shopping; Thursday was the day she usually went. Mann visualised her in the supermarket, putting various items into the basket cart. He wished he were with her instead of starting on another sales trip. Hours of driving yet before he'd reach San Francisco. Three days of hotel sleeping and restaurant eating, hoped-for contacts and likely disappointments. He sighed; then, reaching out impulsively, he switched on the radio. He revolved the tuning knob until he found a station playing soft, innocuous music. He hummed along with it, eyes almost out of focus on the road ahead.

He started as the truck roared past him on the left, causing his car to shudder slightly. He watched the truck and trailer cut in abruptly for the westbound lane and frowned as he had to brake to maintain a safe distance behind it. What's with you? he thought. He eyed the truck with cursory disapproval. It was a huge gasoline tanker pulling a tank trailer, each of them having six pairs of wheels. He could see that it was not a new rig but was dented and in need of renovation, its tanks painted a cheap-looking silvery colour. Mann wondered if the driver had done the painting himself. His gaze shifted from the word FLAMMABLE printed across the back of the trailer tank, red letters on a white background, to the parallel reflector lines painted in red across the bottom of the tank to the massive rubber flaps swaying behind the rear tyres, then back up again. The reflector lines looked as though they'd been clumsily applied with a stencil. The driver must be an independent trucker, he decided, and not too affluent a one, from the looks of his outfit. He glanced at the trailer's licence plate. It was a California issue.

Mann checked his speedometer. He was holding steady at 55 miles an hour, as he invariably did when he drove without thinking on the open highway. The truck driver must have done a good 70 to pass him so quickly. That seemed a little odd. Weren't truck drivers supposed to be a cautious lot?

He grimaced at the smell of the truck's exhaust and looked at the vertical pipe to the left of the cab. It was spewing smoke, which clouded darkly back across the trailer. Christ, he thought. With all the furor about air pollution, why do they keep allowing that sort of thing on the highways?

He scowled at the constant fumes. They'd make him nauseated in a little while, he knew. He couldn't lag back here like this. Either he'd slow down or he'd pass the truck again. He didn't have the time to slow down. He'd gotten a late start. Keeping it at 55 all the way, he'd just about make his afternoon appointment. No, he'd have to pass.

Depressing the gas pedal, he eased his car towards the opposite lane. No sign of anything ahead. Traffic on this route seemed almost nonexistent today. He pushed down harder on the accelerator and steered all the way into the eastbound lane.

As he passed the truck, he glanced at it. The cab was too high for him to see into. All he caught sight of was the back of the truck driver's left hand on the steering wheel. It was darkly tanned and square-looking, with large veins knotted on its surface.

When Mann could see the truck reflected in the rearview mirror, he pulled back over to the proper lane and looked ahead again.

He glanced at the rearview mirror in surprise as the truck driver gave him an extended horn blast. What was that? he wondered; a greeting or a curse? He grunted with amusement, glancing at the mirror as he drove. The front fenders of the truck were a dingy purple colour, the paint faded and chipped; another amateurish job. All he could see was the lower portion of the truck; the rest was cut off by the top of his rear window.

To Mann's right, now, was a slope of shalelike earth with patches of scrub grass growing on it. His gaze jumped to the clapboard house on top of the slope. The television aerial on its roof was sagging at an angle of less than 40 degrees. Must give great reception, he thought.

He looked to the front again, glancing aside abruptly at a sign printed in jagged block letters on a piece of plywood: NIGHT CRAWLERS – BAIT. What the hell is a night crawler? he wondered. It sounded like some monster in a low-grade Hollywood thriller.

The unexpected roar of the truck motor made his gaze jump to the rearview mirror. Instantly, his startled look jumped to the side mirror. By God, the guy was passing him *again*. Mann turned his head to scowl at the leviathan form as it drifted by. He tried to see into the cab but couldn't because of its height. What's with him, anyway? he wondered. What the hell are we having here, a contest? See which vehicle can stay ahead the longer?

He thought of speeding up to stay ahead but changed his mind. When the truck and trailer started back into the westbound lane, he let up on the pedal, voicing a newly incredulous sound as he saw that if he hadn't slowed down, he would have been prematurely cut off again. Jesus Christ, he thought. What's *with* this guy?

His scowl deepened as the odour of the truck's exhaust reached his nostrils again. Irritably, he cranked up the window on his left. Damn it, was he going to have to breathe that crap all the way to San Francisco? He couldn't afford to slow down. He had to meet Forbes at a quarter after three and that was that.

He looked ahead. At least there was no traffic complicating matters. Mann pressed down on the accelerator pedal, drawing close behind the truck. When the highway curved enough to the left to give him a completely open view of the route ahead, he jarred down on the pedal, steering out into the opposite lane.

The truck edged over, blocking his way.

For several moments, all Mann could do was stare at it in blank confusion. Then, with a startled noise, he braked, returning to the proper lane. The truck moved back in front of him.

Mann could not allow himself to accept what apparently had taken place. It had to be a coincidence. The truck driver couldn't have blocked his way on purpose. He waited for more than a minute, then flicked down the turn-indicator lever to make his intentions perfectly clear and, depressing the accelerator pedal, steered again into the eastbound lane.

Immediately, the truck shifted, barring his way.

'*Jesus Christ!*' Mann was astounded. This was unbelievable. He'd never seen such a thing in 26 years of driving. He returned to the westbound lane, shaking his head as the truck swung back in front of him.

He eased up on the gas pedal, falling back to avoid the truck's exhaust. Now what? he wondered. He still had to make San Francisco on schedule. Why in God's name hadn't he gone a little out of his way in the beginning, so he could have travelled by freeway? This damned highway was two lane all the way.

Impulsively, he sped into the eastbound lane again. To his surprise, the truck driver did not pull over. Instead, the driver stuck his left arm out and waved him on. Mann started pushing down on the accelerator. Suddenly, he let up on the pedal with a gasp and jerked the steering wheel around, raking back behind the truck so quickly that his car began to fishtail. He was fighting to control its zigzag whipping when a blue convertible shot by him in the opposite lane. Mann caught a momentary vision of the man inside it glaring at him.

The car came under his control again. Mann was sucking breath in through his mouth. His heart was pounding almost painfully. My God! he thought. *He wanted me to hit that car head on.* The realisation stunned him. True, he should have seen to it himself that the road ahead was clear; that was his failure. But to wave him on . . . Mann felt appalled and sickened. Boy, oh, boy, oh, boy, he thought. This was really one for the books. That son of a bitch had meant for not only him to be killed but a totally uninvolved passer-by as well. The idea seemed beyond his comprehension. On a California highway on a Thursday morning? *Why?*

Mann tried to calm himself and rationalise the incident. Maybe it's the heat, he thought. Maybe the truck driver had a tension headache or an upset stomach; maybe both. Maybe he'd had a fight with his wife. Maybe she'd failed to put out last night. Mann tried in vain to smile. There could be any number of reasons. Reaching out, he twisted off the radio. The cheerful music irritated him.

He drove behind the truck for several minutes, his face a mask of animosity. As the exhaust fumes started putting his stomach on edge, he suddenly forced down the heel of his right hand on the horn bar and held it there. Seeing that the route ahead was clear, he pushed in the accelerator pedal all the way and steered into the opposite lane.

The movement of his car was paralleled immediately by the truck. Mann stayed in place, right hand jammed down on the horn bar. Get out of the way, you son of a bitch! he thought. He felt the muscles of his jaw hardening until they ached. There was a twisting in his stomach.

'*Damn!*' He pulled back quickly to the proper lane, shuddering with fury. 'You miserable son of a bitch,' he muttered, glaring at the truck as it was shifted back in front of him. What the hell is wrong with you? I pass your goddamn rig a couple of times and you go flying off the deep end? Are you nuts or something? Mann nodded tensely. Yes, he thought; he *is*. No other explanation.

He wondered what Ruth would think of all this, how she'd react. Probably, she'd start to honk the horn and would keep on honking it, assuming that, eventually, it would attract the attention of a policeman. He looked around with a scowl. Just where in hell *were* the policemen out here, anyway? He made a scoffing noise. What policemen? Here in the boondocks? They probably had a sheriff on horseback, for Christ's sake.

He wondered suddenly if he could fool the truck driver by passing on the right. Edging his car towards the shoulder, he peered ahead. No chance. There wasn't room enough. The truck driver could shove him through that wire fence if he wanted to. Mann shivered. And he'd want to, sure as hell, he thought.

Driving where he was, he grew conscious of the debris lying beside the highway: beer cans, candy wrappers, icecream containers, newspaper sections browned and rotted by the weather, a FOR SALE sign torn in half. Keep America beautiful, he thought sardonically. He passed a boulder with the name WILL JASPER painted on it in white. Who the hell is Will Jasper? he wondered. What would he think of this situation?

Unexpectedly, the car began to bounce. For several anxious moments, Mann thought that one of his tyres had gone flat. Then he noticed that the paving along this section of highway consisted of pitted slabs with gaps between them. He saw the truck and trailer jolting up and down and thought: I hope it shakes your brains loose. As the truck veered into a sharp left curve, he caught a fleeting glimpse of the driver's face in the cab's side mirror. There was not enough time to establish his appearance.

'Ah,' he said. A long, steep hill was looming up ahead. The truck would have to climb it slowly. There would doubtless be an opportunity to pass somewhere on the grade. Mann pressed down on the accelerator pedal, drawing as close behind the truck as safety would allow.

Halfway up the slope, Mann saw a turnout for the eastbound lane with no oncoming traffic anywhere in sight. Flooring the accelerator pedal, he shot into the opposite lane. The slow-moving truck began to angle out in front of him. Face stiffening, Mann steered his speeding car across the highway edge and curved it sharply on the turnout. Clouds of dust went billowing up behind his car, making him lose sight of the truck. His tyres buzzed and crackled on the dirt, then, suddenly, were humming on the pavement once again.

He glanced at the rearview mirror and a barking laugh erupted from his throat. He'd only meant to pass. The dust had been an unexpected bonus. Let the bastard get a sniff of something rotten smelling in *his* nose for a change! he thought. He honked the horn elatedly, a mocking rhythm of bleats. Screw you, Jack!

He swept across the summit of the hill. A striking vista lay ahead: sunlit hills and flatland, a corridor of dark trees, quadrangles of cleared-off acreage and bright-green vegetable patches; far off, in the distance, a mammoth water tower. Mann felt stirred by the panoramic sight. Lovely, he thought. Reaching out, he turned the radio back on and started humming cheerfully with the music.

Seven minutes later, he passed a billboard advertising CHUCK'S CAFÉ. No thanks, Chuck, he thought. He glanced at a grey house nestled in a hollow. Was that a cemetery in its front yard or a group of plaster statuary for sale?

Hearing the noise behind him, Mann looked at the rearview mirror and felt himself go cold with fear. The truck was hurtling down the hill, pursuing him.

His mouth fell open and he threw a glance at the speedometer. He was doing more than 60! On a curving downgrade, that was not at all a safe speed to be driving. Yet the truck must be exceeding that by a considerable margin, it was closing the distance between them so rapidly. Mann swallowed, leaning to the right as he steered his car around a sharp curve. Is the man *insane*? he thought.

His gaze jumped forward searchingly. He saw a turnoff half a mile ahead and decided that he'd use it. In the rearview mirror, the huge square radiator grille was all he could see now. He stamped down on the gas pedal and his tyres screeched unnervingly as he wheeled around another curve, thinking that, surely, the truck would have to slow down here.

He groaned as it rounded the curve with ease, only the sway of its tanks revealing the outward pressure of the turn. Mann bit trembling lips together as he whipped his car around another curve. A straight descent now. He depressed the pedal farther, glanced at the speedometer. Almost 70 miles an hour! He wasn't used to driving this fast!

In agony, he saw the turnoff shoot by on his right. He couldn't have left the highway at this speed, anyway; he'd have overturned. Goddamn it, what was wrong with that son of a bitch? Mann honked his horn in frightened rage. Cranking down the window suddenly, he shoved his left arm out to wave the truck back.

'*Back!*' he yelled. He honked the horn again. 'Get back, you crazy bastard!'

The truck was almost on him now. He's going to kill me! Mann thought, horrified. He honked the horn repeatedly, then had to use both hands to grip the steering wheel as he swept around another curve. He flashed a look at the rearview mirror. He could see only the bottom portion of the truck's radiator grille. He was going to lose control! He felt the rear wheels start to drift and let up on the pedal quickly. The tyre treads bit in, the car leaped on, regaining its momentum.

Mann saw the bottom of the grade ahead, and in the distance there was a building with a sign that read CHUCK'S CAFÉ. The truck was gaining ground again. This is insane! he thought, enraged and terrified at once. The highway straightened out. He floored the pedal: 74 now – 75. Mann braced himself, trying to ease the car as far to the right as possible.

Abruptly, he began to brake, then swerved to the right, raking his car into the open area in front of the café. He cried out as the car began to fishtail, then careered into a skid. *Steer with it!* screamed a voice in his mind. The rear of the car was lashing from side to side, tyres spewing dirt and raising clouds of dust. Mann pressed harder on the brake pedal, turning further into the skid. The car began to straighten out and he braked harder yet, conscious on the sides of his vision, of the truck and trailer roaring by on the highway. He nearly sideswiped one of the cars parked in front of the café, bounced and skidded by it, going almost straight now. He jammed in the brake pedal as hard as he could. The rear end broke to the right and the car spun half around, sheering sideways to a neck-wrenching halt 30 yards beyond the café.

Mann sat in pulsing silence, eyes closed. His heartbeats felt like club blows in his chest. He couldn't seem to catch his breath. If he were ever going to have a heart attack, it would be now. After a while, he opened his eyes and pressed his right palm against his chest. His heart was still throbbing labouredly. No wonder, he thought. It isn't every day I'm almost murdered by a truck.

He raised the handle and pushed out the door, then started forward, grunting in surprise as the safety belt held him in place. Reaching down with shaking fingers, he depressed the release button and pulled the ends of the belt apart. He glanced at the café. What had its patrons thought of his breakneck appearance? he wondered.

He stumbled as he walked to the front door of the café. TRUCKERS WELCOME, read a sign in the window. It gave Mann a queasy feeling to see it. Shivering, he pulled open the door and went inside, avoiding the sight of its customers. He felt certain they were watching him, but he didn't have the strength to face their looks. Keeping his gaze fixed straight ahead, he moved to the rear of the café and opened the door marked GENTS.

Moving to the sink, he twisted the right-hand faucet and leaned over to cup cold water in his palms and splash it on his face. There was a fluttering of his stomach muscles he could not control.

Straightening up, he tugged down several towels from their dispenser and patted them against his face, grimacing at the smell of the paper. Dropping the soggy towels into a wastebasket beside the sink, he regarded himself in the wall mirror. Still with us, Mann, he thought. He nodded, swallowing. Drawing out his metal comb, he neatened his hair. You never know, he thought. You just never know. You drift along, year after year, presuming certain values to be fixed; like being able to drive on a public thoroughfare without somebody trying to murder you. You come to depend on that sort of thing. Then something occurs and all bets are off. One shocking incident and all the years of logic and acceptance are displaced and, suddenly, the jungle is in front of you again. *Man, part animal, part angel.* Where had he come across that phrase? He shivered.

It was entirely an animal in that truck out there.

His breath was almost back to normal now. Mann forced a smile at his reflection. All right, boy, he told himself. It's over now. It was a goddamned nightmare, but it's over. You are on your way to San Francisco. You'll get yourself a nice hotel room, order a bottle of expensive Scotch, soak your body in a hot bath and forget. Damn right, he thought. He turned and walked out of the washroom.

He jolted to a halt, his breath cut off. Standing rooted, heartbeat hammering at his chest, he gaped through the front window of the café.

The truck and trailer were parked outside.

Mann stared at them in unbelieving shock. It wasn't possible. He'd seen them roaring by at top speed. The driver had won; he'd *won*! He'd had the whole damn highway to himself! *Why had he turned back?*

Mann looked around with sudden dread. There were five men eating, three along the counter, two in booths. He cursed himself for having failed to look at faces when he'd entered. Now there was no way of knowing who it was. Mann felt his legs begin to shake.

Abruptly, he walked to the nearest booth and slid in clumsily behind the table. Now wait, he told himself; just wait. Surely, he could tell which one it was. Masking his face with the menu, he glanced across its top. Was it that one in the khaki work shirt? Mann tried to see the man's hands but couldn't. His gaze flicked nervously across the room. Not that one in the suit, of course. Three remaining. That one in the front booth, square-faced, black-haired? If only he could see the man's hands, it might help. One of the two others at the counter? Mann studied them uneasily. Why hadn't he looked at faces when he'd come in?

Now *wait*, he thought. Goddamn it, *wait*! All right, the truck driver was in here. That didn't automatically signify that he meant to continue the insane duel. Chuck's Café might be the only place to eat for miles around. It *was* lunchtime, wasn't it? The truck driver had probably intended to eat here all the time. He'd just been moving too fast to pull into the parking lot before. So he'd slowed down, turned around and driven back, that was all. Mann forced himself to read the menu. Right, he thought. No point in getting so rattled. Perhaps a beer would help relax him.

The woman behind the counter came over and Mann ordered a ham sandwich on rye toast and a bottle of Coors. As the woman turned away, he wondered, with a sudden twinge of self-reproach, why he hadn't simply left the café, jumped into his car and sped away. He would have known immediately, then, if the truck driver was still out to get him. As it was, he'd have to suffer through an entire meal to find out. He almost groaned at his stupidity.

Still, what if the truck driver *had* followed him out and started after him again? He'd have been right back where he'd started. Even if he'd managed to get a good lead, the truck driver would have overtaken him eventually. It just wasn't in him to drive at 80 and 90 miles an hour in order to stay ahead. True, he might have been intercepted by a California Highway Patrol car. What if he weren't, though?

Mann repressed the plaguing thoughts. He tried to calm himself. He looked deliberately at the four men. Either of two seemed a likely possibility as the driver of the truck: the square-faced one in the front booth and the chunky one in the jump suit sitting at the counter. Mann had an impulse to walk over to them and ask which one it was, tell the man he was sorry he'd irritated him, tell him anything to calm him, since, obviously, he wasn't rational, was a manic-depressive, probably. Maybe buy the man a beer and sit with him awhile to try to settle things.

He couldn't move. What if the truck driver were letting the whole thing drop? Mightn't his approach rile the man all over again? Mann felt drained by indecision. He nodded weakly as the waitress set the sandwich and the bottle in front of him. He took a swallow of the beer, which made him cough. Was the truck driver amused by the sound? Mann felt a stirring of resentment deep inside himself. What right did that bastard have to impose this torment on another human being? It was a free country, wasn't it? Damn it, he had every right to pass the son of a bitch on a highway if he wanted to!

'Oh, hell,' he mumbled. He tried to feel amused. He was making entirely too much of this. Wasn't he? He glanced at the pay telephone on the front wall. What was to prevent him from calling the local police and telling them the situation? But, then, he'd have to stay here, lose time, make Forbes angry, probably lose the sale. And what if the truck driver stayed to face them? Naturally, he'd deny the whole thing. What if the police believed him and didn't do anything about it? After they'd gone, the truck driver would undoubtedly take it out on him again, only worse, *God*! Mann thought in agony.

The sandwich tasted flat, the beer unpleasantly sour. Mann stared at the table as he ate. For God's sake, why was he just *sitting* here like this? He was a grown man, wasn't he? Why didn't he settle this damn thing once and for all?

His left hand twitched so unexpectedly, he spilled beer on his trousers. The man in the jump suit had risen from the counter and was strolling towards the front of the café. Mann felt his heartbeat thumping as the man gave money to the waitress, took his change and a toothpick from the dispenser and went outside. Mann watched in anxious silence.

The man did not get into the cab of the tanker truck.

It had to be the one in the front booth, then. His face took form in Mann's remembrance: square, with dark eyes, dark hair; the man who'd tried to kill him.

Mann stood abruptly, letting impulse conquer fear. Eyes fixed ahead, he started towards the entrance. Anything was preferable to sitting in that booth. He stopped by the cash register, conscious of the hitching of his chest as he gulped in air. Was the man observing him? he wondered. He swallowed, pulling out the clip of dollar bills in his right-hand trouser pocket. He glanced towards the waitress. Come *on*, he thought. He looked at his check and, seeing the amount, reached shakily into his trouser pocket for change. He heard a coin fall onto the floor and roll away. Ignoring it, he dropped a dollar and a quarter onto the counter and thrust the clip of bills into his trouser pocket.

As he did, he heard the man in the front booth get up. An icy shudder spasmed up his neck. Turning quickly to the door, he shoved it open, seeing, on the edges of his vision, the square-faced man approach the cash register. Lurching from the café, he started towards his car with long strides. His mouth was dry again. The pounding of his heart was painful in his chest.

Suddenly, he started running. He heard the café door bang shut and fought away the urge to look across his shoulder. Was that a sound of other running footsteps now? Reaching his car, Mann yanked open the door and jarred in awkwardly behind the steering wheel. He reached into his trouser pocket for the keys and snatched them out, almost dropping them. His hand was shaking so badly he couldn't get the ignition key into its slot. He whined with mounting dread. Come on! he thought.

The key slid in, he twisted it convulsively. The motor started and he raced it momentarily before jerking the transmission shift to drive. Depressing the accelerator pedal quickly, he raked the car around and steered it towards the highway. From the corners of his eyes, he saw the truck and trailer being backed away from the café.

Reaction burst inside him. 'No!' he raged and slammed his foot down on the brake pedal. This was idiotic! Why the hell should he run away? His car slid sideways to a rocking halt and, shouldering out the door, he lurched to his feet and started towards the truck with angry strides. *All right, Jack*, he thought. He glared at the man inside the truck. You want to punch my nose, OK, but no more goddamn tournament on the highway.

The truck began to pick up speed. Mann raised his right arm. 'Hey!' he yelled. He knew the driver saw him. '*Hey!*' He started running as the truck kept moving, engine grinding loudly. It was on the highway now. He sprinted towards it with a sense of martyred outrage. The driver shifted gears, the truck moved faster. 'Stop!' Mann shouted. 'Damn it, *stop!*'

He thudded to a panting halt, staring at the truck as it receded down the highway, moved around a hill and disappeared. 'You son of a bitch,' he muttered. 'You goddamn, miserable son of a bitch.'

He trudged back slowly to his car, trying to believe that the truck driver had fled the hazard of a fistfight. It was possible, of course, but, somehow, he could not believe it.

He got into his car and was about to drive onto the highway when he changed his mind and switched the motor off. That crazy bastard might just be tooling along at 15 miles an hour, waiting for him to catch up. Nuts to that, he thought. So he blew his schedule; screw it. Forbes would have to wait, that was all. And if Forbes didn't care to wait, that was all right, too. He'd sit here for a while and let the nut get out of range, let him think he'd won the day. He grinned. You're the bloody Red Baron, Jack; you've shot me down. Now go to hell with my sincerest compliments. He shook his head. Beyond belief, he thought.

He really should have done this earlier, pulled over, waited. Then the truck driver would have had to let it pass. *Or picked on someone else*, the startling thought occurred to him. Jesus, maybe that was how the crazy bastard whiled away his work hours! Jesus Christ Almighty! was it possible?

He looked at the dashboard clock. It was just past 12.30. Wow, he thought. All that in less than an hour. He shifted on the seat and stretched his legs out. Leaning back against the door, he closed his eyes and mentally perused the things he had to do tomorrow and the following day. Today was shot to hell, as far as he could see.

When he opened his eyes, afraid of drifting into sleep and losing too much time, almost 11 minutes had passed. The nut must be an ample distance off by now, he thought: at least 11 miles and likely more, the way he drove. Good enough. He wasn't going to try to make San Francisco on schedule now, anyway. He'd take it real easy.

Mann adjusted his safety belt, switched on the motor, tapped the transmission pointer into drive position and pulled onto the highway, glancing back across his shoulder. Not a car in sight. Great day for driving. Everybody was staying at home. That nut must have a reputation around here. When Crazy Jack is on the highway, lock your car in the garage. Mann chuckled at the notion as his car began to turn the curve ahead.

Mindless reflex drove his right foot down against the brake pedal. Suddenly, his car had skidded to a halt and he was staring down the highway. The truck and trailer were parked on the shoulder less than 90 yards away.

Mann couldn't seem to function. He knew his car was blocking the westbound lane, knew that he should either make a U-turn or pull off the highway, but all he could do was gape at the truck.

He cried out, legs retracting, as a horn blast sounded behind him. Snapping up his head, he looked at the rearview mirror, gasping as he saw a yellow station wagon bearing down on him at high speed. Suddenly, it veered off towards the eastbound lane, disappearing from the mirror. Mann jerked around and saw it hurtling past his car, its rear end snapping back and forth, its back tyres screeching. He saw the twisted features of the man inside, saw his lips move rapidly with cursing.

Then the station wagon had swerved back into the westbound lane and was speeding off. It gave Mann an odd sensation to see it pass the truck. The man in that station wagon could drive on, unthreatened. Only he had been singled out. What happened was demented. Yet it was happening.

He drove his car onto the highway shoulder and braked. Putting the transmission into neutral, he leaned back, staring at the truck. His head was aching again. There was a pulsing at his temples like the ticking of a muffled clock.

What was he to do? He knew very well that if he left his car to walk to the truck, the driver would pull away and repark farther down the highway. He may as well face the fact that he was dealing with a madman. He felt the tremor in his stomach muscles starting up again. His heartbeat thudded slowly, striking at his chest wall. Now what?

With a sudden, angry impulse, Mann snapped the transmission into gear and stepped down hard on the accelerator pedal. The tyres of the car spun sizzlingly before they gripped; the car shot out onto the highway. Instantly, the truck began to move. He even had the motor on! Mann thought in raging fear. He floored the pedal, then, abruptly, realised he couldn't make it, that the truck would block his way and he'd collide with its trailer. A vision flashed across his mind, a fiery explosion and a sheet of flame incinerating him. He started braking fast, trying to decelerate evenly, so he wouldn't lose control.

When he'd slowed down enough to feel that it was safe, he steered the car onto the shoulder and stopped it again, throwing the transmission into neutral.

Approximately 80 yards ahead, the truck pulled off the highway and stopped.

Mann tapped his fingers on the steering wheel. *Now* what? he thought. Turn around and head east until he reached a cutoff that would take him to San Francisco by another route? How did he know the truck driver wouldn't follow him even then? His cheeks twitched as he bit his lips together angrily. No! He wasn't going to turn around!

His expression hardened suddenly. Well, he wasn't going to *sit* here all day, that was certain. Reaching out, he tapped the gearshift into drive and steered his car onto the highway once again. He saw the massive truck and trailer start to move but made no effort to speed up. He tapped at the brakes, taking a position about 30 yards behind the trailer. He glanced at his speedometer. Forty miles an hour. The truck driver had his left arm out the cab window and was waving him on. What did that mean? Had he changed his mind? Decided, finally, that this thing had gone too far? Mann couldn't let himself believe it.

He looked ahead. Despite the mountain ranges all around, the highway was flat as far as he could see. He tapped a fingernail against the horn bar, trying to make up his mind. Presumably, he could continue all the way to San Francisco at this speed, hanging back just far enough to avoid the worst of the exhaust fumes. It didn't seem likely that the truck driver would stop directly on the highway to block his way. And if the truck driver pulled onto the shoulder to let him pass, he could pull off the highway, too. It would be a draining afternoon but a safe one.

On the other hand, outracing the truck might be worth just one more try. This was obviously what that son of a bitch wanted. Yet, surely, a vehicle of such size couldn't be driven with the same daring as, potentially, his own. The laws of mechanics were against it, if nothing else. Whatever advantage the truck had in mass, it had to lose in stability, particularly that of its trailer. If Mann were to drive at, say, 80 miles an hour and there were a few steep grades – as he felt sure there were – the truck would have to fall behind.

The question was, of course, whether he had the nerve to maintain such a speed over a long distance. He'd never done it before. Still, the more he thought about it, the more it appealed to him; far more than the alternative did.

Abruptly, he decided. *Right*, he thought. He checked ahead, then pressed down hard on the accelerator pedal and pulled into the eastbound lane. As he neared the truck, he tensed, anticipating that the driver might block his way. But the truck did not shift from the westbound lane. Mann's car moved along its mammoth side. He glanced at the cab and saw the name KELLER printed on its door. For a shocking instant, he thought it read KILLER and started to slow down. Then, glancing at the name again, he saw what it really was and depressed the pedal sharply. When he saw the truck reflected in the rearview mirror, he steered his car into the westbound lane.

He shuddered, dread and satisfaction mixed together, as he saw that the truck driver was speeding up. It was strangely comforting to know the man's intentions definitely again. That plus the knowledge of his face and name seemed, somehow, to reduce his stature. Before, he had been faceless, nameless, an embodiment of unknown terror. Now, at least, he was an individual. All right, Keller, said his mind, let's see you beat me with that purple-silver relic now. He pressed down harder on the pedal. *Here we go*, he thought.

He looked at the speedometer, scowling as he saw that he was doing only 74 miles an hour. Deliberately, he pressed down on the pedal, alternating his gaze between the highway ahead and the speedometer until the needle turned past 80. He felt a flickering of satisfaction with himself. All right, Keller, you son of a bitch, top that, he thought.

After several moments, he glanced into the rearview mirror again. Was the truck getting closer? Stunned, he checked the speedometer. Damn it! He was down to 76! He forced in the accelerator pedal angrily. *He mustn't go less than 80!* Mann's chest shuddered with convulsive breath.

He glanced aside as he hurtled past a beige sedan parked on the shoulder underneath a tree. A young couple sat inside it, talking. Already they were far behind, their world removed from his. Had they even glanced aside when he'd passed? He doubted it.

He started as the shadow of an overhead bridge whipped across the hood and windshield. Inhaling raggedly, he glanced at the speedometer again. He was holding at 81. He checked the rearview mirror. Was it his imagination that the truck was gaining ground? He looked forward with anxious eyes. There had to be some kind of town ahead. To hell with time; he'd stop at the police station and tell them what had happened. They'd have to believe him. Why would he stop to tell them such a story if it weren't true? For all he knew, Keller had a police record in these parts. *Oh, sure, we're on to him,* he heard a faceless officer remark. *That crazy bastard's asked for it before and now he's going to get it.*

Mann shook himself and looked at the mirror. The truck *was* getting closer. Wincing, he glanced at the speedometer. Goddamn it, pay attention! raged his mind. He was down to 74 again! Whining with frustration, he depressed the pedal. Eighty! – 80! he demanded of himself. There was a murderer behind him!

His car began to pass a field of flowers; lilacs, Mann saw, white and purple, stretching out in endless rows. There was a small shack near the highway, the words FIELD FRESH FLOWERS painted on it. A brown-cardboard square was propped against the shack, the word FUNERALS printed crudely on it. Mann saw himself, abruptly, lying in a casket, painted like some grotesque mannequin. The overpowering smell of flowers seemed to fill his nostrils. Ruth and the children sitting in the first row, heads bowed. All his relatives –

Suddenly, the pavement roughened and the car began to bounce and shudder, driving bolts of pain into his head. He felt the steering wheel resisting him and clamped his hands around it tightly, harsh vibrations running up his arms. He didn't dare look at the mirror now. He had to force himself to keep the speed unchanged. Keller wasn't going to slow down; he was sure of that. *What if he got a flat tyre, though?* All control would vanish in an instant. He visualised the somersaulting of his car, its grinding, shrieking tumble, the explosion of its gas tank, his body crushed and burned and –

The broken span of pavement ended and his gaze jumped quickly to the rearview mirror. The truck was no closer, but it hadn't lost ground, either. Mann's eyes shifted. Up ahead were hills and mountains. He tried to reassure himself that upgrades were on his side, that he could climb them at the same speed he was going now. Yet all he could imagine were the downgrades, the immense truck close behind him, slamming violently into his car and knocking it across some cliff edge. He had a horrifying vision of dozens of broken, rusted cars lying unseen in the canyons ahead, corpses in every one of them, all flung to shattering deaths by Keller.

Mann's car went rocketing into a corridor of trees. On each side of the highway was a eucalyptus windbreak, each trunk three feet from the next. It was like speeding through a high-walled canyon. Mann gasped, twitching, as a large twig bearing dusty leaves dropped down across the windshield, then slid out of sight. Dear God! he thought. He was getting near the edge himself. If he should lose his nerve at this speed; it was over. Jesus! That would be ideal for Keller! he realised suddenly. He visualised the square-faced driver laughing as he passed the burning wreckage, knowing that he'd killed his prey without so much as touching him.

Mann started as his car shot out into the open. The route ahead was not straight now but winding up into the foothills. Mann willed himself to press down on the pedal even more. Eighty-three now, almost 84.

To his left was a broad terrain of green hills blending into mountains. He saw a black car on a dirt road, moving towards the highway. *Was its side painted white?* Mann's heartbeat lurched. Impulsively, he jammed the heel of his right hand down against the horn bar and held it there. The blast of the horn was shrill and racking to his ears. His heart began to pound. Was it a police car? Was it?

He let the horn bar up abruptly. *No, it wasn't.* Damn! his

mind raged. Keller must have been amused by his pathetic efforts. Doubtless, he was chuckling to himself right now. He heard the truck driver's voice in his mind, coarse and sly. *You think you gonna get a cop to save you, boy? Shee-it. You gonna die.* Mann's heart contorted with savage hatred. *You son of a bitch!* he thought. Jerking his right hand into a fist, he drove it down against the seat. Goddamn you, Keller! I'm going to kill you, if it's the last thing I do!

The hills were closer now. There would be slopes directly, long steep grades. Mann felt a burst of hope within himself. He was sure to gain a lot of distance on the truck. No matter how he tried, that bastard Keller couldn't manage 80 miles an hour on a hill. But I can! cried his mind with fierce elation. He worked up saliva in his mouth and swallowed it. The back of his shirt was drenched. He could feel sweat trickling down his sides. A bath and a drink, first order of the day on reaching San Francisco. A long, hot bath, a long, cold drink. Cutty Sark. He'd splurge, by Christ. He rated it.

The car swept up a shallow rise. Not steep enough, goddamn it! The truck's momentum would prevent its losing speed. Mann felt mindless hatred for the landscape. Already, he had topped the rise and tilted over to a shallow downgrade. He looked at the rearview mirror. *Square*, he thought, everything about the truck was square: the radiator grille, the fender shapes, the bumper ends, the outline of the cab, even the shape of Keller's hands and face. He visualised the truck as some great entity pursuing him, insentient, brutish, chasing him with instinct only.

Mann cried out, horror-stricken, as he saw the ROAD REPAIRS sign up ahead. His frantic gaze leaped down the highway. Both lanes blocked, a huge black arrow pointing towards the alternative route! He groaned in anguish, seeing it was dirt. His foot jumped automatically to the brake pedal and started pumping it. He threw a dazed look at the rearview mirror. The truck was moving as fast as ever! It *couldn't*, though! Mann's expression froze in terror as he started turning to the right.

He stiffened as the front wheels hit the dirt road. For an instant, he was certain that the back part of the car was going to spin; he felt it breaking to the left. 'No, don't!' he cried. Abruptly, he was jarring down the dirt road, elbows braced against his sides, trying to keep from losing control. His tyres battered at the ruts, almost tearing the wheel from his grip. The windows rattled noisily. His neck snapped back and forth with painful jerks. His jolting body surged against the binding of the safety belt and slammed down violently on the seat. He felt the bouncing of the car drive up his spine. His clenching teeth slipped and he cried out hoarsely as his upper teeth gouged deep into his lip.

He gasped as the rear end of the car began surging to the right. He started to jerk the steering wheel to the left, then, hissing, wrenched it in the opposite direction, crying out as the right rear fender cracked into a fence pole, knocking it down. He started pumping at the brakes, struggling to regain control. The car rear yawed sharply to the left, tyres shooting out a spray of dirt. Mann felt a scream tear upward in his throat. He twisted wildly at the steering wheel. The car began careering to the right. He hitched the wheel around until the car was on course again. His head was pounding like his heart now, with gigantic, throbbing spasms. He started coughing as he gagged on dripping blood.

The dirt road ended suddenly, the car regained momentum on the pavement and he dared to look at the rearview mirror. The truck was slowed down but was still behind him, rocking like a freighter on a storm-tossed sea, its huge tyres scouring up a pall of dust. Mann shoved in the accelerator pedal and his car surged forward. A good, steep grade lay just ahead; he'd gain that distance now. He swallowed blood, grimacing at the taste, then fumbled in his trouser pocket and tugged out his handkerchief. He pressed it to his bleeding lip, eyes fixed on the slope ahead. Another 50 yards or so. He writhed his back. His under-shirt was soaking wet, adhering to his skin. He glanced at the rearview mirror. The truck had just regained the highway. *Tough*! he thought with venom. Didn't get me, did you, Keller?

His car was on the first yards of the upgrade when steam began to issue from beneath its hood. Mann stiffened suddenly, eyes widening with shock. The steam increased, became a smoking mist. Mann's gaze jumped down. The red light hadn't flashed on yet but had to in a moment. How could this be happening? Just as he was set to get away! The slope ahead was long and gradual, with many curves. He knew he couldn't stop. Could he U-turn unexpectedly and go back down? the sudden thought occurred. He looked ahead. The highway was too narrow, bound by hills on both sides. There wasn't room enough to make an uninterrupted turn and there wasn't time enough to ease around. If he tried that, Keller would shift direction and hit him head on. 'Oh, my God!' Mann murmured suddenly.

He was going to die.

He stared ahead with stricken eyes, his view increasingly obscured by steam. Abruptly, he recalled the afternoon he'd had the engine steam cleaned at the local car wash. The man who'd done it had suggested he replace the water hoses, because steam-cleaning had a tendency to make them crack. He'd nodded, thinking that he'd do it when he had more time. *More time*! The phrase was like a dagger in his mind. He'd failed to change the hoses and, for that failure he was now about to die.

He sobbed in terror as the dashboard light flashed on. He glanced at it involuntarily and read the word HOT, black on red. With a breathless gasp, he jerked the transmission into low. Why hadn't he done that right away! He looked ahead. The slope seemed endless. Already, he could hear a boiling throb inside the radiator. How much coolant was there left? Steam was clouding faster, hazing up the windshield. Reaching out, he twisted at a dashboard knob. The wipers started flicking back and forth in fan-shaped sweeps. There had to be enough coolant in the radiator to get him to the top. *Then* what? cried his mind. He couldn't drive without coolant, even downhill. He glanced at the rearview mirror. The truck was falling behind. Mann snarled with maddened fury. *If it weren't for that goddamned hose, he'd be escaping now*!

The sudden lurching of the car snatched him back to terror. If he braked now, he could jump out, run and scrabble up that slope. Later, he might not have the time. He couldn't make himself stop the car, though. As long as it kept on running, he felt bound to it, less vulnerable. God knows what would happen if he left it.

Mann stared up the slope with haunted eyes, trying not to see the red light on the edges of his vision. Yard by yard, his car was slowing down. Make it, make it, pleaded his mind, even though he thought that it was futile. The car was running more and more unevenly. The thumping percolation of its radiator filled his ears. Any moment now, the motor would be choked off and the car would shudder to a stop, leaving him a sitting target. No, he thought. He tried to blank his mind.

He was almost to the top, but in the mirror he could see the truck drawing up on him. He jammed down on the pedal and the motor made a grinding noise. He groaned. It had to make the top! Please, God, help me! screamed his mind. The ridge was just ahead. Closer. Closer. Make it. 'Make it.' The car was shuddering and clanking, slowing down – oil, smoke and steam gushing from beneath the hood. The windshield wipers swept from side to side. Mann's head throbbed. Both his hands felt numb. His heartbeat pounded as he stared ahead. Make it, please, God, make it. Make it. *Make it*!

Over! Mann's lips opened in a cry of triumph as the car began descending. Hand shaking uncontrollably, he shoved the transmission into neutral and let the car go into a glide. The triumph strangled in his throat as he saw that there was nothing in sight but hills and more hills. Never mind! He was on a downgrade now, a long one. He passed a sign that read TRUCKS USE LOW GEARS NEXT 12 MILES. Twelve miles! Something would come up. It had to.

The car began to pick up speed. Mann glanced at the speedometer. Forty-seven miles an hour. The red light still burned. He'd save the motor for a long time, too, though; let it cool for 12 miles, if the truck was far enough behind.

His speed increased. Fifty . . . 51. Mann watched the needle turning slowly towards the right. He glanced at the rearview mirror. The truck had not appeared yet. With a little luck, he might still get a good lead. Not as good as he might have if the motor hadn't overheated but enough to work with. There had to be someplace along the way to stop. The needle edged past 55 and started towards the 60 mark.

Again, he looked at the rearview mirror, jolting as he saw that the truck had topped the ridge and was on its way down. He felt his lips begin to shake and crimped them together. His gaze jumped fitfully between the steam-obscured highway and the mirror. The truck was accelerating rapidly. Keller doubtless had the gas pedal floored. it wouldn't be long before the truck caught up to him. Mann's right hand twitched unconsciously towards the gearshift. Noticing, he jerked it back, grimacing, glanced at the speedometer. The car's velocity had just passed 60. Not enough! He had to use the motor now! He reached out desperately.

His right hand froze in mid-air as the motor stalled; then, shooting out the hand, he twisted the ignition key. The motor made a grinding noise but wouldn't start. Mann glanced up, saw that he was almost on the shoulder, jerked the steering wheel around. Again, he turned the key, but there was no response. He looked up at the rearview mirror. The truck was gaining on him swiftly. He glanced at the speedometer. The car's speed was fixed at 62. Mann felt himself crushed in a vice of panic. He stared ahead with haunted eyes.

Then he saw it, several hundred yards ahead: an escape route for trucks with burned-out brakes. There was no alternative now. Either he took the turnout or his car would be rammed from behind. The truck was frighteningly close. He heard the high-pitched wailing of its motor. Unconsciously, he started easing to the right, then jerked the wheel back suddenly. He mustn't give the move away! He had to wait until the last possible moment. Otherwise, Keller would follow him in.

Just before he reached the escape route, Mann wrenched the steering wheel around. The car rear started breaking to the left, tyres shrieking on the pavement. Mann steered with the skid, braking just enough to keep from losing all control. The rear tyres grabbed and, at 60 miles an hour, the car shot up the dirt trail, tyres slinging up a cloud of dust. Mann began to hit the brakes. The rear wheels sideslipped and the car slammed hard against the dirt bank to the right. Mann gasped as the car bounced off and started to fishtail with violent whipping motions, angling towards the trail edge. He drove his foot down on the brake pedal with all his might. The car rear skidded to the right and slammed against the bank again. Mann heard a grinding rend of metal and felt himself heaved downward suddenly, his neck snapped, as the car ploughed to a violent halt.

As in a dream, Mann turned to see the truck and trailer swerving off the highway. Paralysed, he watched the massive vehicle hurtle towards him, staring at it with a blank detachment, knowing he was going to die but so stupefied by the sight of the looming truck that he couldn't react. The gargantuan shape roared closer, blotting out the sky. Mann felt a strange sensation in his throat, unaware that he was screaming.

Suddenly, the truck began to tilt. Mann stared at it in choked-off silence as it started tipping over like some ponderous beast toppling in slow motion. Before it reached his car, it vanished from his rear window. Hands palsied, Mann undid the safety belt and opened the door. Struggling from the car, he stumbled to the trail edge, staring downward. He was just in time to see the truck capsize like a foundering ship. The tanker followed, huge wheels spinning as it overturned.

The storage tank on the truck exploded first, the violence of its detonation causing Mann to stagger back and sit down clumsily on the dirt. A second explosion roared below, its shock wave buffeting across him hotly, making his ears hurt. His glazed eyes saw a fiery column shoot up towards the sky in front of him, then another.

Mann crawled slowly to the trail edge and peered down at the canyon. Enormous gouts of flame were towering upward, topped by thick, black, oily smoke. He couldn't see the truck or trailer, only flames. He gaped at them in shock, all feeling drained from him.

Then, unexpectedly, emotion came. Not dread, at first, and not regret; not the nausea that followed soon. It was a primeval tumult in his mind: the cry of some ancestral beast above the body of its vanquished foe.

THE AUTHOR
Tod Robbins

THE STORY
Spurs

THE MOVIE
Freaks

THE DIRECTOR
Tod Browning

Jacques Courbé was a romanticist. He measured only twenty-eight inches from the soles of his diminutive feet to the crown of his head; but there were times, as he rode into the arena on his gallant charger, St Eustache, when he felt himself a doughty knight of old about to do battle for his lady.

What matter that St Eustache was not a gallant charger except in his master's imagination – not even a pony, indeed, but a large dog of a nondescript breed, with the long snout and upstanding ears of a wolf? What matter that M. Courbé's entrance was invariably greeted with shouts of derisive laughter and bombardments of banana skins and orange peel? What matter that he had no lady, and that his daring deeds were severely curtailed to a mimicry of the bareback riders who preceded him? What mattered all these things to the tiny man who lived in dreams, and who resolutely closed his shoe-button eyes to the drab realities of life?

The dwarf had no friends among the other freaks in Copo's Circus. They considered him ill-tempered and egotistical, and he loathed them for their acceptance of things as they were. Imagination was the armour that protected him from the curious glances of a cruel, gaping world, from the stinging lash of ridicule, from the bombardments of banana skins and orange peel. Without it, he must have shrivelled up and died. But these others? Ah, they had no armour except their own thick hides! The door that opened on the kingdom of imagination was closed and locked to them; and although they did not wish to open this door, although they did not miss what lay beyond it, they resented and mistrusted anyone who possessed the key.

Now it came about, after many humiliating performances in the arena, made palatable only by dreams, that love entered the circus tent and beckoned commandingly to M. Jacques Courbé. In an instant the dwarf was engulfed in a sea of wild, tumultuous passion.

Mlle Jeanne Marie was a daring bareback rider. It made M. Jacques Courbé's tiny heart stand still to see her that first night of her appearance in the arena, performing brilliantly on the broad back of her aged mare, Sappho. A tall, blonde woman of the amazon type, she had round eyes of baby blue which held no spark of her avaricious peasant's soul, carmine lips and cheeks, large white teeth which flashed continually in a smile and hands which, when doubled up, were nearly the size of the dwarf's head.

Her partner in the act was Simon Lafleur, the Romeo of the circus tent – a swarthy, herculean young man with bold black eyes and hair that glistened with grease, like the back of Solon, the trained seal.

From the first performance M. Jacques Courbé loved Mlle Jeanne Marie. All his tiny body was shaken with longing for her. Her buxom charms, so generously revealed in tights and spangles, made him flush and cast down his eyes. The familiarities allowed to Simon Lafleur, the bodily acrobatic contacts of the two performers, made the dwarf's blood boil. Mounted on St Eustache, awaiting his turn at the entrance, he would grind his teeth in impotent rage to see Simon circling round and round the ring, standing proudly on the back of Sappho and holding Mlle Jeanne Marie in an ecstatic embrace, while she kicked one shapely, bespangled leg skywards.

'Ah, the dog!' M. Jacques Courbé would mutter. 'Some day I shall teach this hulking stable-boy his place! *Ma foi*, I will clip his ears for him!'

St Eustache did not share his master's admiration for Mlle Jeanne Marie. From the first he evinced his hearty detestation for her by low growls and a ferocious display of long, sharp fangs. It was little consolation for the dwarf to know that St Eustache showed still more marked signs of rage when Simon Lafleur approached him. It pained M. Jacques Courbé to think that his gallant charger, his sole companion, his bedfellow, should not also love and admire the splendid giantess who each night risked life and limb before the awed populace. Often, when they were alone together, he would chide St Eustache on his churlishness.

'Ah, you devil of a dog!' the dwarf would cry. 'Why must you always growl and show your ugly teeth when the lovely Jeanne Marie condescends to notice you? Have you no feelings under your tough hide? Cur, she is an angel, and you snarl at her! Do you not remember how I found you, a starving puppy in a Paris gutter? And now you must threaten the hand of my princess! So this is your gratitude, great hairy pig!'

M. Jacques Courbé had one living relative – not a dwarf, like himself, but a fine figure of a man, a prosperous farmer living just outside the town of Roubaix. The elder Courbé had never married;

and so one day, when he was found dead from heart failure, his tiny nephew – for whom, it must be confessed, the farmer had always felt an instinctive aversion – fell heir to a comfortable property. When the tidings were brought to him, the dwarf threw both arms about the shaggy neck of St Eustache and cried out:

'Ah, now we can retire, marry and settle down, old friend! I am worth many times my weight in gold!'

That evening, as Mlle Jeanne Marie was changing her gaudy costume after the performance, a light tap sounded on the door.

'Enter!' she called, believing it to be Simon Lafleur, who had promised to take her that evening to the Sign of the Wild Boar for a glass of wine to wash the sawdust out of her throat. 'Enter, *mon chéri!*'

The door swung slowly open; and in stepped M. Jacques Courbé, very proud and upright, in the silks and laces of a courtier, with a tiny gold-hilted sword swinging at his hip. Up he came, his shoe-button eyes all a-glitter to see the more than partially revealed charms of his robust lady. Up he came to within a yard of where she sat; and down on one knee he went and pressed his lips to her red-slippered foot.

'Oh, most beautiful and daring lady,' he cried, in a voice as shrill as a pin scratching on a window-pane, 'will you not take mercy on the unfortunate Jacques Courbé? He is hungry for your smiles, he is starving for your lips! All night long he tosses on his couch and dreams of Jeanne Marie!'

'What play-acting is this, my brave little fellow?' she asked, bending down with the smile of an ogress. 'Has Simon Lafleur sent you to tease me?'

'May the black plague have Simon!' the dwarf cried, his eyes seeming to flash blue sparks. 'I am not play-acting. It is only too true that I love you, mademoiselle; that I wish to make you my lady. And now that I have a fortune, now that – ' He broke off suddenly, and his face resembled a withered apple. 'What is this mademoiselle?' he said, in the low, droning tone of a hornet about to sting. 'Do you laugh at my love? I warn you mademoiselle – do not laugh at Jacques Courbé!'

Mlle Jeanne Marie's large, florid face had turned purple from suppressed merriment. Her lips twitched at the corners. It was all she could do not to burst out into a roar of laughter.

Why, the ridiculous little manikin was serious in his lovemaking! This pocket-sized edition of a courtier was proposing marriage to her! He, this splinter of a fellow, wished to make her his wife! Why, she could carry him about on her shoulder like a trained marmoset!

What a joke this was – what a colossal, corset-creaking joke! Wait till she told Simon Lafleur! She could fairly see him throw back his sleek head, open his mouth to its widest dimensions and shake with silent laughter. But *she* must not laugh – not now. First she must listen to everything the dwarf had to say; draw all the sweetness out of this bonbon of humour before she crushed it under the heel of ridicule.

'I am not laughing,' she managed to say. 'You have taken me by surprise. I never thought, I never even guessed – '

'That is well, mademoiselle,' the dwarf broke in. 'I do not tolerate laughter. In the arena I am paid to make laughter; but those others pay to laugh at *me*. I always make people pay to laugh at me!'

'But do I understand you aright, M. Courbé? Are you proposing an honourable marriage?'

The dwarf rested his hand on his heart and bowed. 'Yes, mademoiselle, an honourable marriage, and the wherewithal to keep the wolf from the door. A week ago my uncle died and left me a large estate. We shall have a servant to wait on our wants, a horse and carriage, food and wine of the best and leisure to amuse ourselves. And you? Why, you will be a fine lady! I will clothe that beautiful big body of yours with silks and laces! You will be as happy, mademoiselle, as a cherry tree in June!'

The dark blood slowly receded from Mlle Jeanne Marie's full cheeks, her lips no longer twitched at the corners, her eyes had narrowed slightly. She had been a bareback rider for years, and she was weary of it. The life of the circus tent had lost its tinsel. She loved the dashing Simon Lafleur; but she knew well enough that this Romeo in tights would never espouse a dowerless girl.

The dwarf's words had woven themselves into a rich mental tapestry. She saw herself a proud lady, ruling over a country estate, and later welcoming Simon Lafleur with all the luxuries that were so near his heart. Simon would be overjoyed to marry into a country estate. These pygmies were a puny lot. They died young! She would do nothing to hasten the end of Jacques Courbé. No, she would be kindness itself to the poor little fellow; but, on the other hand, she would not lose her beauty mourning for him.

'Nothing that you wish shall be withheld from you as long as you love me, mademoiselle,' the dwarf continued. 'Your answer?'

Mlle Jeanne Marie bent forward, and, with a single movement of her powerful arms, raised M. Jacques Courbé and placed him on her knee. For an ecstatic instant she held him thus, as if he were a large French doll, with his tiny sword cocked coquettishly out behind. Then she planted on his cheek a huge kiss that covered his entire face from chin to brow.

'I am yours!' she murmured, pressing him to her ample bosom. 'From the first I loved you, M. Jacques Courbé!'

The wedding of Mlle Jeanne Marie was celebrated in the town of Roubaix, where Copo's Circus had taken up its temporary quarters. Following the ceremony, a feast was served in one of the tents, which was attended by a whole galaxy of celebrities.

The bridegroom, his dark little face flushed with happiness and wine, sat at the head of the board. His chin was just above the tablecloth, so that his head looked like a large orange that had rolled off the fruit-dish. Immediately beneath his dangling feet, St Eustache, who had more than once evinced by deep growls his disapproval of the proceedings, now worried a bone with quick, sly glances from time to time at the plump legs of his new mistress. Papa Copo was on the dwarf's right, his large round face as red and benevolent as a harvest moon. Next to him sat Griffo, the giraffe boy, who was covered with spots, and whose neck was so long that he looked down on all the rest, including M. Hercule Hippo, the giant. The rest of the company included Mlle Lupa, who had sharp white teeth of an incredible length, and who growled when she tried to talk; the tiresome M. Jejongle, who insisted on juggling fruit, plates and knives, although the whole company was heartily sick of his tricks; Mme Samson, with her trained boa constrictors coiled about her neck and peeping out timidly, one above each ear; Simon Lafleur and a score of others.

The bareback rider had laughed silently and almost continually ever since Jeanne Marie had told him of her engagement. Now he sat next to her in his crimson tights. His black hair was brushed back from his forehead and so glistened with grease that it reflected the lights overhead, like a burnished helmet. From time to time he tossed off a brimming goblet of Burgundy, nudged the bride in the ribs with his elbow and threw back his sleek head in another silent outburst of laughter.

'And you sure that you will not forget me, Simon?' she whispered. 'It may be some time before I can get the little ape's money.'

'Forget you, Jeanne?' he muttered. 'By all the dancing devils in champagne, never! I will wait as patiently as Job till you have fed that mouse some poisoned cheese. But what will you do with him in the meantime, Jeanne? You must allow him no liberties. I grind my teeth to think of you in his arms!'

The bride smiled, and regarded her diminutive husband with an appraising glance. What an atom of a man! And yet life might linger in his bones for a long time to come. M. Jacques Courbé had allowed himself only one glass of wine, and yet he was far gone in intoxication. His tiny face was suffused with blood, and he stared at Simon Lafleur belligerently. Did he suspect the truth?

'Your husband is flushed with wine!' the bareback rider whispered. '*Ma foi*, madame, later he may knock you about! Possibly he is a dangerous fellow in his cups. Should he maltreat you, Jeanne, do not forget that you have a protector in Simon Lafleur.'

'You clown!' Jeanne Marie rolled her large eyes roguishly, and laid her hand for an instant on the bareback rider's knee. 'Simon, I could crack his skull between my finger and thumb, like this hickory nut!' She paused to illustrate her example, and then added reflectively: 'And, perhaps, I shall do that very thing, if he attempts any familiarities. Ugh! The little ape turns my stomach!'

By now the wedding guests were beginning to show the effects of their potations. This was especially marked in the case of M. Jacques Courbé's associates in the side-show.

Griffo, the giraffe boy, had closed his large brown eyes, and was swaying his small head languidly above the assembly, while a slightly supercilious expression drew his lips down at the corners. M. Hercule Hippo, swollen out by his libations to even more colossal proportions, was repeating over and over: 'I tell you I am not like other men. When I walk, the earth trembles!' Mlle Lupa, her hairy upper lip lifted above her long white teeth, was gnawing at a bone, growling unintelligible phrases to herself and shooting savage, suspicious glances at her companions. M. Jejongle's hands had grown unsteady, and, as he insisted on juggling the knifes and plates of each new course, broken bits of crockery littered the floor. Mme Samson, uncoiling her necklace of baby boa constrictors, was feeding them lumps of sugar soaked in rum. M. Jacques Courbé had finished his second glass of wine, and was surveying the whispering Simon Lafleur through narrowed eyes.

There can be no genial companionship among great egotists who have drunk too much. Each one of these human oddities thought that he or she alone was responsible for the crowds that daily gathered at Copo's Circus; so now, heated with the good Burgundy, they were not slow in asserting themselves. Their separate egos rattled angrily together, like so many pebbles in a bag. Here was gunpowder which needed only a spark.

'I am a big – a very big man!' M. Hercule Hippo said sleepily. 'Women love me. The pretty little creatures leave their pygmy husbands, so that they may come and stare at Hercule Hippo of Copo's Circus. Ha, and when they return home, they laugh at other men always! "You may kiss me again when you grow up," they tell their sweethearts.'

'Fat bullock, here is one woman who has no love for you!' cried Mlle Lupa, glaring sideways at the giant over her bone. 'That great carcass of yours is only so much food gone to waste. You have cheated the butcher, my friend. Fool, women do not come to see *you*! As well they might stare at the cattle being led through the street. Ah, no, they come from far and near to see one of their own sex who is not a cat!'

'Quite right,' cried Papa Copo in a conciliatory tone, smiling, and rubbing his hands together. 'Not a cat, mademoiselle, but a wolf. Ah, you have a sense of humour! How droll!'

'I *have* a sense of humour,' Mlle Lupa agreed, returning to her bone, 'and also sharp teeth. Let the erring hand not stray too near!'

'You, M. Hippo and Mlle Lupa, are both wrong,' said a voice which seemed to come from the roof. 'Surely it is none other than me whom the people come to stare at!'

All raised their eyes to the supercilious face of Griffo, the giraffe boy, which swayed slowly from side to side on its long, pipe-stem neck. It was he who had spoken, although his eyes were still closed.

'Of all the colossal impudence!' cried the matronly Mme Samson. 'As if my little dears had nothing to say on the subject!' She picked up the two baby boa constrictors, which lay in drunken slumber on her lap; and shook them like whips at the wedding guests. 'Papa Copo knows only too well that it is on account of these little charmers, Mark Antony and Cleopatra, that the side-show is so well attended!'

The circus owner, thus directly appealed to, frowned in perplexity. He felt himself in a quandary. These freaks of his were difficult to handle. Why had he been fool enough to come to M. Jacques Courbé's wedding feast? Whatever he said would be used against him.

As Papa Copo hesitated, his round, red face wreathed in ingratiating smiles, the long deferred spark suddenly alighted in the powder. It all came about on account of the carelessness of M. Jejongle, who had become engrossed in the conversation and wished to put in a word for himself. Absent-mindedly juggling two heavy plates and a spoon, he said in a petulant tone:

'You all appear to forget *me*!'

Scarcely were the words out of his mouth, when one of the heavy plates descended with a crash on the thick skull of M. Hippo; and M. Jejongle was instantly remembered. Indeed he was more than remembered; for the giant, already irritated to boiling point by Mlle Lupa's insults, at this new affront struck out savagely past her and knocked the juggler head-over-heels under the table.

Mlle Lupa, always quick-tempered and especially so when her attention was focused on a juicy chicken bone, evidently considered her dinner companion's conduct far from decorous, and promptly inserted her sharp teeth in the offending hand that had administered the blow. M. Hippo, squealing from rage and pain like a wounded elephant, bounded to his feet, overturning the table.

Pandemonium followed. Every freak's hands, teeth, feet, were turned against the others. Above the shouts, screams, growls and hisses of the combat, Papa Copo's voice could be heard bellowing for peace:

'Ah, my children, my children! This is no way to behave! Calm yourselves, I pray you! Mlle Lupa, remember that you are a lady as well as a wolf!'

There is no doubt that M. Jacques Courbé would have suffered most in this undignified fracas had it not been for St Eustache, who had stationed himself over his tiny master and who now drove off all would-be assailants. As it was, Griffo, the unfortunate giraffe boy, was the most defenceless and therefore became the victim. His small, round head swayed back and forth to blows like a punching bag. He was bitten by Mlle Lupa, buffeted by M. Hippo, kicked by M. Jejongle, clawed by Mme Samson and nearly strangled by both the baby boa constrictors, which had wound themselves about his neck like hangmen's nooses. Undoubtedly he would have fallen victim to circumstances, had it not been for Simon Lafleur, the bride and half a dozen of her acrobatic friends, who Papa Copo had implored to restore peace. Roaring with laughter, they sprang forward and tore the combatants apart.

M. Jacques Courbé was found sitting grimly under a fold of the tablecloth. He held a broken bottle of wine in one hand. The dwarf was very drunk, and in a towering rage. As Simon Lafleur approached with one of his silent laughs, M. Jacques Courbé hurled the bottle at his head.

'Ah, the little wasp!' the bareback rider cried, picking up the dwarf by his waistband. 'Here is your fine husband, Jeanne! Take him away before he does me some mischief. *Parbleu*, he is a bloodthirsty fellow in his cups!'

The bride approached, her blonde face crimson from wine and laughter. Now that she was safely married to a country estate, she took no more pains to conceal her true feelings.

'Oh, *là, là!*' she cried, seizing the struggling dwarf and holding him forcibly on her shoulder. 'What a temper the little ape has! Well, we shall spank it out of him before long!'

'Let me down!' M. Jacques Courbé screamed in a paroxysm of fury. 'You will regret this, madame! Let me down, I say!'

But the stalwart bride shook her head. 'No, no, my little one!' she laughed. 'You cannot escape your wife so easily! What, you would fly from my arms before the honeymoon!'

'Let me down!' he cried again. 'Can't you see that they are laughing at me?'

'And why should they not laugh, my little ape? Let them laugh, if they will; but I will not put you down. No, I will carry you thus, perched on my shoulder, to the farm. It will set a precedent which brides of the future may find a certain difficulty in following!'

'But the farm is quite a distance from here, my Jeanne,' said Simon Lafleur. 'You are as strong as an ox, and he is only a marmoset; still, I will wager a bottle of Burgundy that you set him down by the roadside.'

'Done, Simon!' the bride cried, with a flash of her strong white teeth. 'You shall lose your wager, for I swear that I could carry my little ape from one end of France to the other!'

M. Jacques Courbé no longer struggled. He now sat bolt upright on his bride's broad shoulder. From the flaming peaks of blind passion he had fallen into an abyss of cold fury. His love was dead, but some quiet alien emotion was rearing an evil head from its ashes.

'So, madame, you could carry me from one end of France to the other!' he droned in a monotonous undertone. 'From one end of France to the other! I will remember that always, madame!'

'Come!' cried the bride sullenly. 'I am off. Do you and the others, Simon, follow to see me win my wager.'

They all trooped out of the tent. A full moon rode the heavens and showed the road, lying as white and straight through the meadows as the parting in Simon Lafleur's black, oily hair. The bride, still holding the diminutive bridegroom on her shoulder, burst out into song as she strode forward. The wedding guests followed. Some walked none too steadily. Griffo, the giraffe boy, staggered pitifully on his long, thin legs. Papa Copo alone remained behind.

'What a strange world!' he muttered, standing in the tent door and following them with his round blue eyes. 'Ah, these children of mine are difficult at times – very difficult!'

A year had rolled by since the marriage of Mlle Jeanne Marie and M. Jacques Courbé. Copo's Circus had once more taken up its quarters in the town of Roubaix. For more than a week the country people for miles around had flocked to the side-show to get a peep at Griffo, the giraffe boy; M. Hercule Hippo, the giant; Mlle Lupa, the wolf lady; Mme Samson, with her baby boa constrictors; and M. Jejongle, the famous juggler. Each was still firmly convinced that he or she alone was responsible for the popularity of the circus.

Simon Lafleur sat in his lodgings at the Sign of the Wild Boar. He wore nothing but red tights. His powerful torso, stripped to the waist, glistened with oil. He was kneading his biceps tenderly with some strong-smelling fluid.

Suddenly there came the sound of heavy, laborious footsteps on the stairs. Simon Lafleur looked up. His rather gloomy expression lifted, giving place to the brilliant smile that had won for him the hearts of so many lady acrobats.

'Ah, this is Marcelle!' he told himself. 'Or perhaps it is Rose, the English girl; or, yet again, little Francesca, although she walks more lightly. Well, no matter – whoever it is, I will welcome her!'

But now the lagging, heavy footfalls were in the hall; and, a moment later, they came to a halt outside the door. There was a timid knock.

Simon Lafleur's brilliant smile hardened. 'Perhaps some new admirer who needs encouragement,' he told himself. But aloud he said: 'Enter, mademoiselle!'

The door swung slowly open and revealed the visitor. She was a tall, gaunt woman dressed like a peasant. The wind had blown her hair into her eyes. Now she raised a large, toil-worn hand, brushed it back across her forehead and looked long and attentively at the bareback rider.

'You do not remember me?' she said at length.

Two lines of perplexity appeared above Simon Lafleur's Roman nose; he slowly shook his head. He, who had known so many women in his time, was now at a loss. Was it a fair question to ask a man who was no longer a boy and who had lived? Women change so in a brief time! Now this bag of bones might at one time have appeared desirable to him.

Parbleu! Fate was a conjurer! She waved her wand; and beautiful women were transformed into hags, jewels into pebbles, silks and laces into hempen cords. The brave fellow, who danced tonight at the prince's ball, might tomorrow dance more lightly on the gallows tree. The thing was to live and die with a full belly. To digest all that one could – that was life!

'You do not remember me?' she said again.

Simon Lafleur once more shook his sleek, black head. 'I have a poor memory for faces, madame,' he said politely. 'It is my misfortune, when there are such beautiful faces.'

'Ah, but you should have remembered, Simon!' the woman cried, a sob rising up in her throat. 'We were very close together, you and I. Do you not remember Jeanne Marie?'

'Jeanne Marie!' the bareback rider cried. 'Jeanne Marie, who married a marmoset and a country estate? Don't tell me, madame, that you – '

He broke off and stared at her, open-mouthed. His sharp black eyes wandered from the wisps of wet, straggling hair down her gaunt person till they rested at last on her thick cowhide boots, encrusted with layer on layer of mud from the countryside.

'It is impossible!' he said at last.

'It is indeed Jeanne Marie,' the woman answered, 'or what is left of her. Ah, Simon, what a life he has led me! I have been merely a beast of burden! There are no ignominies which he has not made me suffer!'

'To whom do you refer?' Simon Lafleur demanded. 'Surely you cannot mean that pocket edition husband of yours – that dwarf, Jacques Courbé?'

'Ah, but I do, Simon! Alas, he has broken me!'

'He – that toothpick of a man?' the bareback rider cried, with one of his silent laughs. 'Why, it is impossible! As you once said yourself, Jeanne, you could crack his skull between finger and thumb like a hickory nut!'

'So I thought once. Ah, but I did not know him then, Simon! Because he was small, I thought I could do with him as I liked. It seemed to me that I was marrying a manikin. "I will play Punch and Judy with this little fellow," I said to myself. Simon, you may imagine my surprise when he began playing Punch and Judy with me!'

'But I do not understand, Jeanne. Surely at any time you could have slapped him into obedience!'

'Perhaps,' she assented wearily, 'had it not been for St Eustache.

From the first that wolf dog of his hated me. If I so much as answered his master back, he would show his teeth. Once, at the beginning, when I raised my hand to cuff Jacques Courbé, he sprang at my throat and would have torn me limb from limb, had not the dwarf called him off. I was a strong woman, but even then I was no match for a wolf!'

'There was poison, was there not?' Simon Lafleur suggested.

'Ah, yes, I, too, thought of poison; but it was of no avail. St Eustache would eat nothing that I gave him; and the dwarf forced me to taste first of all the food that was placed before him and his dog. Unless I myself wished to die, there was no way of poisoning either of them.'

'My poor girl!' the bareback rider said, pityingly. 'I begin to understand; but sit down and tell me everything. This is a revelation to me, after seeing you stalking homeward so triumphantly with your bridegroom on your shoulder. You must begin at the beginning.'

'It was just because I carried him thus on my shoulder that I have had to suffer so cruelly,' she said, seating herself on the only other chair the room afforded. 'He has never forgiven me the insult which he says I put upon him. Do you remember how I boasted that I could carry him from one end of France to the other?'

'I remember. Well, Jeanne?'

'Well, Simon, the little demon has figured out the exact distance in leagues. Each morning, rain or shine, we sally out of the house – he on my back, the wolf dog at my heels – and I tramp along the dusty roads till my knees tremble beneath me from fatigue. If I so much as slacken my pace, if I falter, he goads me with his cruel little golden spurs; while, at the same time, St Eustache nips my ankles. When we return home, he strikes so many leagues off a score which he says is the number of leagues from one end of France to the other. Not half that distance has been covered, and I am no longer a strong woman, Simon. Look at these shoes!'

She held up one of her feet for his inspection. The sole of the cowhide boot had worn through; Simon Lafleur caught a glimpse of bruised flesh caked with the mire of the highway.

'This is the third pair that I have had,' she continued hoarsely.

'Now he tells me that the price of shoe leather is too high, that I shall have to finish my pilgrimage barefooted.'

'But why do you put up with all this, Jeanne?' Simon Lafleur asked angrily. 'You, who have a carriage and a servant, should not walk at all!'

'At first there was a carriage and a servant,' she said, wiping the tears from her eyes with the back of her hand, 'but they did not last a week. He sent the servant about his business and sold the carriage at a nearby fair. Now there is no one but me to wait on him and his dog.'

'But the neighbours?' Simon Lafleur persisted. 'Surely you could appeal to them?'

'We have no near neighbours; the farm is quite isolated. I would have run away many months ago, if I could have escaped unnoticed; but they keep a continual watch on me. Once I tried, but I hadn't travelled more than a league before the wolf dog was snapping at my ankles. He drove me back to the farm, and the following day I was compelled to carry the little fiend till I fell from sheer exhaustion.'

'But tonight you got away?'

'Yes,' she said, with a quick, frightened glance at the door. 'Tonight I slipped out while they were both sleeping, and came here to you. I knew that you would protect me, Simon, because of what we have been to each other. Get Papa Copo to take me back in the circus, and I will work my fingers to the bone! Save me, Simon!'

Jeanne Marie could no longer suppress her sobs. They rose in her throat, choking her, making her incapable of further speech.

'Calm yourself, Jeanne,' Simon Lafleur said soothingly. 'I will do what I can for you. I shall have a talk with Papa Copo tomorrow. Of course, you are no longer the same woman that you were a year ago. You have aged since then; but perhaps our good Papa Copo could find you something to do.'

He broke off and eyed her intently. She had stiffened in the chair; her face, even under its coat of grime, had gone a sickly white.

'What troubles you, Jeanne?' he asked a trifle breathlessly.

'Hush!' she said, with a finger to her lips. 'Listen!'

Simon Lafleur could hear nothing but the tapping of the rain on the roof and the sighing of the wind through the trees. An unusual silence seemed to pervade the Sign of the Wild Boar.

'Now don't you hear it?' she cried with an inarticulate gasp. 'Simon, it is in the house – it is on the stairs!'

At last the bareback rider's less sensitive ears caught the sound his companion had heard a full minute before. It was a steady *pit-pat, pit-pat*, on the stairs, hard to dissociate from the drip of the rain from the eaves; but each instant it came nearer, grew more distinct.

'Oh, save me, Simon; save me!' Jeanne Marie cried, throwing herself at his feet and clasping him about the knees. 'Save me! It is St Eustache!'

'Nonsense, woman!' the bareback rider said angrily, but nevertheless he rose. 'There are other dogs in the world. On the second landing there is a blind fellow who owns a dog. Perhaps it is he you hear.'

'No, no – it is St Eustache's step! My God, if you had lived with him a year, you would know it, too! Close the door and lock it!'

'That I will not.' Simon Lafleur said contemptuously. 'Do you think I am frightened so easily? If it is the wolf dog, so much the worse for him. He will not be the first cur I have choked to death with these two hands!'

Pit-pat, pit-pat – it was on the second landing. *Pit-pat, pit-pat* – now it was in the corridor, and coming fast. *Pit-pat* – all at once it stopped.

There was a moment's breathless silence, and then into the room trotted St Eustache. M. Jacques Courbé sat astride the dog's broad back, as he had so often done in the circus ring. He held a tiny drawn sword; his shoe-button eyes seemed to reflect its steely glitter.

The dwarf brought the dog to a halt in the middle of the room, and took in, at a single glance, the prostrate figure of Jeanne Marie. St Eustache, too, seemed to take silent note of it. The stiff hair on his back rose up, he showed his long white fangs hungrily and his eyes glowed like two live coals.

'So I find you *thus*, madame!' M. Jacques Courbé said at last. 'It is fortunate that I have a charger here who can scent out my enemies as well as hunt them down in the open. Without him, I might have had some difficulty in discovering you. Well, the little game is up. I find you with your lover!'

'Simon Lafleur is not my lover!' she sobbed. 'I have not seen him once since I married you until tonight! I swear it!'

'Once is enough,' the dwarf said grimly. 'The impudent stable-boy must be chastised!'

'Oh, spare him!' Jeanne Marie implored. 'Do not harm him, I beg of you! It is not his fault that I came! I – '

But at this point Simon Lafleur drowned her out in a roar of laughter.

'Ho, ho!' he roared, putting his hands on his hips. 'You would chastise me, eh? *Nom d'un chien*! Don't try your circus trick on *me*! Why, hop-o'-my thumb, you who ride on a dog's back like a flea, out of this room before I squash you! Begone, melt, fade away!' He paused, expanded his barrel-like chest, puffed out his cheeks and blew a great breath at the dwarf. 'Blow away, insect,' he bellowed, 'lest I put my heel on you!'

M. Jacques Courbé was unmoved by this torrent of abuse. He sat very upright on St Eustache's back, his tiny sword resting on his tiny shoulder.

'Are you done?' he said at last, when the bareback rider had run dry of invectives. 'Very well, monsieur! Prepare to receive cavalry!' He paused for an instant, then added in a high, clear voice: 'Get him, St Eustache!'

The dog crouched, and, at almost the same moment, sprang at Simon Lafleur. The bareback rider had no time to avoid him and his tiny rider. Almost instantaneously the three of them had come to death grips. It was a gory business.

Simon Lafleur, strong man as he was, was bowled over by the wolf dog's unexpected leap. St Eustache's clashing jaws closed on his right arm and crushed it to the bone. A moment later the dwarf, still clinging to his dog's back, thrust the point of his tiny sword into the body of the prostrate bareback rider.

Simon Lafleur struggled valiantly, but to no purpose. Now he felt the foetid breath of the dog fanning his neck, and the wasp-like sting of the dwarf's blade, which this time found a mortal spot. A convulsive tremor shook him and he rolled over on his back. The circus Romeo was dead.

M. Jacques Courbé cleansed his sword on a kerchief of lace, dismounted and approached Jeanne Marie. She was still crouching on the floor, her eyes closed, her head held tightly between both hands. The dwarf touched her imperiously on the broad shoulder which had so often carried him.

'Madame,' he said, 'we now can return home. You must be more careful hereafter. *Ma foi*, it is an ungentlemanly business cutting the throats of stableboys!'

She rose to her feet, like a large trained animal at the word of command.

'You wish to be carried?' she said between livid lips.

'Ah, that is true, madame,' he murmured. 'I was forgetting our little wager. Ah, yes! Well, you are to be congratulated, madame – you have covered nearly half the distance.'

'Nearly half the distance,' she repeated in a lifeless voice.

'Yes, Madame,' M. Jacques Courbé continued. 'I fancy that you will be quite a docile wife by the time you have done.' He paused, and then added reflectively: 'It is truly remarkable how speedily one can ride the devil out of a woman – with spurs!'

Papa Copo had been spending a convivial evening at the Sign of the Wild Boar. As he stepped out into the street he saw three familiar figures preceding him – a tall woman, a tiny man and a large dog with upstanding ears. The woman carried the man on her shoulder; the dog trotted at her heels.

The circus owner came to a halt and stared after them. His round eyes were full of astonishment.

'Can it be?' he murmured. 'Yes, it is! Three old friends! And so Jeanne Marie still carries him! Ah, but she should not poke fun at M. Jacques Courbé! He is so sensitive; but, alas, they are the kind that are always henpecked!'

THE AUTHOR
Thorp McClusky
THE STORY
While Zombies Walked
THE MOVIE
Revenge of the Zombies
THE DIRECTOR
Steve Sekely

The Packard roadster had left the lowland and was climbing into the hills. It was rough going; this back road was hardly more than two deep, grass-grown ruts – the car barely crawled. Overhead the vivid greenery of the trees nearly met, shrouding, intensifying the heat.

Eileen's letter had brought Anthony Kent down the Atlantic seaboard, his heart leaden, his thoughts troubled. There had been a strangeness in Eileen's brusque dismissal.

'Tony,' the letter had read, 'you must not come to see me this summer. You must not write to me any more. I do not want to see you or hear from you again!'

It had not been like Eileen – that letter; Eileen would at least have been gentle. It was as though that letter had been dictated by a stranger, as though Eileen had been but a puppet, writing words which were not her own. . . .

'Back in the hills aways,' an emaciated, filthy white man, sitting on the steps of a dilapidated shack just off the through highway, had said sourly, in answer to Tony's inquiry. But Tony, glancing at his speedometer, saw that he had already come three and seven-tenths miles. Had the man deliberately misdirected him? After that first startled glance there had been a curious flat opacity in the man's eyes. . . .

Abruptly, rounding a sharp bend in the narrow road, the car came upon a small clearing, in the heart of which nestled a tiny cabin. But at a glance Tony saw that the cabin was deserted. No smoke curled from the rusty iron stovepipe, no dog lay panting in the deep shade, the windows stared bleakly down the road.

Yet a planting of cotton still struggled feebly against the lush weeds! This was the third successive shack on that miserable road that had been, for some strange reason, suddenly abandoned. The peculiarity of this circumstance escaped Tony. His thoughts, leaden, bewildered, full of the dread that Eileen no longer loved him, were turned too deeply inward upon themselves.

It had been absurd of Eileen – throwing up her job with the Lacey-Kent people to rush off down here the instant she heard of her great-uncle's stroke. Absurd, because she could have done more for the old fellow by remaining in New York.

And yet old Robert Perry had raised his dissolute nephew's little girl almost from babyhood, had put her through Brenau College; Tony realised that Eileen's gesture had been the only one compatible with her nature.

But why had she jilted him?

The woebegone shack had merged into the forest. The road, if anything, was growing worse; the car was climbing a gentle grade. Now, as it topped the rise, Tony saw outspread before his eyes a small valley, hemmed in by wooded hills. A rambling, pillared house, half hidden by mimosa and magnolias, flanked by barns, outbuildings, and a tobacco shed, squatted amid broad, level acres lush with cotton.

At first glance the place seemed peculiarly void of life. No person moved in the wide yard surrounding the house; no smoke curled from the field-stone chimney. But as Tony's gaze swept the broad, undulating fields he saw men working, men who were clad in grimy, dirt-greyed garments that were an almost perfect camouflage. Only a hundred feet down the road a man moved slowly through the cotton.

Tony stopped the car opposite the man.

'Is this the Perry place?' he called, his voice sharp and distinct through the afternoon's heat and stillness.

But the grey-clad toiler never lifted his gaze from the cotton beneath his eyes, never so much as turned his head or paused in his work to signify that he had heard.

Tony felt anger rising in him. His nerves were taut with worry, and he had driven many miles without rest. At least the fellow could leave off long enough to give him a civil answer!

But then, the man might be a little deaf. Tony shrugged, jumped from the car and ploughed through the cotton.

'Is this the Perry place?' he bawled.

The man was not more than six feet from Tony, working toward him, with lowered head and shadowed face. But if he heard, he gave no sign.

Sudden, blind rage swept Tony. Had his nerves not been almost at snapping-point he would never have done what he did; he would have let the man's amazing boorishness pass without a word, would have turned back to his car in disgust. But Tony, that day, was not himself.

'Why you – ' he choked. He took a sudden step forward and jerked the man roughly erect.

For an instant Tony glimpsed the man's eyes, grey, sunken, filmed, expressionless as though the man were either blind or an idiot. And then the man, as if nothing had occurred, was once more slumping over the cotton!

'God Almighty!' Tony breathed. And suddenly a chill like ice pressing against his spine swept him, sent his mind swirling and his knees weakly buckling.

The man wore a shapeless, broad-brimmed hat, fastened on his head by a band of elastic beneath his chin. But the savage shaking Tony had given him had jolted it awry.

Above the man's left temple, amid the grey-flecked hair, jagged splinters of bone gleamed through torn and discoloured flesh! And a greyish ribbon of brain-stuff hung down beside the man's left ear!

The man was working in the cotton – with a fractured skull!

Tony's thoughts were reeling, his mind dazed. How that man could continue to work with his brains seeping through a hole in his head was a question so unanswerable he did not even consider it. And yet, dimly, he remembered the almost miraculous stories that had come out of the war, stories of men who had lived with bullet-holes through their heads and with shell fragments imbedded inches deep within their brain-cases. Something like that must have happened to this man. Some horrible accident must have numbed or destroyed every spark of intelligence in him, must have bizarrely left him with only the mechanical impulse to work.

He must be taken to the house at once, Tony knew. Gently Tony grasped his shoulders. And in the mid-afternoon's heat his nerves crawled.

The stooping body beneath the frayed cotton shirt was snake-cold!

'Lord – he's dying – standing on his feet!' Tony mumbled.

The man resisted Tony's efforts to direct him toward the car. As Tony pushed him gently, he resisted as gently, turning back toward the cotton. As Tony, gritting his teeth, grasped those cold shoulders and tugged with all his strength, the man hung back with a strange, weird tenaciousness.

Suddenly Tony released his grip. He was afraid to risk stunning the man with a blow, for a blow might mean death. Yet, strong as he was, he could not budge the man from the path he was chopping along the cotton.

There was only one thing to do. He must go to the house and get help.

Stumbling, his mind vague with horror, Tony made his way to the car, and sent it hurtling the last half-mile down the narrow road to the house.

Only subconsciously, as he plunged up the uneven walk between fragrant, flowering shrubs, did he notice the strange discrepancy between the well-kept appearance of the fields and the dilapidation of the house. His mind was too full of the plodding horror he had seen. But the windows of the house were almost opaque with dirt, and at some of them dusty curtains hung limply while others stared nakedly blank. The screens on the long low porch were torn and rusted as though they had received no attention since spring; the lawn and the shrubbery were unkempt.

Three or four dust-grey wicker chairs stood along the porch. In one of those chairs sat a man.

He was old, and sparsely built. Had he been standing erect he would have measured well over six feet, but he lay back in his chair with his legs extending supinely before him. Tony knew instantly that this was Eileen's great-uncle, Robert Perry.

As he plunged up the dirt-encrusted steps Tony exclaimed hoarsely, 'Mr Perry? I'm Tony Kent. There's a man – '

The old man was leaning slightly forward in his chair. His blue eyes in his deeply lined face suddenly flamed.

'Have you got a gun?' The words were taut and low.

'No.' Tony shook his head impatiently. His mind was full of the horror he had seen working back there in the field. A gun! What did he want with a gun? Did old Robert Perry think he would be dangerous – the story-book rejected-lover type, perhaps? Nonsense. Urgent, staccato words tumbled from his lips as he ignored the question.

'Mr Perry – there's a man back there with the whole top of his head split open. He's stark mad; he wouldn't speak to me or come with me. But – he'll die if he's left where he is! It's a wonder he isn't dead already.'

There was a long silence before the old man answered. 'Where did you see this man?'

'Back there – back in the cotton.'

Old Robert Perry shook his head, spoke in a muttered whisper, as if to himself, 'Die? He can't – die!'

Abruptly he paused. The screen door leading into the house had opened. Two Negroes and a white man had come out on the porch.

The two Negroes were nondescript enough – mere plantation blacks. But the white man!

He was tall and wide as a door. He was so huge that any person attempting to guess his weight would have considered himself lucky if he got the figure within a score of pounds of the truth; he was bigger than any man Tony had ever seen outside sideshow. And he was not a glandular freak; he was muscled like a jungle beast; his whole posture, his whole carriage silently shrieked super-human vitality. His gargantuan face, beneath the broad-brimmed, rusty black hat he wore, was pale as the belly of a dead fish, pale with the pallor of one who shuns the sunlight. His eyes were wide-set, coal-black, and staring; Tony had glimpsed that same intensity of gaze before in the eyes of religious and sociological fanatics. His nose was fleshy and well-muscled at the tip; his lips were thin and straight and tightly compressed. Garbed as he was in a knee-length, clerical coat of greenish, faded black, still wearing a frayed, filthy-white episcopal collar, he looked what he must have been, a pastor without honour, a renegade man of God.

He stood silently there on the porch and looked disapprovingly at Tony. His thin, weak, reformer's lips beneath that powerful, sensual nose tightened. Then, quietly, he spoke, not to Tony but to the paralytic old man:

'Who is this – person, Mr Perry?'

Tony's fists clenched at the man's insolence. His anger turned to astonishment as he heard the old man answer almost cringingly: 'This is Anthony Kent, Reverend Barnes – Anthony Kent, from New York City. Anthony – the Reverend Warren Barnes, who is stopping with us for a while. He has been very kind to us during my – illness.'

Tony nodded coldly. The funereal-clad colossus stared for a long moment at this unexpected guest, and Tony could feel the menace smouldering in him like banked fires. But when he spoke for the second time his words were innocuous enough.

'I'm temporarily in charge here.' His voice was vibrant as a great hollow drum. 'Mr Perry's mind, since he suffered his most unfortunate stroke, has not always been entirely clear, and Miss Eileen too. I am temporarily without a pastorate, and I am glad to help in any way that I can. You understand, I'm sure?' He smiled, the sickeningly pious smile of the chronic hypocrite, and ostentatiously clasped his hands.

Again Tony nodded. 'Yes, I understand, Reverend,' he said quickly, although some obscure sixth sense had already warned him that this man was as slimy and dangerous as a water-moccasin – and as treacherous. But – that man in the field, working in the cotton with the brain-stuff hanging down behind his ear! Hurriedly, Tony went on, 'I spoke to Mr Perry when I came up the steps – something must be done at once – there's a man working out there in the field beside the road with something seriously wrong with his head. My God, I looked at him, and it looked to me as though his skull was fractured!'

With surprising swiftness the colossus turned upon Tony. 'What's that you say? It looked as though *what*?'

Tony rasped, 'A man working in the field with a fractured skull, Reverend! His head looks staved in – bashed open – God knows how he can still work. He's got to be brought to the house.'

The giant's too brilliant, too intense black eyes were suddenly crafty. He laughed, patronisingly, as though humouring a child or a drunkard. 'Oh, come, come, Mr Kent; such things are impossible, you know. A trick of the light, or perhaps your weariness; you've driven a long distance, haven't you? One's eyes play strange tricks upon one.'

He peered at Tony, and suddenly the expression on his face changed. 'But if you're worried, we'll convince you, put your mind at ease. You go and get Cullen, Mose and Job. Jump smart, niggers!' He pointed up the road. 'Jump smart; bring Cullen back here; Mr Kent's got to be shown.' His thin lips curled scornfully.

The two Negroes 'jumped smart'. The Reverend Warren Barnes calmly seated himself in one of the wicker chairs near paralytic old Robert Perry and waved carelessly toward a vacant chair. Tony sat down – glanced inquiringly at Eileen's uncle. But the aged man remained silent, apathetic, indifferent. Obviously, Tony thought, his mind *was* enfeebled; in that, at least, the Reverend Barnes had been truthful.

Almost diffidently, Tony addressed the white-haired old paralytic.

'I've come here to speak with Eileen, Mr Perry. I can't believe that she meant – what she wrote in her last letter. Regardless of whether or not her feelings toward me have changed. I must speak to her. Where is she?'

When the old man spoke his voice was flat and hard. 'Eileen has written to tell you that she wished to terminate whatever had been between you. Perhaps she has decided that she would prefer not to become too deeply involved with a Northerner. Perhaps she has other reasons. But in any case, Mr Kent, you are not acting the gentleman in coming here and attempting to renew an acquaintanceship that has been quite definitely broken off.'

The words were brutal, and not at all the sort of speech Tony would have expected, a moment ago, from a man whose mind had dimmed through age and shock. A sharp, involuntary retort surged to Tony's lips. Suddenly, then, the Reverend Barnes guffawed loudly.

'There, Mr Kent!' he chuckled. It was a sound utterly unministerial, utterly coarse, sardonic and evil. 'There – coming down the road. Is that the man you saw working in the cotton – with the fractured skull?'

Walking into the yard between the two Negroes was the white man Tony had encountered earlier. He was plodding along steadily, almost rapidly, with no assistance from his coloured companions. The straw hat was set tightly down upon his head, shading his face and covering his temples. There was no bit of greyish stuff hanging down beside his left ear.

The three men halted before the porch. The Reverend Barnes,

grinning broadly, showing great, yellowed, decaying teeth, stood up and put his hands on the porch rail. Abruptly he spoke to Tony.

'Is this the man, Mr Kent?'

Tony, his mind numb with amazement, answered, 'It's the man, all right.'

The Reverend Barnes's grin deepened. 'Are you all right, Cullen? Do you feel quite able to work? Not ill, or anything?'

There was a long, long pause before the man answered. And when at last he spoke, his voice was curiously cadenceless, as though speech were an art he seldom practised. But there was no doubt about what he said.

'Ahm all right, Reverend Barnes. Ah feels good.'

The big man chuckled, as though in appreciation of some ghastly joke.

'You haven't any headache?' he persisted. 'No dizziness from the sun, perhaps? You don't want to knock off for the rest of the day?'

After a moment the reply came.

'Ah ain' got no haidache. Ah kin work.'

The Reverend Barnes smiled pontifically. 'Very well, then, Cullen. You may go back to work.'

'Wait!' Tony exclaimed. 'Tell him to take off his hat.'

The big man wheeled slowly; slowly his right hand lifted, like that of some mighty patriarch about to pronounce a benediction – or a damning curse. For an instant Tony glimpsed murder in his eyes. Then his hand fell, and he spoke smoothly, quietly, to Cullen.

'Take off your hat, Cullen.'

With maddening, mechanical slowness the man lifted his hat, and Tony saw a mat of iron-grey hair, caked with dirt.

'Put your hat back on, Cullen. You may go back to work.'

The man turned, was plodding slowly from the yard. And in that instant, striking vaguely against his dazed consciousness, the realisation came to Tony that only the hair on the left side of the man's skull was matted with ground-in dust – the hair above his right ear was relatively clean! He opened his lips to speak. But the Reverend Barnes, as if anticipating him, was saying with amused, contemptuous finality:

'He's gone back to work. Dirty fellows, aren't they – these poor white trash?'

And Tony, wondering if his own reason were tottering, let the man go. . . .

The big man settled comfortably back in his chair.

'You thought you saw something you didn't,' he said. His voice was soft now, soft and tolerant as silk. 'Eye-strain, nervousness that's very close to hysteria. You must look after yourself.'

For an instant Tony cradled his face in his hands. Yes, he must get hold of himself; his mind was overwrought. He raised his head and looked at the old man. 'Eileen,' he said doggedly. 'I must see her.'

Old Robert Perry opened his lips to speak. And suddenly the big man turned in his chair to stare deeply into the aged paralytic's eyes.

'You would like to see Miss Eileen?' he asked Tony, then, with grave courtesy, 'But certainly, Mr Perry. He's come such a distance; it would be a pity – '

'Whatever you say.'

The Reverend Barnes rose from his chair, smiled sorrowfully and pityingly toward Tony.

'Job, Mose,' he said to the two Negroes, 'stay here on the porch, in case Mr Perry has one of his spells.' He nodded significantly to Tony. 'I'll call Miss Eileen. Such a lovely, sweet girl!'

Leisurely, moving on the balls of his feet like some magnificent jungle beast, he rose and stalked across the porch, opened the rusty screen door and disappeared within the house.

Mr Perry did not speak; neither did Tony. There was something in the air that eluded him, Tony knew – some mystery that even Mr Perry himself concealed, some mystery that seemed as elusive as the breeze stirring the magnolias.

Footsteps within the house, and Eileen Perry, small, slender, with the wistful beauty of a spring flower, came onto the porch. Behind her, as if carelessly, his face overspread with a pious smirk, lounged Reverend Barnes.

Tony started up eagerly.

'Eileen!'

For a moment she did not speak. Only her splendid eyes looked at him hungrily, with ill-concealed terror rising in their depths.

'You shouldn't have come, Tony,' she said then, simply.

The words were a rebuff. Yet Tony fancied that he had seen her hands lift toward him. He took a single step forward. But, as if to elude him, she stepped swiftly to the rail, stood with her back toward him.

'I *had* to come, Eileen,' Tony said. His voice sounded oddly choked. 'I love you. I had to know if you meant – those words you wrote, or if it was some strange madness – '

'Madness?' She laughed, and there was sudden hysteria in her low contralto voice. 'Madness? No. I've changed, Tony. You may think what you please about me; you may think that I'm fickle, or that I'm insane – whatever you will. But – above everything else in the world I did not want you to come here. Is that plain enough for you? I thought I tried to tell you that in my letter. And now – I wish that you would go.'

As a man who dreams a nightmare, Tony heard his own voice, muttering, 'But don't you *love me*, Eileen?'

For a moment he believed that she would speak, but she did not. She turned, and, without a backward look, walked into the house.

The giant, Reverend Barnes, was rubbing his hands together – an incongruous, absurd gesture in a man of his physique. And then, after a moment, he laughed, a hoarse, obscene guffaw. But Tony, heartbroken, heard the insulting sound as no more than a disquieting rumble that had no meaning. His lips quivering, his eyes misty with the sudden tears he could not restrain, he walked slowly across the porch.

Then, as though the longing in them could bring her back to him, his tear-dimmed eyes gazed into the emptiness where Eileen had stood, looked unseeingly across the flowering mimosa, stared downward for a second at the porch rail.

A single word had been written on that rail, written in dust with a fingertip. Tony's mind did not register the significance of that word; it was transmitted only to his subconscious. But, as if mechanically, his lax lips moved.

The sombrely clad giant suddenly tensed, took a step forward.

'What was that you said, Mr Kent?'

Mechanically Tony repeated the word.

The big man's eyes swept the rail. The grin had abruptly gone from his face; his muscles knotted beneath his rusty black coat.

And then he leaped. And simultaneously leaped the two Negroes who had lingered, diffidently, down the porch.

Monstrous, spatulate, pasty-white hands clenched into Tony's throat. Abruptly fighting, not with his numbed brain, but with a primitive, involuntary instinct of the flesh for self-preservation, Tony sent his fists lashing into the pair of black faces before him. But the giant renegade minister was on his shoulders like an albino, shrouded leopard; the negroes were tearing at his arms. His knees were buckling.

Like a slender tree stricken by the woodsman's axe, he wavered and plunged headlong. There was a cascade of darting light as his head crashed against the dusty pine boards. Then came oblivion.

Anthony Kent awoke to swirling, throbbing pain. His skull beat and hammered; the dim walls of a small room, barren save for the straw-mattressed cot on which he lay, swooped and gyrated before his eyes.

Slowly he recalled what had occurred. The Reverend Barnes, that magnificent jackal, had struck him down as he stood on the porch. He was in some long-disused room, presumably a servant's bedchamber, within the old Perry house.

A word was struggling upward from deep within his brain. What was that word? Almost he remembered it. It was the word Eileen had written in dust on the porch rail, a word repulsive and hideous.

Eileen had been trying to tell him something, trying to convey some message to him. Eileen, then, loved him!

What was the word?

There was a small, square window in the room, through which a feeble, yellowish light struck high up on the opposite wall. The sun was setting, then; he had been unconscious for hours. But it was not at the window that Tony glanced despairingly. It was at the two-by-six pine beams nailed closely together across that small square space!

Tony stumbled to his feet, reeled to the window and shook those wooden bars with all his strength. But they were solid white pine, and they had been spiked to the house with twenty-penny nails.

Through the narrow apertures between the beams Tony could

see the broad, level fields, and the road, sloping gently upward to disappear within the encircling forest.

People were coming down that road now, grey, dusty people who plodded toward the house. They appeared almost doll-like, for the room in which Tony was imprisoned was on the side of the house, and long before the road swung in toward the yard they passed beyond his vision. But as Tony watched them his nerves crawled.

They walked so slowly, so listlessly, with dragging footsteps! And they stumbled frequently against one another, and against the stones in the road, as though they were almost blind. Almost they walked like soldiers suffering from shell-shock, but recently discharged from some hospital in hell.

For many were maimed. One walked with a deep, broken stoop, as though his chest had been crushed against his backbone. Another's leg was off below the knee, and in place of an artificial limb he wore a stick tied against the leg with rope, a stick that reached from twelve inches beyond the stump to the hip. A third had only one arm; a fourth was skeleton-thin.

In the Name of God whence had these maimed toilers come?

And then a soundless scream rattled in Tony's throat; for, coming down the road alone, walking with the same dragging lifelessness as did the others, was another of the grey toilers. And, as the man turned the wide sweep in the road that would lead him to the house and beyond Tony's vision, Tony glimpsed, in the last yellow rays of the setting sun, the horror that had once been his face!

Had once been his face! For, from beneath the ridge of his nose downward, *the man had no face*! The vertebrate whiteness of his spine, naked save for ragged strings of dessicated flesh, extended with horrid starkness from the throat of his shirt to merge with the shattered base of a bony skull!

Hideous minutes passed, minutes through which Tony fought to retain some semblance of sanity. At last he staggered weakly to the door, only one thought in his mind – to escape that mad place and take Eileen with him.

But the door, like the bars across the window, was made of heavy pine. From its resistance to his assault Tony knew that it was secured by bars slotted through iron sockets. It was impregnable.

Darkness was within that room now. Night had come quickly with the setting of the sun, velvety, semi-tropical night. The window was a purplish square through which a star gleamed brilliantly; the pine bars were invisible in the gloom. Tony was engulfed in blackness.

Yet, in a corner near the floor, there was a lessening of the darkness. Tony, crouching there, saw that the light came through a quarter-inch crack between the planks. Throwing himself down, he glued his eyes to that crack.

He could see only a small portion of the room beneath him, a rectangle roughly three feet by twelve, yet that was enough to tell him that the room was the dining-room of the old house. The middle of an oaken table, littered with dishes and scraps of food, bisected his field of vision.

At that table, his back toward Tony, sat the apostate Reverend Barnes. A little way down the table a black hand and arm appeared and disappeared with irregular frequency. The rumble of voices floated upward through the narrow slit.

'God!' Tony thought. 'If only I had a gun!'

He remembered, then, that the old paralytic had asked him if he had a gun.

From the mutter of voices Tony guessed that there were three men seated about that table; the two Negroes were talking volubly yet with a low, curious tenseness; the Reverend Barnes interrupting only infrequently with monosyllabic grunts. All three seemed to be waiting.

Beside the big man's pallid white hand, on the naked oaken table, sprawling disjointedly amid soggy bits of bread and splotches of grease and chicken bones, lay an incongruous object, a little doll that had been wretchedly sewn together from various bits of cotton cloth. It possessed a face, crudely drawn with black grease or charcoal, and a tuft of kinky hair surmounted the shapeless little bag that represented its head. Obviously it caricatured a Negro.

From time to time, hunching over the table like a great gross idol, his shiny, worn clerical coat taut across his massive shoulders, the renegade minister would pick up the little rag doll, flop its lax arms and legs about, and put it down again.

Suddenly, then, a door, invisible to Tony, opened and closed. The conversation of the two Negroes abruptly ceased. Two black men shuffed slowly across the dining room floor, came close to the table, opposite the colossus. Tony could see them both.

The face of one was rigid and grim, and he held his companion firmly by the arm. The second Negro was swaying drunkenly. His lips were loose and his eyes bleared. Yet there was terror in him.

The Reverend Barnes hunched lower over the table. Tony could see the big muscles in his back ribbing beneath his rusty coat, and the big brass collar-button at the back of his pillar-like neck. 'You're here at last, nigger?' he asked softly. 'You're late. What delayed you? They came from the cotton a long time ago, we have already eaten supper.'

The drunken man mouthed some reply that was unintelligible, terror-ridden.

The giant's shoulders seemed to tighten into a ball of muscle. 'You're drunk, nigger.' he said, and his voice trembled with contemptuous loathing. 'I smell corn liquor on your breath. It stifles me; how any man can so degrade himself – 'Look not upon the wine when it is red.' He paused. 'You fool; I told you not to drink. How can you stay down the road and watch for strangers if you're drunk? You can't be trusted to wave the sheet when you're drunk. You failed today. What have you to say for yourself?'

Words tumbled from the man's slobbering mouth. 'Ahm not drunk. Ah tuk de cawn foh toofache – '

The giant shrugged. 'A stranger came up the road today before we could hide them in the cotton. You're drunk, nigger. I have forgiven you twice. But this is the third time.'

He picked up the little doll.

'This is you, nigger. This is made with your sweat and your hair – '

A scream burst from the man's throat. He had begun to shake horribly.

'Hold him, niggers,' the giant said imperturbably. 'I want to study this; I want to watch it work.'

Black hands grasped the writhing, shuddering man.

The Reverend Barnes picked up a fork. He was holding the little doll in his left hand, looking at it speculatively. And it seemed to Tony – although it may have been a trick of the light – that the lifeless doll writhed and moved of itself, in ghastly synchronisation with the trembling and shuddering of the terror-maddened human it caricatured.

Carefully, the Reverend Barnes stuck a prong of the fork through a leg of the doll. There was a slight rending of cotton.

The shuddering wretch screamed – horribly! And the colossus nodded his head as if in satisfaction.

Again the fork probed into the doll. But this time the big man jabbed all four tines through the little doll's middle.

And this time no scream, but only a gasping, rending moan came from the Negro so firmly held by the strong hands of his kind. And suddenly he was hanging limply there, like a slaughtered thing. . . .

The Reverend Barnes pulled the fork from the doll, tossed the torn doll carelessly on the floor.

'He's dead, niggers,' he said then, callously, 'He's stone dead.'

As Tony lay sprawled on that rough pine flooring, peering down with horrified fascination into the room below, the incredible realisation grew and grew in him that he had witnessed the exercise of powers so primitive, so elemental, so barbaric that descendants of the so-called higher civilisations utterly disbelieve them.

God! Was this voodoo? Perhaps, but the Reverend Barnes was a white man; how had he become an adept? Was it something akin to voodoo but deeper, darker? Had that wretched Negro died through fright, or had there really been some horrible affinity between his living body and the lifeless doll?

What of the thing without a face, walking down the road?

The word that Eileen had written in the dust on the porch rail was hammering at Tony's consciousness. Almost he grasped it, yet it eluded him. An unfamiliar word, reeking of evil. . . .

For a long time there was only silence from the room below – silence, and a thickening haze of bluish smoke. The Negroes, Tony guessed, were smoking, although the big man almost directly beneath his eyes was not. Abruptly, then, the Reverend Barnes rose to his feet. Tony heard him walk across the floor; there was the sound of a door opening, and then a deep, throaty chuckle.

'No need for you to do the dishes tonight, Miss Eileen. Just leave them where they are; we don't need them any more. Come with me; I'm going to take you back to your room.'

Tony heard the man padding heavily yet softly across the floor, and Eileen's reluctant, lighter footsteps. The dining-room door opened and closed.

Tony stumbled to his feet, then shook the door with a despair that was almost madness. Exhausted at last, he clung limply to the iron latch, panting.

Minutes passed – minutes that seemed hours.

Suddenly, from close to his ears, Tony heard muffled sounds of sobbing. Eileen, crying as though her heart was broken, was imprisoned in the next room!

'Eileen!'

Abruptly the sobbing ceased.

'Tony!' The girl's voice came almost clearly into the room, as though she had moved close to the wall. 'You didn't – escape them, Tony?'

'They ganged me,' Tony said grimly. 'I think they were going to let me go, but that big two-faced rattlesnake saw what you wrote on the porch rail, and then they jumped me.'

There was a gasp from beyond the wall and then a long silence. At last Eileen said, softly and penitently, 'I'm sorry, Tony. I thought that you would read it and – understand – and come back later with help. I'm sorry that I got you into this, Tony. I tried to keep you out. But when you came here I-I loved you so, and I wanted so terribly to escape. I had a wild hope that when you got safe away, even though you didn't understand, you would ask someone who knew and could tell you what zombies meant – '

Zombies! That was the word she had written in dust on the porch rail! And instantly, with kaleidoscopic clarity, there flashed across Tony's brain a confusion of mental images he had acquired through the years – an illustration from a book on jungle rites – a paragraph from a voodoo thriller – scenes from one or two fantastic motion pictures he had witnessed. . . .

Zombies! Corpses kept alive by hideous sorcery to work and toil without food or water or pay – mindless, dead things that outraged Nature with every step they took! These were zombies, the books glibly said, grim products of Afro-Haitian superstition. . . .

The men who wrote those books had never suggested that zombies might be real – that the powers which controlled them might be an heritage of the blacks exactly as self-hypnotism is a highly developed faculty among the Hindus. No, the books had been patronisingly written, with more than a hint of amused superiority evident in them; their authors had incredibly failed to understand that even savages could not practise elaborate rites unless there was efficacy in them. . . .

'Zombies!' Tony muttered dazedly. And then, eagerly, 'But – you love me, Eileen I knew it; I knew you couldn't mean those things you wrote – '

'He made me write them,' Eileen whispered. 'He – came here in the spring, Tony. Uncle thinks that they ran him away – from wherever he was – before. He brought four Negroes with him.

'Uncle was old, Tony, and he didn't keep much help here – only six or seven coloured men. The place was run down, Tony; after Uncle had put me through college he didn't have much incentive for keeping it up; he's always told me that I could have it for a sort of country home – after he died.

'But then – this man who said he had been a minister came, and saw all these unworked acres and how isolated the place was.

'He went to Uncle, and told Uncle that he would furnish extra help if Uncle would give him half the crop.

'It was after the – help came that Uncle's Negroes left. Some of them even moved out of their shacks – out of the county. And this man – this Reverend Barnes, had already made a little doll and told Uncle that it was supposed to represent him. He tied the little doll's legs together with Uncle's hair and told Uncle that with stiff legs Uncle wouldn't be able to run away and get help. He told Uncle that any time he wanted to, he could stick a pin through the little doll and Uncle would die.

'And – Uncle can't move his legs! It's true, Tony, every word he said. That man, that – devil, can do anything he says.

'He read all my letters to Uncle, and all of Uncle's letters to me, too, before he sent them down to the post office. He tried to keep me from coming here.

'And when I did come he made another doll, Tony, to represent me. It's stuffed with my hair, Tony; they held me while he cut my hair. He's got little dolls that represent everyone here; he keeps them in a bag inside his shirt.

'*He can kill us all, Tony, whenever he pleases!*'

Hysteria had begun to creep into her voice. She paused for a moment. When she went on, her voice was calmer.

'He keeps one of his coloured men as a lookout in a tree at the top of the hill. The man can see way down to the main road. When he sees anyone turn up this way he opens out a big sheet and they hide the – *helpers* – '

Tony chuckled grimly.

'He didn't open out the sheet today,' he muttered. 'He was drunk.' He tried to make his voice sound confident. 'Eileen, sweetheart – we'll have to get out of this. It shouldn't be impossible, if we can only keep calm and try and think.'

There was a silence. Then Eileen's words came back with quiet, hopeless finality.

'We can't break out of these rooms, Tony. The house is too strongly built. And – I think that tonight he's going to do something dreadful to us. I think that he's afraid to stay here any longer. But before he leaves this place he's going to – Tony, I know that man! He's ruthless, and he's – mad. Sometimes I think that he was really a minister. But not now, not now. He's pure devil now!'

How long Tony and Eileen, with the terrible earnestness of despair, talked to each other through the wall that night, neither ever knew. But it must have been for hours, for they talked of many things, yet never of the horror that menaced them. And they spoke calmly, quietly, with gentle tenderness. . . .

Why should the doomed speak of that which they cannot evade?

Both knew that they were utterly in the giant madman's hands, to do with, save for a miracle, as he pleased. Both knew that the apostate minister was merciless. . . .

There was no moon. But it must have been close to midnight when Tony heard the footsteps of several men on the stairs, the grating of the locks on Eileen's door, the sound of a brief, futile struggle, and then Eileen's despairing cry, 'Good-bye, Tony, sweet – '

Frothing like a rabid beast, he hurled himself at the door, at the barred window, at the walls, beating at them with his naked fists until his knuckles were raw and numb and sweat poured in rivulets from his body.

Grim minutes passed. And then the footsteps returned. There was the sound of pine bars being withdrawn. Tony waited, crouching.

When they entered he leaped. But there was no strength in him – only a terrible, hopeless fury. Quickly they seized his arms, bound his hands firmly behind him with rope, dragged him, struggling impotently, down a steep flight of stairs, through the ground floor hall, and down a second flight of stairs, musty and noisome.

Here they paused for a moment while they fumbled with the latch of a door. At last the door swung open, and they dragged Tony forward into an immense, dimly lit chamber. The door swung shut; the old-fashioned iron latch clicked.

This was the cellar of the plantation-house, an enormous, cavernous place, extending beneath the whole rambling structure. Once designed for the storage of everything necessary to the subsistence of the householders living on the floors above, its vast spaces were broken by immense, mouldy bins. An eight-foot cistern loomed gigantically in a dark corner; wine shelves extended along one entire wall. The whole monstrous place had been dug half from the clayey soil and half from the solid rock; the floor underfoot, rough and uneven, was seamed and stratified rock.

Two oil lanterns, hanging from beams in the cobwebby ceiling, lighted no more than the merest fraction of that great vault; the farther recesses were shrouded in blackness.

The three Negroes – Mose, Job, and the man who had brought in the drunken lookout – waited expectantly, their black hands strong on Tony's arms. And suddenly Tony was a raging fury, tearing madly at those restraining hands . . .

There in the centre of the old cellar, kneeling over a small, fragile form lying still and motionless on the mouldy rock, was the gigantic, black clad Reverend Barnes!

That still, fragile form was Eileen!

At the sound of Tony's struggles the giant looked up, stood erect. Great beads of perspiration bedewed his unnaturally pallid forehead – yet there was a pursy, significant grin on his face.

'Hard work, this, Mr Kent,' he said genially. 'Much harder work than you would think.'

'*What are you doing to her!*'

There was exultant triumph in the booming reply.

'I am binding her with a spell, so that she will always do what I say. This is powerful obeah, Mr Kent. I never dreamed – ' He paused, while a swift dark shadow overspread his huge face, so strong and yet so weak. But the shadow passed as swiftly as it had come, and once again his eyes blazed with evil. Within a few moments I shall put the same spell on you, also, so that you too will always do what I say.'

Chuckling, he spoke to Tony's guards.

'Tie his feet securely and pitch him there by the wine-bin. I'll not want him until later.'

With both his hands and feet tightly bound, the three Negroes dumped Tony down on the jagged rock beside the wine-bin. Tony's face was turned toward where the fallen minister squatted beneath the lanterns, a monstrous, Luciferian image.

'Sit down on the floor, niggers,' he said slowly. 'Relax and rest; there's no need to stand.' The deep, resonant voice throbbed with kindliness. 'I must think.'

Obediently, the three squatted in a row on their haunches and sat looking with silent expectation at this white conjur-man who was their master.

The frock-coated figure shook its head slowly, as though its brain were cobwebby. Then, slowly, it opened the front of its filthy linen shirt, baring the grey-white of its chest – the chest of a powerful and sedentary man, who yet had always shunned the healthful sunlight – the chest of a physical animal whose warped brain had, perhaps through most of its years, abhorred the physical as immoral and unclean. A bag hung there at the figure's chest, suspended by a cord around its neck. Two big hands dipped into that gaping pouch. . . .

Tony was struggling, struggling, rolling his body back and forth in straining jerks, trying to loosen the ropes that bound his feet and hands.

That bag of cotton dolls! One of those dolls represented Eileen.

Tony's shoulder crashed against the beams beneath the wine-bins, leaped with pain as an exposed nail tore the flesh. But the ropes held. . . .

The big man's forearms, beneath the shiny black coat, were suddenly bulging – and in that instant the three Negroes who had been squatting on their haunches were rolling and writhing on the floor, their hands clawing at their throats, their bodies jerking and twisting, their faces purpling, their eyes bulging!

Slow minutes passed. And still the giant, renegade minister crouched there, motionless, his big forearms knotted, his face drawn into a sardonic grimace.

The struggles of the three were becoming feebler. Their arms and legs were beating spasmodically, as though consciousness had gone from them. And at last even that spasmodic twitching ceased and they lay still.

Yet the Reverend Barnes did not stir.

But then, after it seemed to Tony that an eternity had passed, he withdrew his hands from the bag. In his left hand he held by the throat two little cotton dolls, in his right hand, one. With a careless gesture he tossed them to the floor, rose to his feet, and stood slowly flexing and unflexing his fingers. At last he stooped over the three motionless Negroes and grunted with satisfaction.

'Fools, to think that I would ever keep you after your work was done!' He was swaying slightly. Seemingly he had forgotten Tony.

But Tony was stealthily, warily sawing his bound hands back and forth, back and forth across the bit of nail that jutted from the base of the wine-bin. Strand by strand he was breaking the half-inch hemp.

The Reverend Barnes had returned to his position beside Eileen, was once more squatting beside her. She had not moved. But she lay unbound; the colossus was very sure of his sorcery!

For long minutes he sat motionless, his shoulders drooped, his muscles flaccid. At last, with a deep sigh, he raised his head and looked at Eileen.

'Beautiful, beautiful womanhood!' he whispered softly. 'All my life I've wanted a woman like you – '

He reached out a big, splayed and unhealthily colourless hand, touched Eileen's body. Beneath his gentle touch she stirred and moaned.

And suddenly Tony was cursing him wildly.

'Damn you; you hound of hell in priest's clothing!'

The Reverend Barnes's huge hand paused in its caressing.

'You feel jealousy, Mr Kent?'

Tony could not see the expression on the man's face; he was a black-robed bulk against the lantern light. But there was a terrible gentleness in his voice.

'You filthy – ' Tony choked. Words would no longer come to him; his rage was beyond words.

'Mr Kent,' the big man said softly, and Tony sensed that a slow, utterly evil smile was stealing across his face, 'in a little while – such a little while – you'll no longer care what I do with her. You'll be beyond caring.'

He swung about to face Tony.

'But – before I – dispose of you,' he continued, with startling unexpectedness, 'I'm going to tell you the – truth about myself. Why? Perhaps because I want to explain myself, to justify myself to myself. I don't know. Perhaps, in this moment, I have a sudden clear premonition of God's inevitable vengeance – for I am damned, Kent; I know full well that I am damned.

'I have been a preacher for twenty years, Kent. Not the soft-spoken, politically-minded type that ultimately lands the rich city churches; sin was too real to me for that; I fought the Devil tooth and claw.

'Perhaps that was the trouble. My ecclesiastical superiors were never certain of me. They thought of me as a sort of volcano that might explode at any time; I was unpredictable. And they suspected, too, I think, the devil in me – the physical lustiness and the desire for material things I fought so hard to stifle. They gave me only the poorest, back-country churches, they starved me; I was hungry for a mate and I could not even afford a wife. I think they hoped that I would fall into sin, so that they might thus be circumspectly rid of me.

'My last church was a pine shack twenty miles deep in a swamp. My parishioners were almost all Negroes – Negroes and a few whites so poverty-stricken that not one had ever seen a railway train or worn factory-made shoes. And inbreeding, in that disease-ridden country, was the rule, not the exception; you have no idea. . . .

'I worked, there in that earthly hell, like a madman. There was something there, something tangible, for me to fight – and I have always been a literal man. It was a shaman – what you would call a medicine-man or witch doctor. He was, of course, a coloured man.

'It may sound incredible, but I *competed* against that man for almost a year. We were exactly like rival salesmen. I sold faith, and enforced my sales with threats of hell-fire and damnation; he manufactured charms and love-potions, prophesied the future and healed the sick.

'Of course I went after him hammer and tongs. I blasted him in church; I ridiculed him; I told those poor ignorant people that his salves and his potions and his prophecies were no good. Eight months after I arrived there I began to feel that I was winning. . . .

'After about a year had passed he came to see me. We knew each other, of course; I will describe him – a very gentle old man, very tall, very thin and grey. He told me that he wanted me to go away. I think that he knew my weakness, the bitterness in me, better than I knew it myself.

'He raised no religious arguments; in fact, I don't think there were ever any really fundamental differences between us. You know that Holy Writ speaks of witches and warlocks and demons, and my chief objection to this man lay in my private conviction that he was a faker, a mumbo-jumbo expert pulling the wool over the eyes of fools. And, even though I am a fundamentalist, still, this is the twentieth century. The upshot of it was that I laughed at him and listened.

'He merely told me that if I would go away he would teach me his power. What power? I said. I should have known that he was trying to trap me – to strike a bargain. He looked at me. "Among other things, to raise the dead, that they may do your bidding," he said, very slowly and seriously, "although I have never myself done this obeah, because there has never been the need."

'I laughed at him very loudly then, and for a long time.

' "Well," I told him, after I got my breath back, "I am a pretty poor preacher – if the calibre of my parish offers any criterion whatever. Perhaps I am not destined for the life of a minister, after all. Certainly my superiors don't think so. Therefore, if you will teach me these things of which you speak, and if they work, I will never preach another word as long as I live. But, if they do not work, you will come to church on Sunday, and proclaim yourself a faker before the entire congregation."

'I felt very sure of myself, then, and I expected him to attempt to avoid the showdown. But he only answered me, quietly and gravely, "I am the seventh son of a seventh son. I will teach you the obeah my father taught me, and if it works you will go away."

'So – and I will tell you that I kept my tongue in my cheek all the while – I learned the rituals he taught me, learned them word for word, and wrote them down, phonetically, on paper to his dictation.

'But – he had not lied!'

The black-clad giant paused, and Tony saw that he was trembling. Presently the trembling passed, and, in a quiet, colourless monotone, the apostate minister added, 'I knew, then, that I was eternally damned.'

Tony shook his head. 'No. Give up this – madness. No man has ever had the power to – condemn his own soul!'

The colossus shook its head; Tony could see a sneer hardening on its lips.

'I'll – pay! Because I have, now, what I have always wanted – power! Power over other men – and women! Shall I tell you what I am presently going to do with you? I'm going to make you so that you will forget everything; you will walk and talk only when I tell you to; you will do only what I say. You have money; I will make you take your car, and drive Miss Eileen and me to New York. There you will go to the bank, or wherever it is you keep your money, and draw everything out for me. Then, once again, you will get in your car and drive, but this time you will be alone, and while you are driving I will stick a pin into a little doll. "Heart-failure," the doctors will say.'

For a moment Tony did not speak. Then with a strange steadiness, he asked: 'But – Eileen?'

The big man chuckled. 'You ask that question of a man who has denied himself women through all his life? Eileen will belong to me.'

Abruptly, ignoring the bound, suddenly raging man on the floor beside the wine-bin, he turned away. But now, when again he squatted close to Eileen, he did not remain motionless. From somewhere about his clothing he produced a needle and thread, and bits of cloth, and he was sewing. And as he sewed he muttered strange words to himself, in a tongue Tony had never heard before, muttered those words in a cadenceless monotone, as though he himself did not understand them, but was repeating them by rote, as perhaps, they had been taught to him by some aged coloured wizard . . .

Tony's bound wrists rubbed back and forth, back and forth across the nail. Suddenly the strands binding his hands loosed.

Slowly, inch by inch, Tony hunched along the wine-bin, drawing up his feet. Warily he watched the big, crouching man; at any moment the Reverend Barnes might notice. . . .

But seemingly, the colossus was too preoccupied.

In furtive, small strokes, Tony's ankles sawed across the nail.

Suddenly the apostate minister stood up. He was looking at his handiwork, a grotesque little thing of odds and ends, crudely sewn yet unmistakably, with its limp, flopping appendages, a doll. And then he grunted approvingly, came toward Tony with the doll in his left hand.

'I'll have to take a few strands of your hair,' he said grimly. His right hand reached downward toward Tony's scalp.

And then Tony's hands lashed from behind his back, clutched the pillar-like legs, strained. Abruptly the colossus sprawled his length on the uneven rock, his hands out-splayed. The little doll slid unheeded across the cold stone.

Jack-knifing his bound feet beneath him, Tony hurled himself across the floor. And with that tremendous effort the frayed ropes about his ankles ripped away.

Instantly he was atop the big man, his fingers sunk deep into the pasty white throat, his legs locked about giant hips.

But his antagonist's strength seemed superhuman. Only a half hour before those spatulate hands, as surely as though they had been about black throats, had simultaneously strangled three men. Rope-like torso muscles tautened; powerful hands tore at Tony's forearms.

The powerful hands lifted, tightened about Tony's throat. And as those huge talons flexed, a roaring began in Tony's ears, red spots danced madly before his eyes, the dim cellar swirled and heaved.

The colossus, hands still locked about Tony's throat, surged slowly to his feet. Contemptuously he looked into Tony's bloodshot, staring eyes, hurled him reeling across the rock-gouged vault.

And in that instant something hard and sharp split the base of his skull like an intolerable lightning. Bright sparks spun crazily before his eyes – flickered out in utter blackness. He felt himself falling, falling into eternity. . . .

Old Robert Perry, his eyes blazing with inhuman hate, stood above the Reverend Barnes's sprawling corpse, watching the red blood dim the lustre of the axe-blade he had sunk inches deep into the giant's skull!

'That hellish paralysis!' he was babbling, inanely. 'That hellish paralysis – gone just in time!'

Old Robert Perry wheeled. In the feeble yellow light beneath the lantern he saw Eileen, awake now, huddled on the floor, pointing – her eyes pools of horror. And, following with his gaze her outstretched hand, he saw them, coming from the dark bins, the dead things the fallen minister had torn from their graves to toil in the cotton! They came pouring from those great bins with dreadful haste, their faces no longer stony and still, but writhing and tortured. And from the mouths of those that yet possessed mouths poured wild wailings.

Old Robert Perry was trembling – trembling.

'God!' he mumbled. 'Their master's dead, and now they seek their graves!'

Dimly, as one who dreams in fever, he saw them passing him, no longer with stumbling, hopeless footsteps, but hurriedly, eagerly, crowding one another aside in their haste to escape into the night and return to their graves. And the flesh on his back crawled, and loosed, and crawled again. . . .

The zombies, dead things no longer beneath the fallen giant's unholy spell, twisted, broken, rotted by the diseases that had killed them, seeking the graves from which they had been torn!

'God!'

And then they were gone, gone in the night, and the sound of their wailing was a diminishing, scattering thinness in the distance. . . .

Old Robert Perry stared dazedly about, at Eileen, huddled on the floor, sobbing with little, half-mad cries that wrung his heart – at Tony, staggering drunkenly to his feet, stumbling blindly toward his beloved.

'Eileen!'

The name reached out from Tony's heart like the caress of strong arms. Reeling, he followed that cry across the floor to her, dropped to the rock beside her, gathered her in his arms.

Dawn was near when at last old Robert Perry and young Anthony Kent trudged wearily through the purple night toward the plantation house.

The belated moon, preceding the sun by only a few hours, glimmered in the east, a golden, enchanted shield; the woods were still.

The two men did not speak. Their thoughts were full of the horror that had been, of the great pit they had dug in the night and filled with the bodies of the giant renegade and his followers.

Yet, as they drew closer and closer to the rambling old house that nestled, moonbathed and serene, in the valley beneath them, words came at last.

'Anthony Kent,' the old planter said earnestly, 'I have lived on this land through near four generations. I have heard the Negroes talk – of things like this. But I would never have believed – unless the truth had been thrust in my face.'

Tony Kent shifted his spade to his left shoulder before he replied.

'Perhaps it's better,' he said slowly, 'that men are inclined to scepticism. Perhaps, as time goes on, these evil, black arts will die out. It may all be part of some divine plan.'

Their footsteps made little crunching sounds in the road.

'Thank God that the fiend and his niggers were strangers hereabouts!' the old man said fervently. 'They won't be missed. Nobody of course, would ever believe – what really happened.'

'No,' Tony said. 'But it's all over, now. Those dead things have gone – back to their graves.'

They were close to the house. On the long walk, before the low screened porch, a small white-clad figure waited. And then it was running swiftly, eagerly toward them.

'Eileen!'

The name was a pulsing song. And then she was locked in Tony's arms, and he was kissing her upturned, tremulous lips.

THE AUTHOR
Philip K. Dick
THE STORY
*We Can Remember It
For You Wholesale*
THE MOVIE
Total Recall
THE DIRECTOR
Paul Verhoeven

He awoke – and wanted Mars. The valleys, he thought. What would it be like to trudge among them? Great and greater yet: the dream grew as he became fully conscious, the dream and the yearning. He could almost feel the enveloping presence of the other world, which only Government agents and high officials had seen. A clerk like himself? Not likely.

'Are you getting up or not?' his wife Kirsten asked drowsily, with her usual hint of fierce crossness. 'If you are, push the hot coffee button on the darn stove.'

'Okay,' Douglas Quail said, and made his way barefoot from the bedroom of their conapt to the kitchen. There, having dutifully pressed the hot coffee button, he seated himself at the kitchen table, brought out a yellow, small tin of fine Dean Swift snuff. He inhaled briskly, and the Beau Nash mixture stung his nose, burned the roof of his mouth. But still he inhaled; it woke him up and allowed his dreams, his nocturnal desires and random wishes, to condense into a semblance of rationality.

I will go, he said to himself. *Before I die I'll see Mars.*

It was, of course, impossible, and he knew this even as he dreamed. But the daylight, the mundane noise of his wife now brushing her hair before the bedroom mirror – everything conspired to remind him of what he was. A *miserable little salaried employee*, he said to himself with bitterness. Kirsten reminded him of this at least once a day and he did not blame her; it was a wife's job to bring her husband down to Earth. *Down to Earth*, he thought, and laughed. The figure of speech in this was literally apt.

'What are you sniggering about?' his wife asked as she swept into the kitchen, her long busy-pink robe wagging after her. 'A dream, I bet. You're always full of them.'

'Yes,' he said, and gazed out the kitchen window at the hovercars and traffic runnels, and all the little energetic people hurrying to work. In a little while he would be among them. As always.

'I'll bet it has to do with some woman,' Kirsten said witheringly.

'No,' he said. 'A god. The god of war. He has wonderful craters with every kind of plant-life growing deep down in them.'

'Listen.' Kirsten crouched down beside him and spoke earnestly, the harsh quality momentarily gone from her voice. 'The bottom of the ocean – *our* ocean is much more, an infinity of times more beautiful. You know that; everyone knows that. Rent an artificial gill-outfit for both of us, take a week off from work, and we can descend and live down there at one of those year-round aquatic resorts. And in addition – ' She broke off. 'You're not listening. You should be. Here is something a lot better than that compulsion, that obsession you have about Mars, and you don't even listen!' Her voice rose piercingly. 'God in heaven, you're doomed, Doug! What's going to become of you?'

'I'm going to work,' he said, rising to his feet, his breakfast forgotten. 'That's what's going to become of me.'

She eyed him. 'You're getting worse. More fanatical every day. Where's it going to lead?'

'To Mars,' he said, and opened the door to the closet to get down a fresh shirt to wear to work.

Having descended from the taxi Douglas Quail slowly walked across three densely-populated foot runnels and to the modern, attractively inviting doorway. There he halted, impeding mid-morning traffic, and with caution read the shifting-color neon sign. He had, in the past, scrutinized this sign before . . . but never had he come so close. This was very different; what he did now was something else. Something which sooner or later had to happen.

REKAL, INCORPORATED

Was this the answer? After all, an illusion, no matter how convincing, remained nothing more than an illusion. At least objectively. But subjectively – quite the opposite entirely.

And anyhow he had an appointment. Within the next five minutes.

Taking a deep breath of mildly smog-infested Chicago air, he walked through the dazzling polychromatic shimmer of the doorway and up to the receptionist's counter.

The nicely-articulated blonde at the counter, bare-bosomed and tidy, said pleasantly, 'Good morning, Mr Quail.'

'Yes,' he said. 'I'm here to see about a Rekal course. As I guess you know.'

'Not "rekal" but *re*call,' the receptionist corrected him. She picked up the receiver of the vidphone by her smooth elbow and said into it, 'Mr Douglas Quail is here, Mr McClane. May he come inside, now? Or is it too soon?'

'Giz wetwa wum-wum wamp.' the phone mumbled.

'Yes, Mr Quail,' she said. 'You may go in; Mr McClane is expecting you.' As he started off uncertainly she called after him, 'Room D, Mr Quail. To your right.'

After a frustrating but brief moment of being lost he found the proper room. The door hung open and inside, at a big genuine walnut desk, sat a genial-looking man, middle-aged, wearing the latest Martian frog-pelt gray suit; his attire alone would have told Quail that he had come to the right person.

'Sit down, Douglas,' McClane said, waving his plump hand toward a chair which faced the desk. 'So you want to have gone to Mars. Very good.'

Quail seated himself, feeling tense. 'I'm not so sure this is worth the fee,' he said. 'It costs a lot and as far as I can see I really get nothing.' *Costs almost as much as going*, he thought.

'You get tangible proof of your trip,' McClane disagreed emphatically. 'All the proof you'll need. Here; I'll show you.' He dug within a drawer of his impressive desk. 'Ticket stub.' Reaching into a manila folder, he produced a small square of embossed cardboard. 'It proves you went – and returned. Postcards.' He laid out four franked picture 3-D full-color postcards in a neatly-arranged row on the desk for Quail to see. 'Film. Shots you took of local sights on Mars with a rented moving camera.' To Quail he displayed those, too. 'Plus the names of people you met, two hundred poscreds worth of souvenirs, which will arrive – from Mars – within the following month. And passport, certificates listing the shots you received. And more.' He glanced up keenly at Quail. 'You'll know you went, all right,' he said. 'You won't remember us, won't remember me or ever having been here. It'll be a real trip in your mind; we guarantee that. A full two weeks of recall; every last piddling detail. Remember this: if at any time you doubt that you really took an extensive trip to Mars you can return here and get a full refund. You see?'

'But I didn't go,' Quail said. 'I won't have gone, no matter what proofs you provide me with.' He took a deep, unsteady breath. 'And I never was a secret agent with Interplan.' It seemed impossible to him that Rekal, Incorporated's extra-factual memory implant would do its job – despite what he had heard people say.

'Mr Quail,' McClane said patiently. 'As you explained in your letter to us, you have no chance, no possibility in the slightest, of ever actually getting to Mars; you can't afford it, and what is much more important, you could never qualify as an undercover agent for Interplan or anybody else. This is the only way you can achieve your, ahem, life-long dream; am I not correct, sir? You can't be this; you can't actually do this.' He chuckled. 'But you can *have been* and have done. We see to that. And our fee is reasonable; no hidden charges.' He smiled encouragingly.

'Is an extra-factual memory that convincing?' Quail asked.

'More than the real thing, sir. Had you really gone to Mars as an Interplan agent, you would by now have forgotten a great deal; our analysis of true-mem systems – authentic recollections of major events in a person's life – shows that a variety of details are very quickly lost to the person. Forever. Part of the package we offer you is such deep implantation of recall that nothing is forgotten. The packet which is fed to you while you're comatose is the creation of trained experts, men who have spent years on Mars; in every case we verify details down to the last iota. And you've picked a rather easy extra-factual system; had you picked Pluto or wanted to be Emperor of the Inner Planet Alliance we'd have much more difficulty . . . and the charges would be considerably greater.'

Reaching into his coat for his wallet, Quail said, 'Okay. It's been my life-long ambition and so I see I'll never really do it. So I guess I'll have to settle for this.'

'Don't think of it that way,' McClane said severely. 'You're not accepting second-best. The actual memory, with all its vagueness, omissions and ellipses, not to say distortions – that's second-best.' He accepted the money and pressed a button on his desk. 'All right, Mr Quail,' he said, as the door of his office opened and two burly men swiftly entered. 'You're on your way to Mars as a secret agent.' He rose, came over to shake Quail's nervous, moist hand. 'Or rather, you have been on your way. This afternoon at four-thirty you will, um, arrive back here on Terra; a cab will leave you off at your conapt and as I say you will never remember seeing me or coming here; you won't, in fact, even remember having heard of our existence.'

His mouth dry with nervousness, Quail followed the two technicians from the office; what happened next depended on them.

Will I actually believe I've been on Mars? he wondered. *That I
managed to fulfill my lifetime ambition*? He had a strange, lingering
intuition that something would go wrong. But just what – he did
not know.

He would have to wait to find out.

The intercom on McClane's desk, which connected him with the
work-area of the firm, buzzed and a voice said, 'Mr Quail is under
sedation now, sir. Do you want to supervise this one, or shall we go
ahead?'

'It's routine,' McClane observed. 'You may go ahead, Lowe; I
don't think you'll run into any trouble.' Programming an artificial
memory of a trip to another planet – with or without the added fillip
of being a secret agent – showed up on the firm's work-schedule with
monotonous regularity. *In one month*, he calculated wryly, *we must
do twenty of these . . . ersatz interplanetary travel has become our
bread and butter*.

'Whatever you say, Mr McClane,' Lowe's voice came, and there-
upon the intercom shut off.

Going to the vault section in the chamber behind his office,
McClane searched about for a Three packet – trip to Mars – and a
Sixty-two packet: secret Interplan spy. Finding the two packets, he
returned with them to his desk, seated himself comfortably, poured
out the contents – merchandise which would be planted in Quail's
conapt while the lab technicians busied themselves installing false
memory.

A one-poscred sneaky-pete side arm. McClane reflected; *that's the
largest item. Sets us back financially the most*. Then a pellet-sized
transmitter, which could be swallowed if the agent were caught.
Code book that astonishingly resembled the real thing . . . the
firm's models were highly accurate: based, whenever possible, on
actual U.S. military issue. Odd bits which made no intrinsic sense
but which would be woven into the warp and woof of Quail's
imaginary trip, would coincide with his memory: half an ancient
silver fifty cent piece, several quotations from John Donne's sermons
written incorrectly, each on a separate piece of transparent tissue-thin

paper, several match folders from bars on Mars, a stainless steel spoon engraved PROPERTY OF DOME-MARS NATIONAL KIBBUTZIM, a wire tapping coil which –

The intercom buzzed. 'Mr McClane, I'm sorry to bother you but something rather ominous has come up. Maybe it would be better if you were in here after all. Quail is already under sedation; he reacted well to the narkidrine; he's completely unconscious and receptive. But – '

'I'll be in.' Sensing trouble, McClane left his office; a moment later he emerged in the work area.

On a hygienic bed lay Douglas Quail, breathing slowly and regularly, his eyes virtually shut; he seemed dimly – but only dimly – aware of the two technicians and now McClane himself.

'There's no space to insert false memory-patterns?' McClane felt irritation. 'Merely drop out two work weeks; he's employed as a clerk at the West Coast Emigration Bureau, which is a government agency, so he undoubtedly has or had two weeks vacation within the last year. That ought to do it.' Petty details annoyed him. And always would.

'Our problem,' Lowe said sharply, 'is something quite different.' He bent over the bed, said to Quail, 'Tell Mr McClane what you told us.' To McClane he said, 'Listen closely.'

The gray-green eyes of the man lying supine in the bed focused on McClane's face. The eyes, he observed uneasily, had become hard; they had a polished, inorganic quality, like semi-precious tumbled stones. He was not sure that he liked what he saw; the brilliance was too cold. 'What do you want now?' Quail said harshly. 'You've broken my cover. Get out of here before I take you all apart.' He studied McClane. 'Especially you,' he continued. 'You're in charge of this counter-operation.'

Lowe said, 'How long were you on Mars?'

'One month,' Quail said gratingly.

'And your purpose there?' Lowe demanded.

The meager lips twisted; Qauil eyed him and did not speak. At last, drawling the words out so that they dripped with hostility, he said, 'Agent for Interplan. As I already told you. Don't you record everything that's said? Play your vid-aud tape back for your boss and leave me alone.' He shut his eyes, then; the hard brilliance ceased.

McClane felt, instantly, a rushing splurge of relief.

Lowe said quietly, 'This is a tough man, Mr McClane.'

'He won't be,' McClane said, 'after we arrange for him to lose his memory-chain again. He'll be as meek as before.' To Quail he said, 'So *this* is why you wanted to go to Mars so terribly bad.'

Without opening his eyes Quail said, 'I never wanted to go to Mars. I was assigned it – they handed it to me and there I was: stuck. Oh yeah, I admit I was curious about it; who wouldn't be?' Again he opened his eyes and surveyed the three of them, McClane in particular. 'Quite a truth drug you've got here; it brought up things I had absolutely no memory of.' He pondered. 'I wonder about Kirsten,' he said, half to himself. 'Could she be in on it? An Interplan contact keeping an eye on me . . . to be certain I didn't regain my memory? No wonder she's been so derisive about my wanting to go there.' Faintly, he smiled; the smile – one of understanding – disappeared almost at once.

McClane said, 'Please believe me, Mr Quail; we stumbled onto this entirely by accident. In the work we do – '

'I believe you,' Quail said. He seemed tired, now; the drug was continuing to pull him under, deeper and deeper. 'Where did I say I'd been?' he murmured. 'Mars? Hard to remember – I know I'd like to see it; so would everybody else. But me – ' His voice trailed off. 'Just a clerk, a nothing clerk.'

Straightening up, Lowe said to his superior, 'He wants a false memory implanted that corresponds to a trip he actually took. And a false reason which is the real reason. He's telling the truth; he's a long way down in the narkidrine. The trip is very vivid in his mind – at least under sedation. But apparently he doesn't recall it otherwise. Someone, probably at a government military-sciences lab, erased his conscious memories; all he knew was that going to Mars meant something special to him, and so did being a secret agent. They couldn't erase that; it's not a memory but a desire, undoubtedly the same one that motivated him to volunteer for the assignment in the first place.'

The other technician, Keeler, said to McClane, 'What do we do? Graft a false memory-pattern over the real memory? There's no telling what the results would be; he might remember some of the genuine trip, and the confusion might bring on a psychotic interlude.

He'd have to hold two opposite premises in his mind simultaneously: that he went to Mars and that he didn't. That he's a genuine agent for Interplan and he's not, that it's spurious. I think we ought to revive him without any false memory implantation and send him out of here; this is hot.'

'Agreed,' McClane said. A thought came to him. 'Can you predict what he'll remember when he comes out of sedation?'

'Impossible to tell,' Lowe said. 'He probably will have some dim, diffuse memory of his actual trip, now. And he'd probably be in grave doubt as to its validity; he'd probably decide our programming slipped a gear-tooth. And he'd remember coming here; that wouldn't be erased – unless you want it erased.'

'The less we mess with this man,' McClane said, 'the better I like it. This is nothing for us to fool around with; we've been foolish enough to – or unlucky enough to – uncover a genuine Interplan spy who has a cover so perfect that up to now even he didn't know what he was – or rather is.' The sooner they washed their hands of the man calling himself Douglas Quail the better.

'Are you going to plant packets Three and Sixty-two in his conapt?' Lowe said.

'No,' McClane said. 'And we're going to return half his fee.'

'Half! Why half?'

McClane said lamely, 'It seems to be a good compromise.'

As the cab carried him back to his conapt at the residential end of Chicago, Douglas Quail said to himself, *It's sure good to be back on Terra.*

Already the month-long period on Mars had begun to waver in his memory; he had only an image of profound gaping craters, an ever-present ancient erosion of hills, of vitality, of motion itself. A world of dust where little happened, where a good part of the day was spent checking and rechecking one's portable oxygen source. And then the life forms, the unassuming and modest gray-brown cacti and maw-worms.

As a matter of fact he had brought back several moribund examples of Martian fauna; he had smuggled them through customs. After all, they posed no menace; they couldn't survive in Earth's heavy atmosphere.

Reaching into his coat pocket, he rummaged for the container of Martian maw-worms –

And found an envelope instead.

Lifting it out, he discovered to his perplexity, that it contained five hundred and seventy poscreds, in cred bills of low denomination.

Where'd I get this? he asked himself. *Didn't I spend every'cred I had on my trip?*

With the money came a slip of paper marked: *One-half fee ret'd. By McClane*. And then the date. Today's date.

'Recall what, sir or madam?' the robot driver of the cab inquired respectfully.

'Do you have a phone book?' Quail demanded.

'Certainly, sir or madam.' A slot opened; from it slid a microtape phone book for Cook County.

'It's spelled oddly,' Quail said as he leafed through the pages of the yellow section. He felt fear, then; abiding fear. 'Here it is,' he said. 'Take me there, to Rekal, Incorporated. I've changed my mind; I don't want to go home.'

'Yes sir, or madam, as the case may be,' the driver said. A moment later the cab was zipping back in the opposite direction.

'May I make use of your phone?' he asked.

'Be my guest,' the robot driver said. And presented a shiny new emperor 3-D color phone to him.

He dialled his own conapt. And after a pause found himself confronted by a miniature but chillingly realistic image of Kirsten on the small screen. 'I've been to Mars,' he said to her.

'You're drunk.' Her lips writhed scornfully. 'Or worse.'

''s god's truth.'

'When?' she demanded.

'I don't know.' He felt confused. 'A simulated trip, I think. By means of one of those artificial or extra-factual or whatever it is memory places. It didn't take.'

Kirsten said witheringly, 'You *are* drunk.' And broke the connection at her end. He hung up, then, feeling his face flush. *Always the same tone*, he said hotly to himself. *Always the retort, as if she knows everything and I know nothing. What a marriage. Keerist*, he thought dismally.

A moment later the cab stopped at the curb before a modern, very

attractive little pink building, over which a shifting polychromatic neon sign read: REKAL, INCORPORATED.

The receptionist, chic and bare from the waist up, started in surprise, then gained masterful control of herself. 'Oh, hello, Mr Quail,' she said nervously. 'H-how are you? Did you forget something?'

'The rest of my fee back,' he said.

More composed now, the receptionist said, 'Fee? I think you are mistaken, Mr Quail. You were here discussing the feasibility of an extra-factual trip for you, but – ' She shrugged her smooth pale shoulders. 'As I understand it, no trip was taken.'

Quail said, 'I remember everything, miss. My letter to Rekal, Incorporated, which started this whole business off. I remember my arrival here, my visit with Mr McClane. Then the two lab technicians taking me in tow and administering a drug to put me out.' No wonder the firm had returned half his fee. The false memory of his 'trip to Mars' hadn't taken – at least not entirely, not as he had been assured.

'Mr Quail,' the girl said, 'although you are a minor clerk you are a good-looking man and it spoils your features to become angry. If it would make you feel any better, I might, ahem, let you take me out . . .'

He felt furious, then. 'I remember you,' he said savagely. 'For instance the fact that your breasts are sprayed blue; that stuck in my mind. And I remember Mr McClane's promise that if I remembered my visit to Rekal, Incorporated I'd receive my money back in full. Where is Mr McClane?'

After a delay – probably as long as they could manage – he found himself once more seated facing the imposing walnut desk, exactly as he had been an hour or so earlier in the day.

'Some technique you have,' Quail said sardonically. His disappointment – and resentment – was enormous, by now. 'My so-called "memory" of a trip to Mars as an undercover agent for Interplan is hazy and vague and shot full of contradictions. And I clearly remember my dealings here with you people. I ought to take this to the Better Business Bureau.' He was burning angry, at this point; his sense of being cheated had overwhelmed him, had destroyed his customary aversion to participating in a public squabble.

Looking morose, as well as cautious, McClane said, 'We capitu-

late, Quail. We'll refund the balance of your fee. I fully concede the
fact that we did absolutely nothing for you.' His tone was resigned.

Quail said accusingly, 'You didn't even provide me with the
various artifacts that you claimed would "prove" to me I had been on
Mars. All that song-and-dance you went into – it hasn't materialized
into a damn thing. Not even a ticket stub. Nor postcards. Nor
passport. Nor proof of immunization shots. Nor – '

'Listen, Quail,' McClane said. 'Suppose I told you – ' He broke
off. 'Let it go.' He pressed a button on his intercom. 'Shirley, will
you disburse five hundred and seventy more 'creds in the form of a
cashier's check made out to Douglas Quail? Thank you.' He released
the button, then glared at Quail.

Presently the check appeared; the receptionist placed it before
McClane and once more vanished out of sight, leaving the two
men alone, still facing each other across the surface of the massive
walnut desk.

'Let me give you a word of advice,' McClane said as he signed the
check and passed it over. 'Don't discuss your, ahem, recent trip to
Mars with anyone.'

'What trip?'

'Well, that's the thing.' Doggedly, McClane said, 'The trip you
partially remember. Act as if you don't remember; pretend it never
took place. Don't ask me why; just take my advice: it'll be better
for all of us.' He had begun to perspire. Freely. 'Now, Mr Quail,
I have other business, other clients to see.' He rose, showed Quail
to the door.

Quail said, as he opened the door, 'A firm that turns out such
bad work shouldn't have any clients at all.' He shut the door
behind him.

On the way home in the cab Quail pondered the wording of his
letter of complaint to the Better Business Bureau, Terra Division. As
soon as he could get to his typewriter he'd get started; it was clearly
his duty to warn other people away from Rekal, Incorporated.

When he got back to his conapt he seated himself before his
Hermes Rocket portable, opened the drawers and rummaged for
carbon paper – and noticed a small, familiar box. A box which he
had carefully filled on Mars with Martian fauna and later smuggled
through customs.

Opening the box he saw, to his disbelief, six dead maw-worms and several varieties of the unicellular life on which the Martian worms fed. The protozoa were dried-up, dusty, but he recognized them; it had taken him an entire day picking among the vast dark alien boulders to find them. A wonderful, illuminated journey of discovery.

But I didn't go to Mars, he realized.

Yet on the other hand –

Kirsten appeared at the doorway to the room, an armload of pale brown groceries gripped. 'Why are you home in the middle of the day?' Her voice, in an eternity of sameness, was accusing.

'*Did I go to Mars?*' he asked her. 'You would know.'

'No, of course you didn't go to Mars; *you* would know that, I would think. Aren't you always bleating about going?'

He said, 'By God, I think I went.' After a pause he added, 'And simultaneously I think I didn't go.'

'Make up your mind.'

'How can I?' He gestured. 'I have both memory-tracks grafted inside my head; one is real and one isn't but I can't tell which is which. Why can't I rely on you? They haven't tinkered with you.' She could do this much for him at least – even if she never did anything else.

Kirsten said in a level, controlled voice, 'Doug, if you don't pull yourself together, we're through. I'm going to leave you.'

'I'm in trouble.' His voice came out husky and coarse. And shaking. 'Probably I'm heading into a psychotic episode; I hope not, but – maybe that's it. It would explain everything, anyhow.'

Setting down the bag of groceries, Kirsten stalked to the closet. 'I was not kidding,' she said to him quietly. She brought out a coat, got it on, walked back to the door of the conapt. 'I'll phone you one of those days soon,' she said tonelessly. 'This is goodbye, Doug. I hope you pull out of this eventually; I really pray you do. For your sake.'

'Wait,' he said desperately. 'Just tell me and make it absolute; I did go or I didn't – tell me which one.' *But they may have altered your memory-track also*, he realized.

The door closed. His wife had left. Finally!

A voice behind him said, 'Well, that's that. Now put up your hands, Quail. And also please turn around and face this way.'

He turned, instinctively, without raising his hands.

The man who faced him wore the plum uniform of the Interplan Police Agency, and his gun appeared to be UN issue. And, for some odd reason, he seemed familiar to Quail; familiar in a blurred, distorted fashion which he could not pin down. So, jerkily, he raised his hands.

'You remember,' the policeman said, 'your trip to Mars. We know all your actions today and all your thoughts – in particular your very important thoughts on the trip home from Rekal, Incorporated.' He explained, 'We have a telep-transmitter wired within your skull; it keeps us constantly informed.'

A telepathic transmitter; use of a living plasma that had been discovered on Luna. He shuddered with self-aversion. The thing lived inside him, within his own brain, feeding, listening, feeding. But the Interplan police used them; that had come out even in the homeopapes. So this was probably true, dismal as it was.

'Why me?' Quail said huskily. What had he done – or thought? And what did this have to do with Rekal, Incorporated?

'Fundamentally' the Interplan cop said, 'this has nothing to do with Rekal; it's between you and us.' He tapped his right ear. 'I'm still picking up your mentational processes by way of your cephalic transmitter.' In the man's ear Quail saw a small white-plastic plug. 'So I have to warn you: anything you think may be held against you.' He smiled. 'Not that it matters now; you've already thought and spoken yourself into oblivion. What's annoying is the fact that under narkidrine at Rekal, Incorporated you told them, their technicians and the owner, Mr McClane, about your trip – where you went, for whom, some of what you did. They're very frightened. They wish they had never laid eyes on you.' He added reflectively, 'They're right.'

Quail said, 'I never made any trip. It's a false memory-chain improperly planted in me by McClane's technicians.' But then he thought of the box, in his desk drawer, containing the Martian life forms. And the trouble and hardship he had had gathering them. The memory seemed real. And the box of life forms; that certainly was real. Unless McClane had planted it. Perhaps this was one of the 'proofs' which McClane had talked glibly about.

The memory of my trip to Mars, he thought, *doesn't convince me – but unfortunately it has convinced the Interplan Police Agency. They think I really went to Mars and they think I at least partially realize it.*

'We not only know you went to Mars,' the Interplan cop agreed, in answer to his thoughts, 'but we know that you now remember enough to be difficult for us. And there's no use expunging your conscious memory of all this, because if we do you'll simply show up at Rekal, Incorporated again and start over. And we can't do anything about McClane and his operation because we have no jurisdiction over anyone except our own people. Anyhow, McClane hasn't committed any crime.' He eyed Quail. 'Nor, technically, have you. You didn't go to Rekal, Incorporated with the idea of regaining your memory; you went, as we realize, for the usual reason people go there – a love by plain, dull people for adventure.' He added, 'Unfortunately you're not plain, not dull, and you've already had too much excitement; the last thing in the universe you needed was a course from Rekal, Incorporated. Nothing could have been more lethal for you or for us. And, for that matter, for McClane.'

Quail said, 'Why is it "difficult" for you if I remember my trip – my alleged trip – and what I did there?'

'Because,' the Interplan harness bull said, 'what you did is not in accord with our great white all-protecting father public image. You did, for us, what we never do. As you'll presently remember – thanks to narkidrine. That box of dead worms and algae has been sitting in your desk drawer for six months, ever since you got back. And at no time have you shown the slightest curiosity about it. We didn't even know you had it until you remembered it on your way home from Rekal; then we came here on the double to look for it.' He added, unnecessarily, 'Without any luck; there wasn't enough time.'

A second Interplan cop joined the first one; the two briefly conferred. Meanwhile, Qauil thought rapidly. He did remember more, now; the cop had been right about narkidrine. They – Interplan – probably used it themselves. Probably? He knew darn well they did; he had seen them putting a prisoner on it. Where would *that* be? Somewhere on Terra? More likely Luna, he decided, viewing the image rising from his highly defective – but rapidly less so – memory.

And he remembered something else. Their reason for sending him to Mars; the job he had done.

No wonder they had expunged his memory.

'Oh god,' the first of the two Interplan cops said, breaking off his conversation with his companion. Obviously, he had picked up Quail's thoughts. 'Well, this is a far worse problem, now; as bad as it can get.' He walked toward Quail, again covering him with his gun. 'We've got to kill you,' he said. 'And right away.'

Nervously, his fellow officer said. 'Why right away? Can't we simply cart him off to Interplan New York and let them – '

'*He* knows why it has to be right away,' the first cop said; he too looked nervous, now, but Quail realized that it was for an entirely different reason. His memory had been brought back almost entirely, now. And he fully understood the officer's tension.

'On Mars,' Quail said hoarsely, 'I killed a man. After getting past fifteen bodyguards. Some armed with sneaky-pete guns, the way you are.' He had been trained, by Interplan, over a five year period to be an assassin. A professional killer. He knew ways to take out armed adversaries . . . such as these two officers; and the one with the ear-receiver knew it, too.

If he moved swiftly enough –

The gun fired. But he had already moved to one side, and at the same time he chopped down the gun-carrying officer. In an instant he had possession of the gun and was covering the other, confused, officer.

'Picked my thoughts up,' Quail said, panting for breath. 'He knew what I was going to do, but I did it anyhow.'

Half sitting up, the injured officer grated, 'He won't use that gun on you, Sam; I pick that up, too. He knows he's finished, and he knows we know it, too. Come on, Quail.' Laboriously, grunting with pain, he got shakily to his feet. He held out his hand. 'The gun,' he said to Quail. 'You can't use it, and if you turn it over to me I'll guarantee not to kill you; you'll be given a hearing, and someone higher up in Interplan will decide, not me. Maybe they can erase your memory once more; I don't know. But you know the thing I was going to kill you for; I couldn't keep you from remembering it. So my reason for wanting to kill you is in a sense past.'

Quail, clutching the gun, bolted from the conapt, sprinted for the elevator. *If you follow me*, he thought. *I'll kill you. So don't.* He jabbed at the elevator button and, a moment later, the doors slid back.

The police hadn't followed him. Obviously they had picked up his terse, tense thoughts and had decided not to take the chance.

With him inside the elevator descended. He had gotten away – for a time. But what next? Where could he go?

The elevator reached the ground floor; a moment later Quail had joined the mob of peds hurrying along the runnels. His head ached and he felt sick. But at least he had evaded death; they had come very close to shooting him on the spot, back in his own conapt.

And they probably will again, he decided. *When they find me. And with this transmitter inside me, that won't take too long.*

Ironically, he had gotten exactly what he had asked Rekal, Incorporated for. Adventure, peril. Interplan police at work, a secret and dangerous trip to Mars in which his life was at stake – everything he had wanted as a false memory.

The advantages of it being a memory – and nothing more – could now be appreciated.

On a park bench, alone, he sat dully watching a flock of perts: a semi-bird imported from Mars' two moons, capable of soaring flight, even against Earth's huge gravity.

Maybe I can find my way back to Mars, he pondered. But then what? It would be worse on Mars; the political organization whose leader he had assassinated would spot him the moment he stepped from the ship; he would have Interplan and *them* after him, there.

Can you hear me thinking? he wondered. Easy avenue to paranoia; sitting here alone he felt them tuning in on him, monitoring, recording, discussing . . . He shivered, rose to his feet, walked aimlessly, his hands deep in his pockets. *No matter where I go*, he realized. *you'll always be with me. As long as I have this device inside my head.*

I'll make a deal with you, he thought to himself – and to them. *Can you imprint a false-memory template on me again, as you did before, that I lived an average, routine life, never went to Mars? Never saw an Interplan uniform up close and never handled a gun?*

A voice inside his brain answered, 'As has been carefully explained to you: that would not be enough.'

Astonished, he halted.

'We formerly communicated with you in this manner,' the voice continued. 'When you were operating in the field, on Mars. It's been months since we've done it; we assumed, in fact, that we'd never have to do so again. Where are you?'

'Walking,' Quail said, 'to my death.' *By your officers' guns*, he added as an afterthought. 'How can you be sure it wouldn't be enough?' he demanded. 'Don't the Rekal techniques work?'

'As we said. If you're given a set of standard, average memories you get – restless. You'd inevitably seek out Rekal or one of its competitors again. We can't go through this a second time.'

'Suppose,' Quail said, 'once my authentic memories have been canceled, something more vital than standard memories are implanted. Something which would act to satisfy my craving,' he said. 'That's been proved; that's probably why you initially hired me. But you ought to be able to come up with something else – something equal. I was the richest man on Terra but I finally gave all my money to educational foundations. Or I was a famous deep-space explorer. Anything of that sort; wouldn't one of those do?'

Silence.

'Try it,' he said desperately. 'Get some of your top-notch military psychiatrists; explore my mind. Find out what my most expansive daydream is.' He tried to think. 'Women,' he said. 'Thousands of them, like Don Juan had. An interplanetary playboy – a mistress in every city on Earth, Luna and Mars. Only I gave that up, out of exhaustion. Please,' he begged. 'Try it.'

'You'd voluntarily surrender, then?' the voice inside his head asked. 'If we agreed, to arrange such a solution? If it's possible?'

After an interval of hesitation he said, 'Yes.' *I'll take the risk*, he said to himself, *that you don't simply kill me.*

'You make the first move,' the voice said presently. 'Turn yourself over to us. And we'll investigate that line of possibility. If we can't do it, however, if your authentic memories begin to crop up again as they've done at this time, then – ' There was silence and then the voice finished, 'We'll have to destroy you. As you must understand. Well, Quail, you still want to try?'

'Yes,' he said. Because the alternative was death now – and for certain. At least this way he had a chance, slim as it was.

'You present yourself at our main barracks in New York,' the voice of the Interplan cop resumed. 'At 580 Fifth Avenue, floor twelve. Once you've surrendered yourself we'll have our psychiatrists begin on you; we'll have personality-profile tests made. We'll attempt to determine your absolute, ultimate fantasy wish – then we'll bring you back to Rekal, Incorporated, here; get them in on it, fulfilling that wish in vicarious surrogate retrospection. And – good luck. We do owe you something; you acted as a capable instrument for us.' The voice lacked malice; if anything, they – the organization – felt sympathy toward him.

'Thanks,' Quail said. And began searching for a robot cab.

'Mr Quail,' the stern-faced, elderly Interplan psychiatrist said, 'you possess a most interesting wish-fulfilment dream fantasy. Probably nothing such as you consciously entertain or suppose. This is commonly the way; I hope it won't upset you too much to hear about it.'

The senior ranking Interplan officer present said briskly, 'He better not be too much upset to hear about it, not if he expects not to get shot.'

'Unlike the fantasy of wanting to be an Interplan under-cover agent,' the psychiatrist continued, 'which, being relatively speaking a product of maturity, had a certain plausibility to it, this production is a grotesque dream of your childhood; it is no wonder you fail to recall it. Your fantasy is this: you are nine years old, walking alone down a rustic lane. An unfamiliar variety of space vessel from another star system lands directly in front of you. No one on Earth but you, Mr Quail, sees it. The creatures within are very small and helpless, somewhat on the order of field mice, although they are attempting to invade Earth; tens of thousands of other such ships will soon be on their way, when this advance party gives the go-ahead signal.'

'And I suppose I stop them,' Quail said, experiencing a mixture of amusement and disgust. 'Single-handed I wipe them out. Probably by stepping on them with my foot.'

'No,' the psychiatrist said patiently. 'You halt the invasion, but not by destroying them. Instead, you show them kindness and mercy, even though by telepathy – their mode of communication – you know why they have come. They have never seen such humane traits exhibited by any sentient organism, and to show their appreciation they make a covenant with you.'

Quail said, 'They won't invade Earth as long as I'm alive.'

'Exactly.' To the Interplan officer the psychiatrist said, 'You can see it does fit his personality, despite his feigned scorn.'

'So by merely existing,' Quail said, feeling a growing pleasure, 'by simply being alive, I keep Earth safe from alien rule. I'm in effect, then, the most important person on Terra. Without lifting a finger.'

'Yes, indeed, sir,' the psychiatrist said. 'And this is bedrock in your psyche; this is a life-long childhood fantasy. Which, without depth and drug therapy, you never would have recalled. But it has always existed in you; it went underneath, but never ceased.'

To McClane, who sat intently listening, the senior police official said, 'Can you implant an extra-factual memory pattern that extreme in him?'

'We get handed every possible type of wish-fantasy there is,' McClane said. 'Frankly, I've heard a lot worse than this. Certainly we can handle it. Twenty-four hours from now he won't just *wish* he'd saved Earth; he'll devoutly believe it really happened.'

The senior police official said, 'You can start the job, then. In preparation we've already once again erased the memory in him of his trip to Mars.'

Quail said, 'What trip to Mars?'

No one answered him, so reluctantly, he shelved the question. And anyhow a police vehicle had now put in its appearance; he, McClane and the senior police officer crowded into it, and presently they were on their way to Chicago and Rekal, Incorporated.

'You had better make no errors this time,' the police officer said to heavy-set, nervous-looking McClane.

'I can't see what could go wrong,' McClane mumbled, perspiring. 'This has nothing to do with Mars or Interplan. Single-handedly stopping an invasion of Earth from another star-system.' He shook his head at that. 'Wow, what a kid dreams up. And by pious virtue, too; not by force. It's sort of quaint.' He dabbed at his forehead with a large linen pocket handkerchief.

Nobody said anything.

'In fact,' McClane said, 'it's touching.'

'But arrogant,' the police official said starkly. 'Inasmuch as when he dies the invasion will resume. No wonder he doesn't recall it; it's the most grandiose fantasy I ever ran across.' He eyed Quail with disapproval. 'And to think we put this man on our payroll.'

When they reached Rekal, Incorporated the receptionist, Shirley, met them breathlessly in the outer office. 'Welcome back, Mr Quail,' she fluttered, her melon-shaped breasts – today painted an incandescent orange – bobbing with agitation. 'I'm sorry everything worked out so badly before; I'm sure this time it'll go better.'

Still repeatedly dabbing at his shiny forehead with his neatly-folded Irish linen handkerchief, McClane said, 'It better.' Moving with rapidity he rounded up Lowe and Keeler, escorted them and Douglas Quail to the work area, and then, with Shirley and the senior police officer, returned to his familiar office. To wait.

'Do we have a packet made up for this, Mr McClane?' Shirley asked, bumping against him in her agitation, then coloring modestly.

'I think we do.' He tried to recall, then gave up and consulted the formal chart. 'A combination,' he decided aloud, 'of packets Eighty-one, Twenty, and Six.' From the vault section of the chamber behind his desk he fished out the appropriate packets, carried them to his desk for inspection. 'From Eighty-one,' he explained, 'a magic healing rod given him – the client in question, this time Mr Quail – by the race of beings from another system. A token of their gratitude.'

'Does it work?' the police officer asked curiously.

'It did once,' McClane explained. 'But he, ahem, you see, used it up years ago, healing right and left. Now it's only a memento. But he remembers it working spectacularly.' He chuckled, then opened packet Twenty. 'Document from the UN Secretary General thanking him for saving Earth; this isn't precisely appropriate, because part of Quail's fantasy is that no one knows of the invasion except himself, but for the sake of verisimilitude we'll throw it in.' He inspected packet Six, then. What came from this? He couldn't recall; frowning, he dug into the plastic bag as Shirley and the Interplan police officer watched intently.

'Writing,' Shirley said. 'In a funny language.'

'This tells who they were,' McClane said, 'and where they came from. Including a detailed star map logging their flight here and the system of origin. Of course it's in *their* script, so he can't read it. But he remembers them reading it to him in his own tongue.' He placed the three artifacts in the center of the desk. 'These should be taken to Quail's conapt,' he said to the police officer. 'So that when he gets home he'll find them. And it'll confirm his fantasy. SOP – standard operating procedure.' He chuckled apprehensively, wondering how matters were going with Lowe and Keeler.

The intercom buzzed. 'Mr McClane, I'm sorry to bother you.' It was Lowe's voice; he froze as he recognized it, froze and became mute. 'But something's come up. Maybe it would be better if you came in here and supervised. Like before, Quail reacted well to the narkidrine; he's unconscious, relaxed and receptive. But – '

McClane sprinted for the work area.

On a hygienic bed Douglas Quail lay breathing slowly and regularly, eyes half-shut, dimly conscious of those around him.

'We started interrogating him,' Lowe said, white-faced. To find out exactly when to place the fantasy-memory of him single-handedly having saved Earth. And strangely enough – '

'They told me not to tell,' Douglas Quail mumbled in a dull drug-saturated voice. 'That was the agreement. I wasn't even supposed to remember. But how could I forget an event like that?'

I guess it would be hard, McClane reflected. *But you did – until now.*

'They even gave me a scroll,' Quail mumbled, 'of gratitude. I have it hidden in my conapt; I'll show it to you.'

To the Interplan officer who had followed after him, McClane said, 'Well, I offer the suggestion that you better not kill him. If you do they'll return.'

'They also gave me a magic invisible destroying rod,' Quail mumbled, eyes totally shut now. 'That's how I killed that man on Mars you sent me to take out. It's in my drawer along with the box of Martian maw-worms and dried-up plant life.'

Wordlessly, the Interplan officer turned and stalked from the work area.

I might as well put those packets of proof-artifacts away, McClane said to himself resignedly. He walked, step by step, back to his office. *Including the citation from the UN Secretary General. After all –*

The real one probably would not be long in coming.

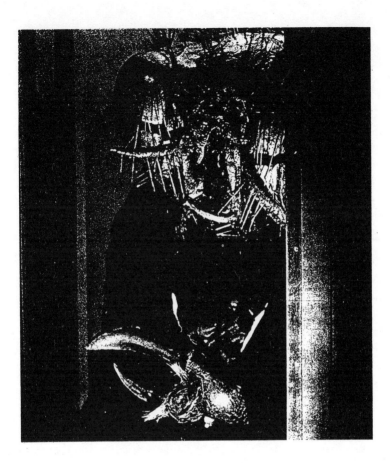

THE AUTHOR
George Langelaan

THE STORY
The Fly

THE MOVIE
The Fly

THE DIRECTOR
Kurt Newmann

Telephones and telephone bells have always made me uneasy. Years ago, when they were mostly wall fixtures, I disliked them, but nowadays, when they are planted in every nook and corner, they are a downright intrusion. We have a saying in France that a coalman is master in his own house; with the telephone that is no longer true, and I suspect that even the Englishman is no longer king in his own castle.

At the office, the sudden ringing of the telephone annoys me. It means that, no matter what I am doing, in spite of the switchboard operator, in spite of my secretary, in spite of doors and walls, some unknown person is coming into the room and onto my desk to talk right into my very ear, confidentially – and that whether I like it or not. At home, the feeling is still more disagreeable, but the worst is when the telephone rings in the dead of night. If anyone could see me turn on the light and get up blinking to answer it, I suppose I would look like any other sleepy man annoyed at being disturbed. The truth in such a case, however, is that I am struggling against panic, fighting down a feeling that a stranger has broken into the house and is in my bedroom. By the time I manage to grab the receiver and say: *'Ici Monsieur Delambre. Je vous écoute,'* I am outwardly calm, but I only get back to a more normal state when I recognize the voice at the other end and when I know what is wanted of me.

This effort at dominating a purely animal reaction and fear had become so effective that when my sister-in-law called me at two in the morning, asking me to come over, but first to warn the police that she had just killed my brother, I quietly asked her how and why she had killed André.

'But, François! . . . I can't explain all that over the telephone. Please call the police and come quickly.'

'Maybe I had better see you first, Hélène?'

'No, you'd better call the police first; otherwise they will start asking you all sorts of awkward questions. They'll have enough trouble as it is to believe that I did it alone. . . . And, by the way, I suppose you ought to tell them that André . . . André's body, is down at the factory. They may want to go there first.'

'Did you say that André is at the factory?'

'Yes . . . under the steam-hammer.'

'Under the what!'

'The steam-hammer! But don't ask so many questions. Please come quickly, François! Please understand that I'm afraid . . . that my nerves won't stand it much longer!'

Have you ever tried to explain to a sleepy police officer that your sister-in-law has just phoned to say that she has killed your brother with a steam-hammer? I repeated my explanation, but he would not let me.

'*Oui, Monsieur, oui*, I hear . . . but who are you? What is your name? Where do you live? I said, where do you live!'

It was then that Commissaire Charas took over the line and the whole business. He at least seemed to understand everything. Would I wait for him? Yes, he would pick me up and take me over to my brother's house. When? In five or ten minutes.

I had just managed to pull on my trousers, wriggle into a sweater and grab a hat and coat, when a black Citroën, headlights blazing, pulled up at the door.

'I assume you have a night watchman at your factory, Monsieur Delambre. Has he called you?' asked Commissaire Charas, letting in the clutch as I sat down beside him and slammed the door of the car.

'No, he hasn't. Though of course my brother could have entered the factory through his laboratory where he often works late at night . . . all night sometimes.'

'Is Professor Delambre's work connected with your business?'

'No, my brother is, or was, doing research work for the *Ministère de l'Air*. As he wanted to be away from Paris and yet within reach of where skilled workmen could fix up or make gadgets big and small for his experiments, I offered him one of the old workshops of the factory and he came to live in the first house built by our grandfather on the top of the hill at the back of the factory.'

'Yes, I see. Did he talk about his work? What sort of research work?'

'He rarely talked about it, you know; I suppose the Air Ministry could tell you. I only know that he was about to carry out a number of experiments he had been preparing for some months, something to do with the disintegration of matter, he told me.'

Barely slowing down, the Commissaire swung the car off the

road, slid it through the open factory gate and pulled up sharp by a policeman apparently expecting him.

I did not need to hear the policeman's confirmation. I knew now that my brother was dead, it seemed that I had been told years ago. Shaking like a leaf, I scrambled out after the Commissaire.

Another policeman stepped out of a doorway and led us toward one of the shops where all the lights had been turned on. More policemen were standing by the hammer, watching two men setting up a camera. It was tilted downward, and I made an effort to look.

It was far less horrid than I had expected. Though I had never seen my brother drunk, he looked just as if he were sleeping off a terrific binge, flat on his stomach across the narrow line on which the white-hot slabs of metal were rolled up to the hammer. I saw at a glance that his head and arm could only be a flattened mess, but that seemed quite impossible; it looked as if he had somehow pushed his head and arm right into the metallic mass of the hammer.

Having talked to his colleagues, the Commissaire turned toward me:

'How can we raise the hammer, Monsieur Delambre?'

'I'll raise it for you.'

'Would you like us to get one of your men over?'

'No, I'll be all right. Look, here is the switchboard. It was originally a steam-hammer, but everything is worked electrically here now. Look, Commissaire, the hammer has been set at fifty tons and its impact at zero.'

'At zero . . .?'

'Yes, level with the ground if you prefer. It is also set for single strokes, which means that it has to be raised after each blow. I don't know what Hélène, my sister-in-law, will have to say about all this, but one thing I am sure of: she certainly did not know how to set and operate the hammer.'

'Perhaps it was set that way last night when work stopped?'

'Certainly not. The drop is never set at zero, Monsieur le Commissaire.'

'I see. Can it be raised gently?'

'No. The speed of the upstroke cannot be regulated. But in any case it is not very fast when the hammer is set for single strokes.'

'Right. Will you show me what to do? It won't be very nice to watch, you know.'

'No, no, Monsieur le Commissaire. I'll be all right.'

'All set?' asked the Commissaire of the others. 'All right then, Monsieur Delambre. Whenever you like.'

Watching my brother's back, I slowly but firmly pushed the upstroke button.

The unusual silence of the factory was broken by the sigh of compressed air rushing into the cylinders, a sigh that always makes me think of a giant taking a deep breath before solemnly socking another giant, and the steel mass of the hammer shuddered and then rose swiftly. I also heard the sucking sound as it left the metal base and thought I was going to panic when I saw André's body heave forward as a sickly gush of blood poured all over the ghastly mess bared by the hammer.

'No danger of it coming down again, Monsieur Delambre?'

'No, none whatever,' I mumbled as I threw the safety switch and, turning around, I was violently sick in front of a young green-faced policeman.

For weeks after, Commissaire Charas worked on the case, listening, questioning, running all over the place, making out reports, telegraphing and telephoning right and left. Later, we became quite friendly and he owned that he had for a long time considered me as suspect number one, but had finally given up that idea because, not only was there no clue of any sort, but not even a motive.

Hélène, my sister-in-law, was so calm throughout the whole business that the doctors finally confirmed what I had long considered the only possible solution: that she was mad. That being the case, there was of course no trial.

My brother's wife never tried to defend herself in any way and even got quite annoyed when she realized that people thought her mad, and this of course was considered proof that she was indeed mad. She owned up to the murder of her husband and proved easily that she knew how to handle the hammer; but she would never say why, exactly how, or under what circumstances she had killed my brother. The great mystery was how and why had my brother so obligingly stuck his head under the hammer, the only possible explanation for his part in the drama.

The night watchman had heard the hammer all right; he had even heard it twice, he claimed. This was very strange, and the stroke-counter which was always set back to naught after a job, seemed to prove him right, since it marked the figure two. Also, the foreman in charge of the hammer confirmed that after cleaning up the day before the murder, he had as usual turned the stroke-counter back to naught. In spite of this, Hélène maintained that she had only used the hammer once, and this seemed just another proof of her insanity.

Commissaire Charas who had been put in charge of the case at first wondered if the victim were really my brother. But of that there was no possible doubt, if only because of the great scar running from his knee to his thigh, the result of a shell that had landed within a few feet of him during the retreat in 1940; and there were also the fingerprints of his left hand which corresponded to those found all over his laboratory and his personal belongings up at the house.

A guard had been put on his laboratory and the next day half a dozen officials came down from the Air Ministry. They went through all his papers and took away some of his instruments, but before leaving, they told the Commissaire that the most interesting documents and instruments had been destroyed.

The Lyons police laboratory, one of the most famous in the world, reported that André's head had been wrapped up in a piece of velvet when it was crushed by the hammer, and one day Commissaire Charas showed me a tattered drapery which I immediately recognized as the brown velvet cloth I had seen on a table in my brother's laboratory, the one on which his meals were served when he could not leave his work.

After only a very few days in prison, Hélène had been transferred to a near-by asylum, one of the three in France where insane criminals are taken care of. My nephew Henri, a boy of six, the very image of his father, was entrusted to me, and eventually all legal arrangements were made for me to become his guardian and tutor.

Hélène, one of the quietest patients of the asylum, was allowed visitors and I went to see her on Sundays. Once or twice the Commissaire had accompanied me and, later, I learned that he had also visited Hélène alone. But we were never able to obtain any information from my sister-in-law who seemed to have become utterly indifferent. She rarely answered my questions and hardly ever those of the Commissaire. She spent a lot of her time sewing, but her favourite pastime seemed to be catching flies which she invariably released unharmed after having examined them carefully.

Hélène only had one fit of raving – more like a nervous breakdown than a fit said the doctor who had administered morphia to quieten her – the day she saw a nurse swatting flies.

The day after Hélène's one and only fit, Commissaire Charas came to see me.

'I have a strange feeling that there lies the key to the whole business, Monsieur Delambre,' he said.

I did not ask him how it was that he already knew all about Hélène's fit.

'I do not follow you, Commissaire. Poor Madame Delambre could have shown an exceptional interest for anything else, really. Don't you think that flies just happen to be the border-subject of her tendency to raving?'

'Do you believe she is really mad?' he asked.

'My dear Commissaire, I don't see how there can be any doubt. Do you doubt it?'

'I don't know. In spite of all the doctors say, I have the impression that Madame Delambre has a very clear brain . . . even when catching flies.'

'Supposing you were right, how would you explain her attitude with regard to her little boy? She never seems to consider him as her own child.'

'You know, Monsieur Delambre, I have thought about that also. She may be trying to protect him. Perhaps she fears the boy or, for all we know, hates him?'

'I'm afraid I don't understand, my dear Commissaire.'

'Have you noticed, for instance, that she never catches flies when the boy is there?'

'No. But come to think of it, you are quite right. Yes, that is strange . . . Still, I fail to understand.'

'So do I, Monsieur Delambre. And I'm very much afraid that we shall never understand, unless perhaps your sister-in-law should *get better.*'

'The doctors seem to think that there is no hope of any sort, you know.'

'Yes. Do you know if your brother ever experimented with flies?'

'I really don't know, but I shouldn't think so. Have you asked the Air Ministry people? They knew all about the work.'

'Yes, and they laughed at me.'

'I can understand that.'

'You are very fortunate to understand anything, Monsieur Delambre. I do not . . . but I hope to some day.'

'Tell me, Uncle, do flies live a long time?'

We were just finishing our lunch and, following an established tradition between us, I was just pouring some wine into Henri's glass for him to dip a biscuit in.

Had Henri not been staring at his glass gradually being filled to the brim, something in my look might have frightened him.

This was the first time that he had ever mentioned flies, and I shuddered at the thought that Commissaire Charas might quite easily have been present. I could imagine the glint in his eye as he would have answered my nephew's question with another question. I could almost hear him saying:

'I don't know, Henri. Why do you ask?'

'Because I have again seen the fly that *Maman* was looking for.'

And it was only after drinking off Henri's own glass of wine that I realized that he had answered my spoken thought.

'I did not know that your mother was looking for a fly.'

'Yes, she was. It has grown quite a lot, but I recognized it all right.'

'Where did you see this fly, Henri, and . . . how did you recognize it?'

'This morning on your desk, Uncle François. It's head is white instead of black, and it has a funny sort of leg.'

Feeling more and more like Commissaire Charas, but trying to look unconcerned, I went on:

'And when did you see this fly for the first time?'

'The day that Papa went away. I had caught it, but *Maman* made me let it go. And then after, she wanted me to find it again. She changed her mind.' And shrugging his shoulders just as my brother used to, he added, 'You know what women are.'

'I think that fly must have died long ago, and you must be mistaken, Henri,' I said, getting up and walking to the door.

But as soon as I was out of the dining room, I ran up the stairs to my study. There was no fly anywhere to be seen.

I was bothered, far more than I cared to even think about. Henri had just proved that Charas was really closer to a clue than had seemed when he told me about his thoughts concerning Hélène's pastime.

For the first time I wondered if Charas did not really know much more than he let on. For the first time also, I wondered about Hélène. Was she really insane? A strange, horrid feeling was growing on me, and the more I thought about it, the more I felt that, somehow, Charas was right: Hélène was *getting away with it*!

What could possibly have been the reason for such a monstrous crime? What had led up to it? Just what had happened?

I thought of all the hundreds of questions that Charas had put to Hélène, sometimes gently like a nurse trying to soothe, sometimes stern and cold, sometimes barking them furiously. Hélène had answered very few, always in a calm quiet voice and never seeming to pay any attention to the way in which the question had been put. Though dazed, she had seemed perfectly sane then.

Refined, well-bred and well-read, Charas was more than just an intelligent police official. He was a keen psychologist and had an amazing way of smelling out a fib or an erroneous statement even before it was uttered. I knew that he had accepted as true the few answers she had given him. But then there had been all those questions which she had never answered: the most direct and important ones. From the very beginning, Hélène had adopted a very simple system. 'I cannot answer that question,' she would say in her low quiet voice. And that was that! The repetition of the same question never seemed to annoy her. In all the hours of questioning that she underwent, Hélène did not once point out to the Commissaire that he had already asked her this or that. She would simply say, 'I cannot answer that question,' as though it

were the very first time that that particular question had been asked
and the very first time she had made that answer.

This cliché had become the formidable barrier beyond which
Commissaire Charas could not even get a glimpse, an idea of
what Hélène might be thinking. She had very willingly answered
all questions about her life with my brother – which seemed a
happy and uneventful one – up to the time of his end. About his
death however, all that she would say was that she had killed him
with the steam-hammer, but she refused to say why, what had led
up to the drama and how she got my brother to put his head under
it. She never actually refused outright; she would just go blank and,
with no apparent emotion, would switch over to, 'I cannot answer
that question.'

Hélène, as I have said, had shown the Commissaire that she knew
how to set and operate the steam-hammer.

Charas could only find one single fact which did not coincide
with Hélène's declarations, the fact that the hammer had been used
twice. Charas was no longer willing to attribute this to insanity. That
evident flaw in Hélène's stonewall defence seemed a crack which the
Commissaire might possibly enlarge. But my sister-in-law finally
cemented it by acknowledging:

'All right, I lied to you. I did use the hammer twice. But do not
ask me why, because I cannot tell you.'

'Is that your only . . . misstatement, Madame Delambre?' had
asked the Commissaire, trying to follow up what looked at last like
an advantage.

'It is . . . and you know it, Monsieur le Commissaire.'

And, annoyed, Charas had seen that Hélène could read him like
an open book.

I had thought of calling on the Commissaire, but the knowledge
that he would inevitably start questioning Henri made me hesitate.
Another reason also made me hesitate, a vague sort of fear that he
would look for and find the fly Henri had talked of. And that
annoyed me a good deal because I would find no satisfactory
explanation for that particular fear.

André was definitely not the absent-minded sort of professor who
walks about in pouring rain with a rolled umbrella under his arm. He
was human, had a keen sense of humour, loved children and animals

and could not bear to see anyone suffer. I had often seen him drop his work to watch a parade of the local fire brigade, or see the *Tour de France* cyclists go by, or even follow a circus parade all around the village. He liked games of logic and precision, such as billiards and tennis, bridge and chess.

How was it then possible to explain his death? What could have made him put his head under that hammer? It could hardly have been the result of some stupid bet or a test of his courage. He hated betting and had no patience with those who indulged in it. Whenever he heard a bet proposed, he would invariably remind all present that, after all, a bet was but a contract between a fool and a swindler, even if it turned out to be a toss-up as to which was which.

It seemed there were only two possible explanations to André's death. Either he had gone mad, or else he had a reason for letting his wife kill him in such a strange and terrible way. And just what could have been his wife's role in all this? They surely could not have been both insane?

Having finally decided not to tell Charas about my nephew's innocent revelations, I thought I myself would question Hélène.

She seemed to have been expecting my visit for she came into the parlor almost as soon as I had made myself known to the matron and been allowed inside.

'I wanted to show you my garden,' explained Hélène as I looked at the coat slung over her shoulders.

As one of the 'reasonable' inmates, she was allowed to go into the garden during certain hours of the day. She had asked for and obtained the right to a little patch of ground where she could grow flowers, and I had sent her seeds and some rosebushes out of my garden.

She took me straight to a rustic wooden bench which had been made in the men's workshop and only just set up under a tree close to her little patch of ground.

Searching for the right way to broach the subject of André's death, I sat for a while tracing vague designs on the ground with the end of my umbrella.

'François, I want to ask you something,' said Hélène after a while.

'Anything I can do for you, Hélène?'

'No, just something I want to know. Do flies live very long?'

Staring at her, I was about to say that her boy had asked the very same question a few-hours earlier when I suddenly realized that here was the opening I had been searching for and perhaps even the possibility of striking a great blow, a blow perhaps powerful enough to shatter her stonewall defence, be it sane or insane.

Watching her carefully, I replied:

'I don't really know, Hélène; but the fly you were looking for was in my study this morning.'

No doubt about it, I had struck a shattering blow. She swung her head round with such force that I heard the bones crack in her neck. She opened her mouth, but said not a word; only her eyes seemed to be screaming with fear.

Yes, it was evident that I had crashed through something, but what? Undoubtedly, the Commissaire would have known what to do with such an advantage; I did not. All I knew was that he would never have given her time to think, to recuperate, but all I could do, and even that was a strain, was to maintain my best poker-face, hoping against hope that Hélène's defences would go on crumbling.

She must have been quite a while without breathing, because she suddenly gasped and put both hands over her still open mouth.

'François . . . Did you kill it?' she whispered, her eyes no longer fixed, but searching every inch of my face.

'No.'

'You have it then . . . You have it on you! Give it to me!' she almost shouted touching me with both her hands, and I knew that had she felt strong enough, she would have tried to search me.

'No. Hélène, I haven't got it.'

'But you know now . . . You have guessed, haven't you?'

'No, Hélène. I only know one thing, and that is that you are not insane. But I mean to know all, Hélène, and, somehow, I am going to find out. You can choose: either you tell me everything and I'll see what is to be done, or . . .'

'Or what? Say it!'

'I was going to say it, Hélène . . . or I assure you that your friend the Commissaire will have that fly first thing tomorrow morning.'

She remained quite still, looking down at the palms of her hands on her lap and, although it was getting chilly, her forehead and hands were moist.

Without even brushing aside a wisp of long brown hair blown across her mouth by the breeze, she murmured:

'If I tell you . . . will you promise to destroy that fly before doing anything else?'

'No, Hélène. I can make no such promise before knowing.'

'But François, you must understand. I promised André that fly would be destroyed. That promise must be kept and I can say nothing until it is.'

I could sense the deadlock ahead. I was not yet losing ground, but I was losing the initiative. I tried a shot in the dark.

'Hélène, of course you understand that as soon as the police examine that fly, they will know that you are not insane, and then . . .'

'François, no! For Henri's sake! Don't you see? I was expecting that fly; I was hoping it would find me here but it couldn't know what had become of me. What else could it do but go to others it loves, to Henri, to you . . . you who might know and understand what was to be done!'

Was she really mad, or was she simulating again? But mad or not, she was cornered. Wondering how to follow up and how to land the knockout blow without running the risk of seeing her slip away out of reach, I said very quietly:

'Tell me all, Hélène. I can then protect your boy.'

'Protect my boy from what? Don't you understand that if I am here, it is merely so that Henri won't be the son of a woman who was guillotined for having murdered his father? Don't you understand that I would by far prefer the guillotine to the living death of this lunatic asylum?'

'I understand, Hélène, and I'll do my best for the boy whether you tell me or not. If you refuse to tell me, I'll still do the best I can to protect Henri, but you must understand that the game will be out of my hands, because Commissaire Charas will have the fly.'

'But why must you know?' said, rather than asked, my sister-in-law, struggling to control her temper.

'Because I must and will know how and why my brother died, Hélène.'

'All right. Take me back to the . . . house. I'll give you what your Commissaire would call my "Confession."'

'Do you mean to say that you have written it!'

'Yes. It was not really meant for you, but more likely for *your friend*, the Commissaire. I had foreseen that, sooner or later, he would get too close to the truth.'

'You then have no objection to his reading it?'

'You will act as you think fit, François. Wait for me a minute.'

Leaving me at the door of the parlor, Hélène ran upstairs to her room. In less than a minute she was back with a large brown envelope.

'Listen, François; you are not nearly as bright as was your poor brother, but you are not unintelligent. All I ask is that you read this alone. After that, you may do as you wish.'

'That I promise you, Hélène,' I said taking the precious envelope. 'I'll read it tonight and although tomorrow is not a visiting day, I'll come down to see you.'

'Just as you like,' said my sister-in-law without even saying good-bye as she went back upstairs.

It was only on reaching home, as I walked from the garage to the house, that I read the inscription on the envelope:

TO WHOM IT MAY CONCERN
(Probably Commissaire Charas)

Having told the servants that I would have only a light supper to be served immediately in my study and that I was not to be disturbed after, I ran upstairs, threw Hélène's envelope on my desk and made another careful search of the room before closing the shutters and drawing the curtains. All I could find was a long since dead mosquito stuck to the wall near the ceiling.

Having motioned to the servant to put her tray down on a table by the fireplace, I poured myself a glass of wine and locked the door behind her. I then disconnected the telephone – I always did this now at night – and turned out all the lights but the lamp on my desk.

Slitting open Hélène's fat envelope, I extracted a thick wad of closely written pages. I read the following lines neatly centered in the middle of the top page:

This is not a confession because, although I killed my husband, I am not a murderess. I simply and very faithfully carried out his last wish by crushing his head and right arm under the steam-hammer of his brother's factory.

Without even touching the glass of wine by my elbow, I turned the page and started reading.

For very nearly a year before his death (*the manuscript began*), my husband had told me of some of his experiments. He knew full well that his colleagues of the Air Ministry would have forbidden some of them as too dangerous, but he was keen on obtaining positive results before reporting his discovery.

Whereas only sound and pictures had been, so far, transmitted through space by radio and television, André claimed to have discovered a way of transmitting matter. Matter, any solid object, placed in his 'transmitter' was instantly disintegrated and reintegrated in a special receiving set.

André considered his discovery as perhaps the most important since that of the wheel sawn off the end of a tree trunk. He reckoned that the transmission of matter by instantaneous 'disintegration – reintegration' would completely change life as we had known it so far. It would mean the end of all means of transport, not only of goods including food, but also of human beings. André, the practical scientist who never allowed theories or day dreams to get the better of him, already foresaw the time when there would no longer be any airplanes, ships, trains or cars and, therefore, no longer any roads or railway lines, ports, airports or stations. All that would be replaced by matter-transmitting and receiving stations throughout the world. Travellers and goods would be placed in special cabins and at a given signal, would simply disappear and reappear almost immediately at the chosen receiving station.

André's receiving set was only a few feet away from his transmitter, in an adjoining room of his laboratory, and he at first ran into all sorts of snags. His first successful experiment was carried out with an ash tray taken from his desk, a souvenir we had brought back from a trip to London.

That was the first time he told me about his experiments and I had no idea of what he was talking about the day he came dashing into the house and threw the ash tray in my lap.

'Hélène, look! For a fraction of a second, a bare ten millionth of a second, that ash tray has been completely disintegrated. For one little moment it no longer existed! Gone! Nothing left, absolutely nothing! Only atoms travelling through space at the speed of light! And the moment after, the atoms were once more gathered together in the shape of an ash tray!'

'André, please . . . please! What on earth are you raving about?'

He started sketching all over a letter I had been writing. He laughed at my wry face, swept all my letters off the table and said:

'You don't understand? Right. Let's start all over again. Hélène, do you remember I once read you an article about the mysterious flying stones that seem to come from nowhere in particular, and which are said to occasionally fall in certain houses in India? They come flying in as though thrown from outside and that, in spite of closed doors and windows.'

'Yes, I remember. I also remember that Professor Augier, your friend of the *Collège de France*, who had come down for a few days, remarked that if there was no trickery about it, the only possible explanation was that the stones had been disintegrated after having been thrown from outside, come through the walls, and then been reintegrated before hitting the floor or the opposite walls.'

'That's right. And I added that there was, of course, one other possibility, namely the momentary and partial disintegration of the walls as the stone or stones came through.'

'Yes, André. I remember all that, and I suppose you also remember that I failed to understand, and that you got quite annoyed. Well, I still do not understand why and how, even disintegrated, stones should be able to come through a wall or a closed door.'

'But it is possible, Hélène, because the atoms that go to make up matter are not close together like the bricks of a wall. They are separated by relative immensities of space.'

'Do you mean to say that you have disintegrated that ash tray, and then put it together again after pushing it through something?'

'Precisely, Hélène. I projected it through the wall that separates my transmitter from my receiving set.'

'And would it be foolish to ask how humanity is to benefit from ash trays that can go through walls?'

André seemed quite offended, but he soon saw that I was only teasing and again waxing enthusiastic, he told me of some of the possibilities of his discovery.

'Isn't it wonderful, Hélène?' he finally gasped, out of breath.

'Yes, André. But I hope you won't ever transmit me; I'd be too much afraid of coming out at the other end like your ash tray.'

'What do you mean?'

'Do you remember what was written under that ash tray?'

'Yes, of course: Made in Japan. That was the great joke of our typically British souvenir.'

'The words are still there, André; but . . . look!'

He took the ash tray out of my hands, frowned, and walked over to the window. Then he went quite pale, and I knew that he had seen what had proved to me that he had indeed carried out a strange experiment.

The three words were still there, but reversed and reading:

Made in Japan

Without a word, having completely forgotten me, André rushed off to his laboratory. I only saw him the next morning, tired and unshaven after a whole night's work.

A few days later André had a new reverse which put him out of sorts and made him fussy and grumpy for several weeks. I stood it patiently enough for a while, but being myself bad tempered one evening, we had a silly row over some futile thing, and I reproached him for his moroseness.

'I'm sorry, *chérie*. I've been working my way through a maze of problems and have given you all a very rough time. You see, my very first experiment with a live animal proved a complete fiasco.'

'André! You tried that experiment with Dandelo, didn't you?'

'Yes. How did you know?' he answered sheepishly. 'He disintegrated perfectly, but he never reappeared in the receiving set.'

'Oh, André! What became of him then?'

'Nothing . . . there is just no more Dandelo; only the dispersed atoms of a cat wandering, God knows where, in the universe.'

Dandelo was a small white cat the cook had found one morning in the garden and which we had promptly adopted. Now I knew how it had disappeared and was quite angry about the whole thing, but my husband was so miserable over it all that I said nothing.

I saw little of my husband during the next few weeks. He had most of his meals sent down to the laboratory. I would often wake up in the morning and find his bed unslept in. Sometimes, if he had come in very late, I would find that storm-swept appearance which only a man can give a bedroom by getting up very early and fumbling around in the dark.

One evening he came home to dinner all smiles, and I knew that his troubles were over. His face dropped, however, when he saw I was dressed for going out.

'Oh. Were you going out, Hélène?'

'Yes, the Drillons invited me for a game of bridge, but I can easily phone them and put it off.'

'No. it's all right.'

'It isn't all right. Out with it, dear!'

'Well, I've at last got everything perfect and I wanted you to be the first to see the miracle.'

'*Magnifique*, André! Of course I'll be delighted.'

Having telephoned our neighbours to say how sorry I was and so forth, I ran down to the kitchen and told the cook that she had exactly ten minutes in which to prepare a 'celebration dinner.'

'An excellent idea, Hélène,' said my husband when the maid appeared with the champagne after our candlelight dinner. 'We'll celebrate with reintegrated champagne!' and taking the tray from the maid's hands, he led the way down to the laboratory.

'Do you think it will be as good as before its disintegration?' I asked, holding the tray while he opened the door and switched on the lights.

'Have no fear. You'll see! Just bring it here, will you,' he said, opening the door of a telephone call-box he had bought and which had been transformed into what he called a transmitter. 'Put it down on that now,' he added, putting a stool inside the box.

Having carefully closed the door, he took me to the other end of the room and handed me a pair of very dark sun glasses. He put on another pair and walked back to a switchboard by the transmitter.

'Ready, Hélène?' said my husband, turning out all the lights. 'Don't remove your glasses till I give the word.'

'I won't budge, André. Go on,' I told him, my eyes fixed on the tray which I could just see in a greenish shimmering light through the glass panelled door of the telephone booth.

'Right,' said André throwing a switch.

The whole room was brilliantly illuminated by an orange flash. Inside the booth I had seen a crackling ball of fire and felt its heat on my face, neck and hands. The whole thing lasted but the fraction of a second, and I found myself blinking at green-edged black holes like those one sees after having stared at the sun.

'*Et voilà*! You can take off your glasses, Hélène.'

A little theatrically perhaps, my husband opened the door of the booth. Though André had told me what to expect, I was astonished to find that the champagne, glasses, tray and stool were no longer there.

André ceremoniously led me by the hand into the next room in a corner of which stood a second telephone booth. Opening the door wide, he triumphantly lifted the champagne tray off the stool.

Feeling somewhat like the good-natured kind-member-of-the-audience who has been dragged onto the music hall stage by the magician, I refrained from saying, 'All done with mirrors,' which I knew would have annoyed my husband.

'Sure it's not dangerous to drink?' I asked as the cork popped.

'Absolutely sure, Hélène,' he said handing me a glass. 'But that was nothing. Drink this off and I'll show you something much more astounding.'

We went back into the other room.

'Oh, André! Remember poor Dandelo!'

'This is only a guinea pig, Hélène. But I'm positive it will go through all right.'

He set the furry little beast down on the green enamelled floor of the booth and quickly closed the door. I again put on my dark glasses and saw and felt the vivid crackling flash.

Without waiting for André to open the door, I rushed into the

next room where the lights were still on and looked into the
receiving booth.

'Oh, André! *Chéri*! He's there all right!' I shouted excitedly,
watching the little animal trotting round and round. 'It's wonderful,
André. It works! You've succeeded!'

'I hope so, but I must be patient. I'll know for sure in a few
weeks' time.'

'What do you mean? Look! He's as full of life as when you put
him in the other booth.'

'Yes, so he seems. But we'll have to see if all his organs are intact,
and that will take some time. If that little beast is still full of life in
a month's time, we then consider the experiment a success.'

I begged André to let me take care of the guinea pig.

'All right, but don't kill it by overfeeding,' he agreed with a grin
for my enthusiasm.

Though not allowed to take Hop-la – the name I had given the
guinea pig – out of its box in the laboratory, I tied a pink ribbon
round its neck and was allowed to feed it twice a day.

Hop-là soon got used to its pink ribbon and became quite a tame
little pet, but that month of waiting seemed a year.

And then one day, André put Miquette, our cocker spaniel, into
his 'transmitter.' He had not told me beforehand, knowing full well
that I would never have agreed to such an experiment with our dog.
But when he did tell me, Miquette had been successfully transmitted
half a dozen times and seemed to be enjoying the operation thoroughly; no sooner was she let out of the 'reintegrator' than she
dashed madly into the next room, scratching at the 'transmitter'
door to have 'another go,' as André called it.

I now expected that my husband would invite some of his
colleagues and Air Ministry specialists to come down. He usually did
this when he had finished a research job and, before handing them
long detailed reports which he always typed himself, he would carry
out an experiment or two before them. But this time, he just went
on working. Once morning I finally asked him when he intended
throwing his usual 'surprise party,' as we called it.

'No, Hélène; not for a long while yet. This discovery is much too
important. I have an awful lot of work to do on it still. Do you realize
that there are some parts of the transmission proper which I do not

yet myself fully understand? It works all right, but you see, I can't just say to all these eminent professors that I do this and that and, poof, it works! I must be able to explain how and why it works. And what is even more important, I must be ready and able to refute every destructive argument they will not fail to trot out, as they usually do when faced with anything really good.'

I was occasionally invited down to the laboratory to witness some new experiment, but I never went unless André invited me, and only talked about his work if he broached the subject first. Of course it never occurred to me that he would, at that stage at least, have tried an experiment with a human being; though, had I thought about it – knowing André – it would have been obvious that he would never have allowed anyone into the 'transmitter' before he had been through to test it first. It was only after the accident that I discovered he had duplicated all his switches inside the disintegration booth, so that he could try it out by himself.

The morning André tried this terrible experiment, he did not show up for lunch. I sent the maid down with a tray, but she brought it back with a note she had found pinned outside the laboratory door: *Do not disturb me, I am working.*

He did occasionally pin such notes on his door and, though I noticed it, I paid no particular attention to the unusually large handwriting of his note.

It was just after that, as I was drinking my coffee, that Henri came bouncing into the room to say that he had caught a funny fly, and would I like to see it. Refusing even to look at his closed fist, I ordered him to release it immediately.

'But, *Maman*, it has such a funny white head!'

Marching the boy over to the open window, I told him to release the fly immediately, which he did. I knew that Henri had caught the fly merely because he thought it looked curious or different from other flies, but I also knew that his father would never stand for any form of cruelty to animals, and that there would be a fuss should he discover that our son had put a fly in a box or a bottle.

At dinner time that evening, André had still not shown up and, a little worried, I ran down to the laboratory and knocked at the door.

He did not answer my knock, but I heard him moving around

and a moment later he slipped a note under the door. It was typewritten:

HELENE, I AM HAVING TROUBLE. PUT THE BOY TO BED AND COME BACK IN AN HOUR'S TIME. A.

Frightened, I knocked and called, but André did not seem to pay any attention and, vaguely reassured by the familiar noise of his typewriter, I went back to the house.

Having put Henri to bed, I returned to the laboratory where I found another note slipped under the door. My hand shook as I picked it up because I knew by then that something must be radically wrong. I read:

HELENE, FIRST OF ALL I COUNT ON YOU NOT TO LOSE YOUR NERVE OR DO ANYTHING RASH BECAUSE YOU ALONE CAN HELP ME. I HAVE HAD A SERIOUS ACCIDENT. I AM NOT IN ANY PARTICULAR DANGER FOR THE TIME BEING THOUGH IT IS A MATTER OF LIFE AND DEATH. IT IS USELESS CALLING TO ME OR SAYING ANYTHING, I CANNOT ANSWER, I CANNOT SPEAK. I WANT YOU TO DO EXACTLY AND VERY CAREFULLY ALL THAT I ASK. AFTER HAVING KNOCKED THREE TIMES TO SHOW THAT YOU UNDERSTAND AND AGREE, FETCH ME A BOWL OF MILK LACED WITH RUM. I HAVE HAD NOTHING ALL DAY AND CAN DO WITH IT.

Shaking with fear, not knowing what to think and repressing a furious desire to call André and bang away until he opened, I knocked three times as requested and ran all the way home to fetch what he wanted.

In less than five minutes I was back. Another note had been slipped under the door:

HELENE, FOLLOW THESE INSTRUCTIONS CAREFULLY. WHEN YOU KNOCK I'LL OPEN THE DOOR. YOU ARE TO WALK OVER TO MY DESK AND PUT DOWN THE BOWL OF MILK. YOU WILL THEN GO INTO THE OTHER ROOM WHERE THE RECEIVER IS. LOOK CAREFULLY AND TRY TO FIND A FLY WHICH OUGHT TO BE THERE BUT WHICH I AM UNABLE TO FIND. UNFORTUNATELY I CANNOT SEE SMALL THINGS VERY EASILY.

before you come in you must promise to obey me implicitly. DO NOT LOOK AT ME AND REMEMBER THAT TALKING IS QUITE USELESS. I CANNOT ANSWER. KNOCK AGAIN THREE TIMES AND THAT WILL MEAN I HAVE YOUR PROMISE. MY LIFE DEPENDS ENTIRELY ON THE HELP YOU CAN GIVE ME.

I had to wait a while to pull myself together, and then I knocked slowly three times.

I heard André shuffling behind the door, then his hand fumbling with the lock, and the door opened.

Out of the corner of my eye, I saw that he was standing behind the door, but without looking round, I carried the bowl of milk to his desk. He was evidently watching me and I must at all costs appear calm and collected.

'*Chéri*, you can count on me,' I said gently, and putting the bowl down under his desk lamp, the only one alight, I walked into the next room where all the lights were blazing.

My first impression was that some sort of hurricane must have blown out of the receiving booth. Papers were scattered in every direction, a whole row of test tubes lay smashed in a corner, chairs and stools were upset and one of the window curtains hung half torn from its bent rod. In a large enamel basin on the floor a heap of burned documents was still smouldering.

I knew that I would not find the fly André wanted me to look for. Women know things that men only suppose by reasoning and deduction; it is a form of knowledge very rarely accessible to them and which they disparagingly call intuition. I already knew that the fly André wanted was the one which Henri had caught and which I had made him release.

I heard André shuffling around in the next room, and then a strange gurgling and sucking as though he had trouble in drinking his milk.

'André, there is no fly here. Can you give me any sort of indication that might help? If you can't speak, rap or something . . . you know: once for yes, twice for no.'

I had tried to control my voice and speak as though perfectly calm, but I had to choke down a sob of desperation when he rapped twice for 'no.'

'May I come to you, André? I don't know what can have happened, but whatever it is, I'll be courageous, dear.'

After a moment of silent hesitation, he tapped once on his desk.

At the door I stopped aghast at the sight of André standing with his head and shoulders covered by the brown velvet cloth he had taken from a table by his desk, the table on which he usually ate when he did not want to leave his work. Suppressing a laugh that might easily have turned to sobbing, I said:

'André, we'll search thoroughly tomorrow, by daylight. Why don't you go to bed? I'll lead you to the guest room if you like, and won't let anyone else see you.'

His left hand tapped the desk twice.

'Do you need a doctor, André?'

'No,' he rapped.

'Would you like me to call up Professor Augier? He might be of more help . . .'

Twice he rapped 'no' sharply. I did not know what to do or say. And then I told him:

'Henri caught a fly this morning which he wanted to show me, but I made him release it. Could it have been the one you are looking for? I didn't see it, but the boy said its head was white.'

André emitted a strange metallic sigh, and I just had time to bite my fingers fiercely in order not to scream. He had let his right arm drop, and instead of his long-fingered muscular hand, a grey stick with little buds on it like the branch of a tree, hung out of his sleeve almost down to his knee.

'André, *mon chéri*, tell me what happened. I might be of more help to you if I knew. André . . . oh, it's terrible!' I sobbed, unable to control myself.

Having rapped once for yes, he pointed to the door with his left hand.

I stepped out and sank down crying as he locked the door behind me. He was typing again and I waited. At last he shuffled to the door and slid a sheet of paper under it.

HELENE, COME BACK IN THE MORNING. I MUST THINK AND WILL HAVE TYPED OUT AN EXPLANATION FOR YOU. TAKE ONE OF MY SLEEPING TABLETS AND GO STRAIGHT TO BED. I NEED YOU FRESH and strong tomorrow, MA PAUVRE CHERIE. A.

'Do you want anything for the night, André?' I shouted through the door.

He knocked twice for no, and a little later I heard the typewriter again.

The sun full on my face woke me up with a start. I had set the alarm-clock for five but had not heard it, probably because of the sleeping tablets. I had indeed slept like a log, without a dream. Now I was back in my living nightmare and crying like a child I sprang out of bed. It was just on seven!

Rushing into the kitchen, without a word for the startled servants, I rapidly prepared a trayload of coffee, bread and butter with which I ran down to the laboratory.

André opened the door as soon as I knocked and closed it again as I carried the tray to his desk. His head was still covered, but I saw from his crumpled suit and his open camp-bed that he must have at least tried to rest.

On his desk lay a typewritten sheet for me which I picked up. André opened the other door, and taking this to mean that he wanted to be left alone, I walked into the next room. He pushed the door to and I heard him pouring out the coffee as I read:

DO YOU REMEMBER THE ASH TRAY EXPERIMENT? I HAVE HAD A SIMILAR ACCIDENT. I 'TRANSMITTED' MYSELF SUCCESSFULLY THE NIGHT BEFORE LAST. DURING A SECOND EXPERIMENT YESTERDAY A FLY WHICH I DID NOT SEE MUST HAVE GOT INTO THE 'DISINTE-GRATOR.' MY ONLY HOPE IS TO FIND THAT FLY AND GO THROUGH AGAIN WITH IT. PLEASE SEARCH FOR IT CAREFULLY SINCE, IF IT IS NOT FOUND, I SHALL HAVE TO FIND A WAY OF PUTTING AN END TO ALL THIS.

If only André had been more explicit! I shuddered at the thought that he must be terribly disfigured and then cried softly as I imagined his face inside-out, or perhaps his eyes in place of his ears, or his mouth at the back of his neck, or worse! André must be saved! For that, the fly must be found! Pulling myself together, I said:

'André, may I come in?'

He opened the door.

'André, don't despair, I am going to find that fly. It is no longer in the laboratory, but it cannot be very far. I suppose you're disfigured, perhaps terribly so, but there can be no question of putting an end to all this, as you say in your note; that I will never stand for. If necessary, if you do not wish to be seen, I'll make you a mask or a cowl so that you can go on with your work until you get well again. If you cannot work, I'll call Professor Augier, and he and all your other friends will save you, André.'

Again I heard that curious metallic sigh as he rapped violently on his desk.

'André, don't be annoyed; please be calm. I won't do anything without first consulting you, but you must rely on me, have faith in me and let me help you as best I can. Are you terribly disfigured, dear? Can't you let me see your face? I won't be afraid . . . I am your wife you know.'

But my husband again rapped a decisive 'no' and pointed to the door.

'All right. I am going to search for the fly now, but promise me you won't do anything foolish; promise you won't do anything rash or dangerous without first letting me know all about it!'

He extended his left hand, and I knew I had his promise.

I will never forget that ceaseless day-long hunt for a fly. Back home, I turned the house inside-out and made all the servants join in the search. I told them that a fly had escaped from the Professor's laboratory and that it must be captured alive, but it was evident they already thought me crazy. They said so to the police later, and that day's hunt for a fly most probably saved me from the guillotine later.

I questioned Henri and as he failed to understand right away what I was talking about, I shook him and slapped him, and made him cry in front of the round-eyed maids. Realizing that I must not let myself go, I kissed and petted the poor boy and at last made him understand what I wanted of him. Yes, he remembered, he had found the fly just by the kitchen window; yes, he had released it immediately as told to.

Even in summer time we had very few flies because our house is on the top of a hill and the slightest breeze coming across the valley blows round it. In spite of that, I managed to catch dozens of flies that day. On all the window sills and all over the garden I had put saucers of milk, sugar, jam, meat – all the things likely to attract flies. Of all those we caught, and many others which we failed to catch but which I saw, none resembled the one Henri had caught the day before. One by one, with a magnifying glass, I examined every unusual fly, but none had anything like a white head.

At lunch time, I ran down to André with some milk and mashed potatoes. I also took some of the flies we had caught, but he gave me to understand that they could be of no possible use to him.

'If that fly has not been found tonight, André, we'll have to see what is to be done. And this is what I propose: I'll sit in the next room. When you can't answer by the yes-no method of rapping, you'll type out whatever you want to say and then slip it under the door. Agreed?'

'Yes,' rapped André.

By nightfall we had still not found the fly. At dinner time, as I prepared André's tray, I broke down and sobbed in the kitchen in front of the silent servants. My maid thought that I had had a row with my husband, probably about the mislaid fly, but I learned later that the cook was already quite sure that I was out of my mind.

Without a word, I picked up the tray and then put it down again as I stopped by the telephone. That this was really a matter of life and death for André, I had no doubt. Neither did I doubt that he fully intended committing suicide, unless I could make him change his mind, or at least put off such a drastic decision. Would I be strong enough? He would never forgive me for not keeping a promise, but under the circumstances, did that really matter? To the devil with promises and honour! At all costs André must be saved! And having thus made up my mind, I looked up and dialled Professor Augier's number.

'The Professor is away and will not be back before the end of the week,' said a polite neutral voice at the other end of the line.

That was that! I would have to fight alone and fight I would. I would save André come what may.

All my nervousness had disappeared as André let me in and, after putting the tray of food down on his desk, I went into the other room, as agreed.

'The first thing I want to know,' I said as he closed the door behind me, 'is what happened exactly. Can you please tell me, André?'

I waited patiently while he typed an answer which he pushed under the door a little later.

HELENE, I WOULD RATHER NOT TELL YOU. SINCE GO I MUST, I WOULD RATHER YOU REMEMBER ME AS I WAS BEFORE. I MUST DESTROY MYSELF IN SUCH A WAY THAT NONE CAN POSSIBLY KNOW WHAT HAS HAPPENED TO ME. I HAVE OF COURSE THOUGHT OF SIMPLY DISINTEGRATING MYSELF IN MY TRANSMITTER, BUT I HAD BETTER NOT BECAUSE, SOONER OR LATER, I MIGHT FIND MYSELF REINTEGRATED. SOME DAY, SOMEWHERE, SOME SCIENTIST IS SURE TO MAKE THE SAME DISCOVERY. I HAVE THEREFORE THOUGHT OF A WAY WHICH IS NEITHER SIMPLE NOR EASY, BUT YOU CAN AND WILL HELP ME.

For several minutes I wondered if André had not simply gone stark raving mad.

'André,' I said at last, 'whatever you may have chosen or thought of, I cannot and will never accept such a cowardly solution. No matter how awful the result of your experiment or accident, you are alive, you are a man, a brain . . . and you have a soul. You have no right to destroy yourself! You know that!'

The answer was soon typed and pushed under the door.

I AM ALIVE ALL RIGHT, BUT I AM ALREADY NO LONGER A MAN. AS TO MY BRAIN OR INTELLIGENCE, IT MAY DISAPPEAR AT ANY MOMENT. AS IT IS, IT IS NO LONGER INTACT, AND THERE CAN BE NO SOUL WITHOUT INTELLIGENCE . . . AND YOU KNOW THAT!

'Then you must tell the other scientists about your discovery. They will help you and save you, André!'

I staggered back frightened as he angrily thumped the door twice.

'André . . . why? Why do you refuse the aid you know they would give you with all their hearts?'

A dozen furious knocks shook the door and made me understand that my husband would never accept such a solution. I had to find other arguments.

For hours, it seemed, I talked to him about our boy, about me, about his family, about his duty to us and to the rest of humanity. He made no reply of any sort. At last I cried:

'André . . . do you hear me?'

'Yes,' he knocked very gently.

'Well, listen then. I have another idea. You remember your first experiment with the ash tray? . . . Well, do you think that if you had put it through again a second time, it might possibly have come out with the letters turned back the right way?'

Before I had finished speaking, André was busily typing and a moment later I read his answer:

I HAVE ALREADY THOUGHT OF THAT. AND THAT WAS WHY I NEEDED THE FLY. IT HAS TO GO THROUGH WITH ME. THERE IS NO HOPE OTHERWISE.

'Try all the same, André. You never know!'

I HAVE TRIED SEVEN TIMES ALREADY, was the typewritten reply I got to that.

'André! Try again, please!'

The answer this time gave me a flutter of hope, because no woman has ever understood, or will ever understand, how a man about to die can possibly consider anything funny.

I DEEPLY ADMIRE YOUR DELICIOUS FEMININE LOGIC. WE COULD GO ON DOING THIS EXPERIMENT UNTIL DOOMSDAY. HOWEVER, JUST TO GIVE YOU THAT PLEASURE, PROBABLY THE VERY LAST I SHALL EVER BE ABLE TO GIVE YOU, I WILL TRY ONCE MORE. IF YOU CANNOT FIND THE DARK GLASSES, TURN YOUR BACK TO THE MACHINE AND PRESS YOUR HANDS OVER YOUR EYES. LET ME KNOW WHEN YOU ARE READY.

'Ready, André!' I shouted, without even looking for the glasses and following his instructions.

I heard him move around and then open and close the door of his 'disintegrator.' After what seemed a very long wait, but probably was not more than a minute or so, I heard a violent crackling noise and perceived a bright flash through my eyelids and fingers.

I turned around as the booth door opened.

His head and shoulders still covered with the brown velvet cloth, André was gingerly stepping out of it.

'How do you feel, André? Any difference?' I asked, touching his arm.

He tried to step away from me and caught his foot in one of the stools which I had not troubled to pick up. He made a violent effort to regain his balance, and the velvet cloth slowly slid off his shoulders and head as he fell heavily backward.

The horror was too much for me, too unexpected. As a matter of fact, I am sure that, even had I known, the horror-impact could hardly have been less powerful. Trying to push both hands into my mouth to stifle my screams and although my fingers were bleeding, I screamed again and again. I could not take my eyes off him, I could not even close them, and yet I knew that if I looked at the horror much longer, I would go on screaming for the rest of my life.

Slowly, the monster, the thing that had been my husband, covered its head, got up and groped its way to the door and passed it. Though still screaming, I was able to close my eyes.

I who had ever been a true Catholic, who believed in God and another, better life hereafter, have today but one hope: that when I die, I really die, and that there may be no after-life of any sort because, if there is, then I shall never forget! Day and night, awake or asleep, I see it, and I know that I am condemned to see it forever, even perhaps into oblivion!

Until I am totally extinct, nothing can, nothing will ever make me forget that dreadful white hairy head with its low flat skull and its two pointed ears. Pink and moist, the nose was also that of a cat, a huge cat. But the eyes! Or rather, where the eyes should have been were two brown bumps the size of saucers. Instead of a mouth, animal or human, was a long hairy vertical slit from which hung a black quivering trunk that widened at the end, trumpet-like, and from which saliva kept dripping.

I must have fainted, because I found myself flat on my stomach on the cold cement floor of the laboratory, staring at the closed door behind which I could hear the noise of André's typewriter.

Numb, numb and empty, I must have looked as people do

immediately after a terrible accident, before they fully understand what has happened. I could only think of a man I had once seen on the platform of a railway station, quite conscious, and looking stupidly at his leg still on the line where the train had just passed.

My throat was aching terribly, and that made me wonder if my vocal cords had not perhaps been torn, and whether I would ever be able to speak again.

The noise of the typewriter suddenly stopped and I felt I was going to scream again as something touched the door and a sheet of paper slid from under it.

Shivering with fear and disgust, I crawled over to where I could read it without touching it:

NOW YOU UNDERSTAND. THAT LAST EXPERIMENT WAS A NEW DISASTER, MY POOR HELENE. I SUPPOSE YOU RECOGNIZED PART OF DANDELO'S HEAD. WHEN I WENT INTO THE DISINTEGRATOR JUST NOW, MY HEAD WAS ONLY THAT OF A FLY. I NOW ONLY HAVE EYES AND MOUTH LEFT. THE REST HAS BEEN REPLACED BY PARTS OF THE CAT'S HEAD. POOR DANDELO WHOSE ATOMS HAD NEVER COME TOGETHER. YOU SEE NOW THAT THERE CAN ONLY BE ONE POSSIBLE SOLUTION, DON'T YOU? I MUST DISAPPEAR. KNOCK ON THE DOOR WHEN YOU ARE READY AND I SHALL EXPLAIN WHAT YOU HAVE TO DO.

Of course he was right, and it had been wrong and cruel of me to insist on a new experiment. And I knew that there was now no possible hope, that any further experiments could only bring about worse results.

Getting up dazed, I went to the door and tried to speak, but no sound came out of my throat . . . so I knocked once!

You can of course guess the rest. He explained his plan in short typewritten notes, and I agreed, I agreed to everything!

My head on fire, but shivering with cold, like an automaton, I followed him into the silent factory. In my hand was a full page of explanations: what I had to know about the steam-hammer.

Without stopping or looking back, he pointed to the switchboard that controlled the steam-hammer as he passed it. I went no farther and watched him come to a halt before the terrible instrument.

He knelt down, carefully wrapped the cloth round his head, and then stretched out flat on the ground.

It was not difficult. I was not killing my husband. André, poor André, had gone long ago, years ago it seemed. I was merely carrying out his last wish . . . and mine.

Without hesitating, my eyes on the long still body, I firmly pushed the 'stroke' button right in. The great metallic mass seemed to drop slowly. It was not so much the resounding clang of the hammer that made me jump as the sharp cracking which I had distinctly heard at the same time. My hus . . . the thing's body shook a second and then lay still.

It was then I noticed that he had forgotten to put his right arm, his fly-leg, under the hammer. The police would never understand but the scientists would, and they must not! That had been André's last wish, also!

I had to do it and quickly, too; the night watchman must have heard the hammer and would be round any moment. I pushed the other button and the hammer slowly rose. Seeing but trying not to look, I ran up, leaned down, lifted and moved forward the right arm which seemed terribly light. Back at the switchboard, again I pushed the red button, and down came the hammer a second time. Then I ran all the way home.

You know the rest and can now do whatever you think right.

So ended Hélene's manuscript.

The following day I telephoned Commissaire Charas to invite him to dinner.

'With pleasure, Monsieur Delambre. Allow me, however, to ask: is it the Commissaire you are inviting, or just Monsieur Charas?'

'Have you any preference?'

'No, not at the present moment.'

'Well, then, make it whichever you like. Will eight o'clock suit you?'

Although it was raining, the Commissaire arrived on foot that evening.

'Since you did not come tearing up to the door in your black Citroën, I take it you have opted for Monsieur Charas, off duty?'

'I left the car up a side-street,' mumbled the Commissaire with a grin as the maid staggered under the weight of his raincoat.

'*Merci.*' he said a minute later as I handed him a glass of Pernod into which he tipped a few drops of water, watching it turn the golden amber liquid to pale blue milk.

'You heard about my poor sister-in-law?'

'Yes, shortly after you telephoned me this morning. I am sorry, but perhaps it was all for the best. Being already in charge of your brother's case, the inquiry automatically comes to me.'

'I suppose it was suicide.'

'Without a doubt. Cyanide the doctors say quite rightly; I found a second tablet in the unstitched hem of her dress.'

'*Monsieur est servi,*' announced the maid.

'I would like to show you a very curious document afterward, Charas.'

'Ah, yes. I heard that Madame Delambre had been writing a lot, but we could find nothing beyond the short note informing us that she was committing suicide.'

During our tête-à-tête dinner, we talked politics, books and films, and the local football club of which the Commissaire was a keen supporter.

After dinner, I took him up to my study where a bright fire – a habit I had picked up in England during the war – was burning.

Without even asking him, I handed him his brandy and mixed myself what he called 'crushed-bug juice in soda water' – his appreciation of whisky.

'I would like you to read this, Charas; first because it was partly intended for you and, secondly, because it will interest you. If you think Commissaire Charas has no objection, I would like to burn it after.'

Without a word, he took the wad of sheets Hélène had given me the day before and settled down to read them.

'What do you think of it all?' I asked some twenty minutes later as he carefully folded Hélène's manuscript, slipped it into the brown envelope, and put it into the fire.

Charas watched the flames licking the envelope from which wisps of grey smoke were escaping, and it was only when it burst into flames that he said slowly raising his eyes to mine:

'I think it proves very definitely that Madame Delambre was quite insane.'

For a long time we watched the fire eating up Hélène's 'confession.'

'A funny thing happened to me this morning, Charas. I went to the cemetery where my brother is buried. It was quite empty and I was alone.'

'Not quite, Monsieur Delambre. I was there, but I did not want to disturb you.'

'Then you saw me . . .'

'Yes. I saw you bury a matchbox.'

'Do you know what was in it?'

'A fly, I suppose.'

'Yes. I had found it early this morning, caught in a spider's web in the garden.'

'Was it dead?'

'No, not quite. I . . . crushed it . . . between two stones. Its head was . . . white . . . all white.'

THE AUTHOR
John Cheever

THE STORY
The Swimmer

THE MOVIE
The Swimmer

THE DIRECTOR
Sydney Pollack

It was one of those midsummer Sundays when everyone sits around saying, 'I *drank* too much last night.' You might have heard it whispered by the parishioners leaving church, heard it from the lips of the priest himself, struggling with his cassock in the *vestiarium*, heard it from the golf links and the tennis courts, heard it from the wildlife preserve where the leader of the Audubon group was suffering from a terrible hangover. 'I *drank* too much,' said Donald Westerhazy. 'We all *drank* too much,' said Lucinda Merrill. 'It must have been the wine,' said Helen Westerhazy. 'I *drank* too much of that claret.'

This was at the edge of the Westerhazys' pool. The pool, fed by an artesian well with a high iron content, was a pale shade of green. It was a fine day. In the west there was a massive stand of cumulus cloud so like a city seen from a distance – from the bow of an approaching ship – that it might have had a name. Lisbon. Hackensack. The sun was hot. Neddy Merrill sat by the green water, one hand in it, one around a glass of gin. He was a slender man – he seemed to have the especial slenderness of youth – and while he was far from young he had slid down his banister that morning and given the bronze backside of Aphrodite on the hall table a smack, as he jogged toward the smell of coffee in his dining room. He might have been compared to a summer's day, particularly the last hours of one, and while he lacked a tennis racket or a sail bag the impression was definitely one of youth, sport, and clement weather. He had been swimming and now he was breathing deeply, stertorously as if he could gulp into his lungs the components of that moment, the heat of the sun, the intenseness of his pleasure. It all seemed to flow into his chest. His own house stood in Bullet Park, eight miles to the south, where his four beautiful daughters would have had their lunch and might be playing tennis. Then it occurred to him that by taking a dogleg to the southwest he could reach his home by water.

His life was not confining and the delight he took in this observation could not be explained by its suggestion of escape. He seemed to see, with a cartographer's eye, that string of swimming pools, that quasi-subterranean stream that curved across the county. He had made a discovery, a contribution to modern geography; he would name the stream Lucinda after his wife. He was not a practical joker nor was he a fool but he was determinedly original and had a vague and modest idea of himself as a legendary figure. The day was beautiful and it seemed to him that a long swim might enlarge and celebrate its beauty.

He took off a sweater that was hung over his shoulders and dove in. He had an inexplicable contempt for men who did not hurl themselves into pools. He swam a choppy crawl, breathing either with every stroke or every fourth stroke and counting somewhere well in the back of his mind the one-two one-two of a flutter kick. It was not a serviceable stroke for long distances but the domestication of swimming had saddled the sport with some customs and in his part of the world a crawl was customary. To be embraced and sustained by the light green water was less a pleasure, it seemed, than the resumption of a natural condition, and he would have liked to swim without trunks, but this was not possible, considering his project. He hoisted himself up on the far curb – he never used the ladder – and started across the lawn. When Lucinda asked where he was going he said he was going to swim home.

The only maps and charts he had to go by were remembered or imaginary but these were clear enough. First there were the Grahams, the Hammers, the Lears, the Howlands, and the Crosscups. He would cross Ditmar Street to the Bunkers and come, after a short portage, to the Levys, the Welchers, and the public pool in Lancaster. Then there were the Hallorans, the Sachses, the Biswangers, Shirley Adams, the Gilmartins, and the Clydes. The day was lovely, and that he lived in a world so generously supplied with water seemed like a clemency, a beneficence. His heart was high and he ran across the grass. Making his way home by an uncommon route gave him the feeling that he was a pilgrim, an explorer, a man with a destiny, and he knew that he would find friends all along the way; friends would line the banks of the Lucinda River.

He went through a hedge that separated the Westerhazys' land from the Grahams', walked under some flowering apple trees, passed the shed that housed their pump and filter, and came out at the Grahams' pool. 'Why, Neddy,' Mrs Graham said, 'what a marvelous surprise. I've been trying to get you on the phone all morning. Here, let me get you a drink.' He saw then, like any explorer, that the hospitable customs and traditions of the natives would have to be handled with diplomacy if he was ever going to reach his destination. He did not want to mystify or seem rude to the Grahams nor did he have the time to linger there. He swam the length of their pool and joined them in the sun and was rescued, a few minutes later, by the arrival of two carloads of friends from Connecticut. During the uproarious reunions he was able to slip away. He went down by the front of the Grahams' house, stepped over a thorny hedge, and crossed a vacant lot to the Hammers'. Mrs Hammer, looking up from her roses, saw him swim by although she wasn't quite sure who it was. The Lears heard him splashing past the open windows of their living room. The Howlands and the Crosscups were away. After leaving the Howlands' he crossed Ditmar Street and started for the Bunkers', where he could hear, even at that distance, the noise of a party.

The water refracted the sound of voices and laughter and seemed to suspend it in midair. The Bunkers' pool was on a rise and he climbed some stairs to a terrace where twenty-five or thirty men and women were drinking. The only person in the water was Rusty Towers, who floated there on a rubber raft. Oh, how bonny and lush were the banks of the Lucinda River! Prosperous men and women gathered by the sapphire-colored waters while caterer's men in white coats passed them cold gin. Overhead a red de Haviland trainer was circling around and around and around in the sky with something like the glee of a child in a swing. Ned felt a passing affection for the scene, a tenderness for the gathering, as if it was something he might touch. In the distance he heard thunder. As soon as Enid Bunker saw him she began to scream: 'Oh, look who's here! What a marvelous surprise! When Lucinda said that you couldn't come I thought I'd *die*.' She made her way to him through the crowd, and when they had finished kissing she led him to the bar, a progress that was slowed by the fact that he stopped to kiss eight or ten other women and shake the hands of as many men. A smiling bartender he had seen at a hundred parties gave him a gin and tonic and he stood by the bar for a moment, anxious not to get stuck in any conversation that would delay his voyage. When he seemed about to be surrounded he dove in and swam close to the side to avoid colliding with Rusty's raft. At the far end of the pool he bypassed the Tomlinsons with a broad smile and jogged up the garden path.

The gravel cut his feet but this was the only unpleasantness. The party was confined to the pool, and as he went toward the house he heard the brilliant, watery sound of voices fade, heard the noise of a radio from the Bunkers' kitchen, where someone was listening to a ball game. Sunday afternoon. He made his way through the parked cars and down the grassy border of their driveway to Alewives Lane. He did not want to be seen on the road in his bathing trunks but there was no traffic and he made the short distance to the Levys' driveway, marked with a PRIVATE PROPERTY sign and a green tube for *The New York Times*. All the doors and windows of the big house were open but there were no signs of life; not even a dog barked. He went around the side of the house to the pool and saw that the Levys had only recently left. Glasses and bottles and dishes of nuts were on a table at the deep end, where there was a bathhouse or gazebo, hung with Japanese lanterns. After swimming the pool he got himself a glass and poured a drink. It was his fourth or fifth drink and he had swum nearly half the length of the Lucinda River. He felt tired, clean, and pleased at that moment to be alone; pleased with everything.

It would storm. The stand of cumulus cloud – that city – had risen and darkened, and while he sat there he heard the percussiveness of thunder again. The de Haviland trainer was still circling overhead and it seemed to Ned that he could almost hear the pilot laugh with pleasure in the afternoon; but when there was another peal of thunder he took off for home. A train whistle blew and he wondered what time it had gotten to be. Four? Five? He thought of the provincial station at that hour, where a waiter, his tuxedo concealed by a raincoat, a dwarf with some flowers wrapped in newspaper, and a woman who had been crying would be waiting for the local. It was suddenly growing dark; it was that moment when the pin-headed birds seem to organize their song into some acute and knowledgeable recognition of the storm's approach. Then there was a fine noise of rushing water from the crown of an oak at his back, as if a spigot there had been turned. Then the noise of fountains came from the crowns of all the tall trees. Why did he love storms, what was the meaning of his excitement when the door sprang open and the rain wind fled rudely up the stairs, why had the simple task of shutting the windows of an old house seemed fitting and urgent, why did the first watery notes of a storm wind have for him the unmistakable sound of good news, cheer, glad tidings? Then there was an explosion, a smell of cordite, and rain lashed the Japanese lanterns that Mrs Levy had bought in Kyoto the year before last, or was it the year before that?

He stayed in the Levys' gazebo until the storm had passed. The rain had cooled the air and he shivered. The force of the wind had stripped a maple of its red and yellow leaves and scattered them over the grass and the water. Since it was midsummer the tree must be blighted, and yet he felt a peculiar sadness at this sign of autumn. He braced his shoulders, emptied his glass, and started for the Welchers' pool. This meant crossing the Lindleys' riding ring and he was surprised to find it overgrown with grass and all the jumps dismantled. He wondered if the Lindleys had sold their horses or gone away for the summer and put them out to board. He seemed to remember having heard something about the Lindleys and their horses but the memory was unclear. On he went, barefoot through the wet grass, to the Welchers', where he found their pool was dry.

This breach in his chain of water disappointed him absurdly, and he felt like some explorer who seeks a torrential headwater and finds a dead stream. He was disappointed and mystified. It was common enough to go away for the summer but no one ever drained his pool. The Welchers had definitely gone away. The pool furniture was folded, stacked, and covered with a tarpaulin. The bathhouse was locked. All the windows of the house were shut, and when he went around to the driveway in front he saw a FOR SALE sign nailed to a tree. When had he last heard from the Welchers – when, that is, had he and Lucinda last regretted an invitation to dine with them? It seemed only a week or so ago. Was his memory failing or had he so disciplined it in the repression of unpleasant facts that he had damaged his sense of the truth? Then in the distance he heard the sound of a tennis game. This cheered him, cleared away all his apprehensions and let him regard the overcast sky and the cold air with indifference. This was the day that Neddy Merrill swam across the county. That was the day! He started off then for his most difficult portage.

HAD YOU GONE for a Sunday afternoon ride that day you might have seen him, close to naked, standing on the shoulders of Route 424, waiting for a chance to cross. You might have wondered if he was the victim of foul play, had his car broken down, or was he merely a fool. Standing barefoot in the deposits of the highway – beer cans, rags, and blowout patches – exposed to all kinds of ridicule, he seemed pitiful. He had known when he started that this was a part of his journey – it had been on his maps – but confronted with the lines of traffic, worming through the summery light, he found himself unprepared. He was laughed at, jeered at, a beer can was thrown at him, and he had no dignity or humor to bring to the situation. He could have gone back, back to the Westerhazys', where Lucinda would still be sitting in the sun. He had signed nothing, vowed nothing, pledged nothing, not even to himself. Why, believing as he did, that all human obduracy was susceptible to common sense, was he unable to turn back? Why was he determined to complete his journey even if it meant putting his life in danger? At what point had this prank, this joke, this piece of horseplay become serious? He could not go back, he could not even recall with any clearness the green water at the Westerhazys', the sense of inhaling the day's components, the friendly and relaxed voices saying that they had *drunk* too much. In the space of an hour, more or less, he had covered a distance that made his return impossible.

An old man, tooling down the highway at fifteen miles an hour, let him get to the middle of the road, where there was a grass divider. Here he was exposed to the ridicule of the northbound traffic, but after ten or fifteen minutes he was able to cross. From here he had only a short walk to the Recreation Center at the edge of the village of Lancaster, where there were some handball courts and a public pool.

The effect of the water on voices, the illusion of brilliance and suspense, was the same here as it had been at the Bunkers' but the sounds here were louder, harsher, and more shrill, and as soon as he entered the crowded enclosure he was confronted with regimentation. 'ALL SWIMMERS MUST TAKE A SHOWER BEFORE USING THE POOL. ALL SWIMMERS MUST USE THE FOOTBATH. ALL SWIMMERS MUST WEAR THEIR IDENTIFICATION DISKS.' He took a shower, washed his feet in a cloudy and bitter solution, and made his way to the edge of the water. It stank of chlorine and looked to him like a sink. A pair of lifeguards in a pair of towers blew police whistles at what seemed to be regular intervals and abused the swimmers through a public address system. Neddy remembered the sapphire water at the Bunkers' with longing and thought that he might contaminate himself – damage his own prosperousness and charm – by swimming in this murk, but he reminded himself that he was an explorer, a pilgrim, and that this was merely a stagnant bend in the Lucinda River. He dove, scowling with distaste, into the chlorine and had to swim with his head above water to avoid collisions, but even so he was bumped into, splashed, and jostled. When he got to the shallow end both lifeguards were shouting at him: 'Hey, you, you without the identification disk, get outa the water.' He did, but they had no way of pursuing him and he went through the reek of suntan oil and chlorine out through the hurricane fence and passed the handball courts. By crossing the road he entered the wooded part of the Halloran estate. The woods were not cleared and the footing was treacherous and difficult until he reached the lawn and the clipped beech hedge that encircled their pool.

The Hallorans were friends, an elderly couple of enormous wealth who seemed to bask in the suspicion that they might be Communists. They were zealous reformers but they were not Communists, and yet when they were accused, as they sometimes were, of subversion, it seemed to gratify and excite them. Their beech hedge was yellow and he guessed this had been blighted like the Levys' maple. He called hullo, hullo, to warn the Hallorans of his approach, to palliate his invasion of their privacy. The Hallorans, for reasons that had never been explained to him, did not wear bathing suits. No explanations were in order, really. Their nakedness was a detail in their uncompromising zeal for reform and he stepped politely out of his trunks before he went through the opening in the hedge.

Mrs Halloran, a stout woman with white hair and a serene face, was reading *The Times*. Mr Halloran was taking beech leaves out of the water with a scoop. They seemed not surprised or displeased to see him. Their pool was perhaps the oldest in the country, a fieldstone rectangle, fed by a brook. It had no filter or pump and its waters were the opaque gold of the stream.

'I'm swimming across the country,' Ned said.

'Why, I didn't know one could,' exclaimed Mrs Halloran.

'Well, I've made it from the Westerhazys',' Ned said. 'That must be about four miles.'

He left his trunks at the deep end, walked to the shallow end, and swam this stretch. As he was pulling himself out of the water he heard Mrs Halloran say, 'We've been *terribly* sorry to hear about all your misfortunes, Neddy.'

'My misfortunes?' Ned asked. 'I don't know what you mean.'

'Why, we heard that you'd sold the house and that your poor children . . .'

'I don't recall having sold the house,' Ned said, 'and the girls are at home.'

'Yes,' Mrs Halloran sighed. 'Yes . . .' Her voice filled the air with an unseasonable melancholy and Ned spoke briskly. 'Thank you for the swim.'

'Well, have a nice trip,' said Mrs Halloran.

Beyond the hedge he pulled on his trunks and fastened them. They were loose and he wondered if, during the space of an afternoon, he could have lost some weight. He was cold and he was tired and the naked Hallorans and their dark water had depressed him. The swim was too much for his strength but how could he have guessed this, sliding down the banister that morning and sitting in the Westerhazys' sun? His arms were lame. His legs felt rubbery and ached at the joints. The worst of it was the cold in his bones and the feeling that he might never be warm again. Leaves were falling down around him and he smelled wood smoke on the wind. Who would be burning wood at this time of year?

He needed a drink. Whiskey would warm him, pick him up, carry him through the last of his journey, refresh his feeling that it was original and valorous to swim across the county. Channel swimmers took brandy. He needed a stimulant. He crossed the lawn in front of the Hallorans' house and went down a little path to where they had built a house for their only daughter, Helen, and her husband, Eric Sachs. The Sachses' pool was small and he found Helen and her husband there.

'Oh, *Neddy*,' Helen said. 'Did you lunch at Mother's?'

'Not *really*,' Ned said. 'I *did* stop to see your parents.' This seemed to be explanation enough. 'I'm terribly sorry to break in on you like this but I've taken a chill and I wonder if you'd give me a drink.'

'Why, I'd *love* to,' Helen said, 'but there hasn't been any-thing in this house to drink since Eric's operation. That was three years ago.'

Was he losing his memory, had his gift for concealing painful facts let him forget that he had sold his house, that his children were in trouble, and that his friend had been ill? His eyes slipped from Eric's face to his abdomen, where he saw three pale, sutured scars, two of them at least a foot long. Gone was his navel, and what, Neddy thought, would the roving hand, bed-checking one's gifts at 3 A.M., make of a belly with no navel, no link to birth, this breach in the succession?

'I'm sure you can get a drink at the Biswangers',' Helen said. 'They're having an enormous do. You can hear it from here. Listen!'

She raised her head and from across the road, the lawns, the gardens, the woods, the fields, he heard again the brilliant noise of voices over water. 'Well, I'll get wet,' he said, still feeling that he had no freedom of choice about his means of travel. He dove into the Sachses' cold water and, gasping, close to drowning, made his way from one end of the pool to the other. 'Lucinda and I want *terribly* to see you,' he said over his shoulder, his face set toward the Biswangers'. 'We're sorry it's been so long and we'll call you *very* soon.'

He crossed some fields to the Biswangers' and the sounds of revelry there. They would be honored to give him a drink, they would be happy to give him a drink. The Biswangers invited him and Lucinda for dinner four times a year, six weeks in advance. They were always rebuffed and yet they continued to send out their invitations, unwilling to comprehend the rigid and undemocratic realities of their society. They were the sort of people who discussed the price of things at cocktails, exchanged market tips during dinner, and after dinner told dirty stories to mixed company. They did not belong to Neddy's set – they were not even on Lucinda's Christmas-card list. He went toward their pool with feelings of indifference, charity, and some unease, since it seemed to be getting dark and these were the longest days of the year. The party when he joined it was noisy and large. Grace Biswanger was the kind of hostess who asked the optometrist, the veterinarian, the real-estate dealer, and the dentist. No one was swimming and the twilight, reflected on the water of the pool, had a wintry gleam. There was a bar and he started for this. When Grace Biswanger saw him she came toward him, not affectionately as he had every right to expect, but bellicosely.

'Why, this party has everything,' she said loudly, 'including a gate crasher.'

She could not deal him a social blow – there was no question about this and he did not flinch. 'As a gate crasher,' he asked politely, 'do I rate a drink?'

'Suit yourself,' she said. 'You don't seem to pay much attention to invitations.'

She turned her back on him and joined some guests, and he went to the bar and ordered a whiskey. The bartender served him but he served him rudely. His was a world in which the caterer's men kept the social score, and to be rebuffed by a part-time barkeep meant that he had suffered some loss of social esteem. Or perhaps the man was new and uninformed. Then he heard Grace at his back say: 'They went for broke overnight – nothing but income – and he showed up drunk one Sunday and asked us to loan him five thousand dollars. . . .' She was always talking about money. It was worse than eating your peas off a knife. He dove into the pool, swam its length and went away.

The next pool on his list, the last but two, belonged to his old mistress, Shirley Adams. If he had suffered any injuries at the Biswangers' they would be cured here. Love – sexual roughhouse in fact – was the supreme elixir, the pain killer, the brightly colored pill that would put the spring back into his step, the joy of life in his heart. They had had an affair last week, last month, last year. He couldn't remember. It was he who had broken it off, his was the upper hand, and he stepped through the gate of the wall that surrounded her pool with nothing so considered as self-confidence. It seemed in a way to be his pool, as the lover, particularly the illicit lover, enjoys the possessions of his mistress with an authority unknown to holy matrimony. She was there, her hair the colour of brass, but her figure, at the edge of the lighted, cerulean water, excited in him no profound memories. It had been, he thought, a lighthearted affair, although she had wept when he broke it off. She seemed confused to see him and he wondered if she was still wounded. Would she, God forbid, weep again?

'What do you want?' she asked.

'I'm swimming across the county.'

'Good Christ. Will you ever grow up?'

'What's the matter?'

'If you've come here for money,' she said, 'I won't give you another cent.'

'You could give me a drink.'

'I could but I won't. I'm not alone.'

'Well, I'm on my way.'

He dove in and swam the pool, but when he tried to haul himself up onto the curb he found that the strength in his arms and shoulders had gone, and he paddled to the ladder and climbed out. Looking over his shoulder he saw, in the lighted bathhouse, a young man. Going out onto the dark lawn he smelled chrysanthemums or marigolds – some stubborn autumnal fragrance – on the night air, strong as gas. Looking overhead he saw that the stars had come out, but why should he seem to see Andromeda, Cepheus, and Cassiopeia? What had become of the constellations of midsummer? He began to cry.

It was probably the first time in his adult life that he had ever cried, certainly the first time in his life that he had ever felt so miserable, cold, tired, and bewildered. He could not understand the rudeness of the caterer's barkeep or the rudeness of a mistress who had come to him on her knees and showered his trousers with tears. He had swum too long, he had been immersed too long, and his nose and his throat were sore from the water. What he needed then was a drink, some company, and some clean, dry clothes, and while he could have cut directly across the road to his home he went on to the Gilmartins' pool. Here, for the first time in his life, he did not dive but went down the steps into the icy water and swam a hobbled sidestroke that he might have learned as a youth. He staggered with fatigue on his way to the Clydes' and paddled the length of their pool, stopping again and again with his hand on the curb to rest. He climbed up the ladder and wondered if he had the strength to get home. He had done what he wanted, he had swum the county, but he was so stupefied with exhaustion that his triumph seemed vague. Stooped, holding on to the gateposts for support, he turned up the driveway of his own house.

The place was dark. Was it so late that they had all gone to bed? Had Lucinda stayed at the Westerhazys' for supper? Had the girls joined her there or gone someplace else? Hadn't they agreed, as they usually did on Sunday, to regret all their invitations and stay at home? He tried the garage doors to see what cars were in but the doors were locked and rust came off the handles onto his hands. Going toward the house, he saw that the force of the thunderstorm had knocked one of the rain gutters loose. It hung down over the front door like an umbrella rib, but it could be fixed in the morning. The house was locked, and he thought that the stupid cook or the stupid maid must have locked the place up until he remembered that it had been some time since they had employed a maid or a cook. He shouted, pounded on the door, tried to force it with his shoulder, and then, looking in at the windows, saw that the place was empty.

THE AUTHOR
William Fryer Harvey
THE STORY
The Beast With Five Fingers
THE MOVIE
The Beast With Five Fingers
THE DIRECTOR
Robert Florey

The story, I suppose, begins with Adrian Borlsover, whom I met when I was a little boy and he an old man. My father had called to appeal for a subscription, and before he left, Mr Borlsover laid his right hand in blessing on my head. I shall never forget the awe in which I gazed up at his face and realized for the first time that eyes might be dark and beautiful and shining, and yet not able to see.

For Adrian Borlsover was blind.

He was an extraordinary man, who came of an eccentric stock. Borlsover sons for some reason always seemed to marry very ordinary women; which perhaps accounted for the fact that no Borlsover had been a genius, and only one Borlsover had been mad. But they were great champions of little causes, generous patrons of odd sciences, founders of querulous sects, trustworthy guides to the bypath meadows of erudition.

Adrian was an authority on the fertilization of orchids. He had held at one time the family living at Borlsover Conyers, until a congenital weakness of the lungs obliged him to seek a less rigorous climate in the sunny south-coast watering-place where I had seen him. Occasionally he would relieve one or other of the local clergy. My father described him as a fine preacher, who gave long and inspiring sermons from what many men would have considered unprofitable texts. 'An excellent proof,' he would add, 'of the truth of the doctrine of direct verbal inspiration.'

Adrian Borlsover was exceedingly clever with his hands. His penmanship was exquisite. He illustrated all his scientific papers, made his own wood-cuts, and carved the reredos that is at present the chief feature of interest in the church at Borlsover Conyers. He had an exceedingly clever knack in cutting silhouettes for young ladies and paper pigs and cows for little children, and made more than one complicated wind-instrument of his own devising.

When he was fifty years old Adrian Borlsover lost his sight. In a wonderfully short time he adapted himself to the new conditions of life. He quickly learnt to read Braille. So marvellous indeed was his sense of touch, that he was still able to maintain his interest in botany. The mere passing of his long supple fingers over a flower was sufficient means for its identification, though occasionally he would use his lips. I have found several letters of his among my father's correspondence; in no case was there anything to show that he was afflicted with blindness, and this in spite of the fact that he exercised undue economy in the spacing of lines. Towards the close of his life Adrian Borlsover was credited with powers of touch that seemed almost uncanny. It has been said that he could tell at once the colour of a ribbon placed between his fingers. My father would neither confirm nor deny the story.

Adrian Borlsover was a bachelor. His elder brother, Charles, had married late in life, leaving one son, Eustace, who lived in the gloomy Georgian mansion at Borlsover Conyers, where he could work undisturbed in collecting material for his great book on heredity.

Like his uncle, he was a remarkable man. The Borlsovers had always been born naturalists, but Eustace possessed in a special degree the power of systematizing his knowledge. He had received his university education in Germany; and then, after post-graduate work in Vienna and Naples, had travelled for four years in South America and the East, getting together a huge store of material for a new study into the processes of variation.

He lived alone at Borlsover Conyers with Saunders, his secretary, a man who bore a somewhat dubious reputation in the district, but whose powers as a mathematician, combined with his business abilities, were invaluable to Eustace.

Uncle and nephew saw little of each other. The visits of Eustace were confined to a week in the summer or autumn – tedious weeks, that dragged almost as slowly as the bath-chair in which the old man was drawn along the sunny sea-front. In their way the two men were fond of each other, though their intimacy would, doubtless, have been greater, had they shared the same religious views. Adrian held to the old-fashioned evangelical dogmas of his early manhood; his nephew for many years had been thinking of embracing Buddhism. Both men possessed, too, the reticence the Borlsovers had always shown, and which their enemies sometimes called hypocrisy. With Adrian it was a reticence as to the things he had left undone; but with Eustace it seemed that the curtain which he was so careful to leave undrawn hid something more than a half-empty chamber.

Two years before his death, Adrian Borlsover developed, unknown to himself, the not uncommon power of automatic writing.

Eustace made the discovery by accident. Adrian was sitting reading in bed, the forefinger of his left hand tracing the Braille characters, when his nephew noticed that a pencil the old man held in his right hand was moving slowly along the opposite page. He had left his seat in the window and sat down beside the bed. The right hand continued to move, and now he could see plainly that they were letters and words which it was forming.

'Adrian Borlsover,' wrote the hand, 'Eustace Borlsover, Charles Borlsover, Francis Borlsover, Sigismund Borlsover, Adrian Borlsover, Eustace Borlsover, Saville Borlsover. B for Borlsover. Honesty Is the Best Policy. Beautiful Belinda Borlsover.'

'What curious nonsense!' said Eustace to himself.

'King George ascended the throne in 1760,' wrote the hand. 'Crowd, a noun of multitude; a collection of individuals. Adrian Borlsover, Eustace Borlsover.'

'It seems to me,' said his uncle, closing the book, 'that you had much better make the most of the afternoon sunshine and take your walk now.'

'I think perhaps I will,' Eustace answered as he picked up the volume. 'I won't go far, and when I come back, I can read to you those articles in *Nature* about which we were speaking.'

He went along the promenade, but stopped at the first shelter, and, seating himself in the corner best protected from the wind, he examined the book at leisure. Nearly every page was scored with a meaningless jumble of pencil-marks; rows of capital letters, short words, long words, complete sentences, copy-book tags. The whole thing, in fact, had the appearance of a copy-book, and, on a more careful scrutiny, Eustace thought that there was ample evidence to show that the handwriting at the beginning of the book, good though it was, was not nearly so good as the handwriting at the end.

He left his uncle at the end of October with a promise to return early in December. It seemed to him quite clear that the old man's power of automatic writing was developing rapidly, and for the first time he looked forward to a visit that would combine duty with interest.

But on his return he was at first disappointed. His uncle, he thought, looked older. He was listless, too, preferring others to read to him and dictating nearly all his letters. Not until the day before he left had Eustace an opportunity of observing Adrian Borlsover's newfound faculty.

The old man, propped up in bed with pillows, had sunk into a light sleep. His two hands lay on the coverlet, his left hand tightly clasping his right. Eustace took an empty manuscript book and placed a pencil within reach of the fingers of the right hand. They snatched at it eagerly, then dropped the pencil to loose the left hand from its restraining grasp.

'Perhaps to prevent interference I had better hold that hand,' said Eustace to himself, as he watched the pencil. Almost immediately it began to write.

'Blundering Borlsovers, unnecessarily unnatural, extraordinarily eccentric, culpably curious.'

'Who are you?' asked Eustace in a low voice.

'Never you mind,' wrote the hand of Adrian.

'Is it my uncle who is writing?'

'O my prophetic soul, mine uncle!'

'Is it anyone I know?'

'Silly Eustace, you'll see me very soon.'

'When shall I see you?'

'When poor old Adrian's dead.'

'Where shall I see you?'

'Where shall you not?'

Instead of speaking his next question, Eustace wrote it. 'What is the time?'

The fingers dropped the pencil and moved three or four times across the paper. Then, picking up the pencil, they wrote: 'Ten minutes before four. Put your book away, Eustace. Adrian mustn't find us working at this sort of thing. He doesn't know what to make of it, and I won't have poor old Adrian disturbed. Au revoir!'

Adrian Borlsover awoke with a start.

'I've been dreaming again,' he said; 'such queer dreams of lea-guered cities and forgotten towns. You were mixed up in this one, Eustace, though I can't remember how. Eustace, I want to warn you. Don't walk in doubtful paths. Choose your friends well. Your poor grandfather . . .'

A fit of coughing put an end to what he was saying, but Eustace saw that the hand was still writing. He managed unnoticed to draw the book away. 'I'll light the gas,' he said, 'and ring for tea.' On the other side of the bed-curtain he saw the last sentence that had been written.

'It's too late, Adrian,' it said. 'We're friends already, aren't we, Eustace Borlsover?'

On the following day Eustace left. He thought his uncle looked ill when he said good-bye, and the old man spoke despondently of the failure his life had been.

'Nonsense, uncle,' said his nephew. 'You have got over your difficulties in a way not one in a hundred thousand would have done. Every one marvels at your splendid perseverance in teaching your hand to take the place of your lost sight. To me it's been a revelation of the possibilities of education.'

'Education,' said his uncle dreamily, as if the word had started a new train of thought. 'Education is good so long as you know to whom and for what purpose you give it. But with the lower orders of men, the base and more sordid spirits, I have grave doubts as to its results. Well, good-bye Eustace; I may not see you again. You are a true Borlsover, with all the Borlsover faults. Marry, Eustace. Marry some good, sensible girl. And if by any chance I don't see you again, my will is at my solicitor's. I've not left you any legacy, because I know you're well provided for; but I thought you might like to have my books. Oh, and there's just another thing. You know, before the end, people often lose control over themselves and make absurd requests. Don't pay any attention to them, Eustace. Good-bye!' and he held out his hand. Eustace took it. It remained in his a fraction of a second longer than he had expected and gripped him with a virility that was surprising. There was, too, in its touch a subtle sense of intimacy.

'Why, uncle,' he said, 'I shall see you alive and well for many long years to come.'

Two months later Adrian Borlsover died.

Eustace Borlsover was in Naples at the time. He read the obituary notice in the *Morning Post* on the day announced for the funeral.

'Poor old fellow!' he said. 'I wonder whether I shall find room for all his books.'

The question occurred to him again with greater force when, three days later, he found himself standing in the library at Borlsover Conyers, a huge room built for use and not for beauty in the year of Waterloo by a Borlsover who was an ardent admirer of the great Napoleon. It was arranged on the plan of many college libraries, with tall projecting bookcases forming deep recesses of dusty silence, fit graves for the old hates of forgotten controversy, the dead passions of forgotten lives. At the end of the room, behind the bust of some unknown eighteenth-century divine, an ugly iron corkscrew stair led to a shelf-lined gallery. Nearly every shelf was full.

'I must talk to Saunders about it,' said Eustace. 'I suppose that we shall have to have the billiard-room fitted up with bookcases.'

The two men met for the first time after many weeks in the dining-room that evening.

'Hallo!' said Eustace, standing before the fire with his hands in his pockets. 'How goes the world, Saunders? Why these dress togs?'

He himself was wearing an old shooting-jacket. He did not believe in mourning, as he had told his uncle on his last visit; and, though he usually went in for quiet-coloured ties, he wore this evening one of an ugly red, in order to shock Morton the butler, and to make them thrash out the whole question of mourning for themselves in the servants' hall. Eustace was a true Borlsover. 'The world,' said Saunders, 'goes the same as usual, confoundedly slow. The dress togs are accounted for by an invitation from Captain Lockwood to bridge.'

'How are you getting there?'

'There's something the matter with the car, so I've told Jackson to drive me round in the dogcart. Any objection?'

'Oh dear me, no! We've had all things in common for far too many years for me to raise objections at this hour of the day.'

'You'll find your correspondence in the library,' went on Saunders. 'Most of it I've seen to. There are a few private letters I haven't opened. There's also a box with a rat or something inside it that came by the evening post. Very likely it's the six-toed beast Terry was sending us to cross with the four-toed albino. I didn't look because I didn't want to mess up my things; but I should gather from the way it's jumping about that it's pretty hungry.'

'Oh, I'll see to it,' said Eustace, 'while you and the captain earn an honest penny.'

Dinner over and Saunders gone, Eustace went into the library. Though the fire had been lit, the room was by no means cheerful.

'We'll have all the lights on, at any rate,' he said, as he turned the switches. 'And, Morton,' he added, when the butler brought the coffee, 'get me a screwdriver or something to undo this box. Whatever the animal is, he's kicking up the deuce of a row. What is it? Why are you dawdling?'

'If you please, sir, when the postman brought it, he told me that they'd bored the holes in the lid at the post office. There were no breathing holes in the lid, sir, and they didn't want the animal to die. That is all, sir.'

'It's culpably careless of the man, whoever he was,' said Eustace, as he removed the screws, 'packing an animal like this in a wooden box with no means of getting air. Confound it all! I meant to ask Morton to bring me a cage to put it in. Now I suppose I shall have to get one myself.'

He placed a heavy book on the lid from which the screws had been removed, and went into the billiard-room. As he came back into the library with an empty cage in his hand, he heard the sound of something falling, and then of something scuttling along the floor.

'Bother it! The beast's got out. How in the world am I to find it again in this library?'

To search for it did indeed seem hopeless. He tried to follow the sound of the scuttling in one of the recesses, where the animal seemed to be running behind the books in the shelves; but it was impossible to locate it. Eustace resolved to go on quietly reading. Very likely the animal might gain confidence and show itself. Saunders seemed to have dealt in his usual methodical manner with most of the correspondence. There were still the private letters.

What was that? Two sharp clicks and the lights in the hideous candelabras that hung from the ceiling suddenly went out.

'I wonder if something has gone wrong with the fuse,' said Eustace, as he went to the switches by the door. Then he stopped. There was a noise at the other end of the room, as if something was crawling up the iron corkscrew stair. 'If it's gone into the gallery,' he said, 'well and good.' He hastily turned on the lights, crossed the room, and climbed up the stair. But he could see nothing. His grandfather had placed a little gate at the top of the stair, so that children could run and romp in the gallery without fear of accident. This Eustace closed, and, having considerably narrowed the circle of his search, returned to his desk by the fire.

How gloomy the library was! There was no sense of intimacy about the room. The few busts that an eighteenth-century Borlsover had brought back from the grand tour might have been in keeping in the old library. Here they seemed out of place. They made the room feel cold in spite of the heavy red damask curtains and great gilt cornices.

With a crash two heavy books fell from the gallery to the floor; then, as Borlsover looked, another, and yet another.

'Very well. You'll starve for this, my beauty!' he said. 'We'll do some little experiments on the metabolism of rats deprived of water. Go on! Chuck them down! I think I've got the upper hand.' He turned once more to his correspondence. The letter was from the family solicitor. It spoke of his uncle's death, and of the valuable collection of books that had been left to him in the will.

There was one request [he read] which certainly came as a surprise to me. As you know, Mr Adrian Borlsover had left instructions that his body was to be buried in as simple a manner as possible at Eastbourne. He expressed a desire that there should be neither wreaths nor flowers of any kind, and hoped that his friends and relatives would not consider it necessary to wear mourning. The day before his death we received a letter cancelling these instructions. He wished the body to be embalmed (he gave us the address of the man we were to employ – Pennifer, Ludgate Hill), with orders that his right hand should be sent to you, stating that it was at your special request. The other arrangements about the funeral remained unaltered.

Good Lord,' said Eustace, 'what in the world was the old boy driving at? And what in the name of all that's holy is that?'

Someone was in the gallery. Someone had pulled the cord attached to one of the blinds, and it had rolled up with a snap. Someone must be in the gallery, for a second blind did the same. Someone must be walking round the gallery, for one after the other the blinds sprang up, letting in the moonlight.

'I haven't got to the bottom of this yet,' said Eustace, 'but I will do, before the night is very much older'; and he hurried up the corkscrew stair. He had just got to the top, when the lights went out a second time, and he heard again the scuttling along the floor. Quickly he stole on tiptoe in the dim moonshine in the direction of the noise, feeling, as he went, for one of the switches. His fingers touched the metal knob at last. He turned on the electric light.

About ten yards in front of him, crawling along the floor, was a man's hand. Eustace stared at it in utter amazement. It was moving quickly in the manner of a geometer caterpillar, the fingers humped up one moment, flattened out the next; the thumb appeared to give a crablike motion to the whole. While he was looking, too surprised to stir, the hand disappeared round the corner. Eustace ran forward. He no longer saw it, but he could hear it, as it squeezed its way behind the books on one of the shelves. A heavy volume had been displaced. There was a gap in the row of books, where it had got in. In his fear lest it should escape him again, he seized the first book that came to his hand and plugged it into the hole. Then, emptying two shelves of their contents, he took the wooden boards and propped them up in front to make his barrier doubly sure. 'I wish Saunders was back,' he said; 'one can't tackle this sort of thing alone.' It was after eleven, and there seemed little likelihood of Saunders returning before twelve. He did not dare to leave the shelf unwatched, even to run downstairs to ring the bell. Morton, the butler, often used to come round about eleven to see that the windows were fastened, but he might not come. Eustace was thoroughly unstrung. At last he heard steps down below.

'Morton!' he shouted. 'Morton!'

'Sir?'

'Has Mr Saunders got back yet?'

'Not yet, sir.'

'Well, bring me some brandy, and hurry up about it. I'm up in the gallery, you duffer.'

'Thanks,' said Eustace, as he emptied the glass. 'Don't go to bed yet, Morton. There are a lot of books that have fallen down by accident. Bring them up and put them back in their shelves.'

Morton had never seen Borlsover in so talkative a mood as on that night. 'Here,' said Eustace, when the books had been put back and dusted, 'you might hold up these boards for me, Morton. That beast in the box got out, and I've been chasing it all over the place.'

'I think I can hear it clawing at the books, sir. They're not valuable, I hope? I think that's the carriage, sir; I'll go and call Mr Saunders.'

It seemed to Eustace that he was away for five minutes, but it could hardly have been more than one, when he returned with Saunders. 'All right, Morton, you can go now. I'm up here, Saunders.'

'What's all the row?' asked Saunders, as he lounged forward with his hands in his pockets. The luck had been with him all the evening. He was completely satisfied, both with himself and with Captain Lockwood's taste in wines. 'What's the matter? You look to me to be in an absolutely blue funk.'

'That old devil of an uncle of mine,' began Eustace – 'Oh, I can't explain it all. It's his hand that's been playing Old Harry all the evening. But I've got it cornered behind these books. You've got to help me to catch it.'

'What's up with you, Eustace? What's the game?'

'It's no game, you silly idiot! If you don't believe me, take out one of those books and put your hand in and feel.'

'All right,' said Saunders; 'but wait till I've rolled up my sleeve. The accumulated dust of centuries, eh?' He took off his coat, knelt down, and thrust his arm along the shelf.

'There's something there right enough,' he said. 'It's got a funny, stumpy end to it, whatever it is, and nips like a crab. Ah! no, you don't!' He pulled his hand out in a flash. 'Shove in a book quickly. Now it can't get out.'

'What was it?' asked Eustace.

'Something that wanted very much to get hold of me. I felt what seemed like a thumb and forefinger. Give me some brandy.'

'How are we to get it out of there?'

'What about a landing-net?'

'No good. It would be too smart for us. I tell you, Saunders, it can cover the ground far faster than I can walk. But I think I see how we can manage it. The two books at the end of the shelf are big ones, that go right back against the wall. The others are very thin. I'll take out one at a time, and you slide the rest along, until we have it squashed between the end two.'

It certainly seemed to be the best plan. One by one as they took out the books, the space behind grew smaller and smaller. There was something in it that was certainly very much alive. Once they caught sight of fingers feeling for a way of escape. At last they had it pressed between the two big books.

'There's muscle there, if there isn't warm flesh and blood,' said Saunders, as he held them together. 'It seems to be a hand right enough, too. I suppose this is a sort of infectious hallucination. I've read about such cases before.'

'Infectious fiddlesticks!' said Eustace, his face white with anger; 'bring the thing downstairs. We'll get it back into the box.'

It was not altogether easy, but they were successful at last. 'Drive in the screws,' said Eustace; 'we won't run any risks. Put the box in this old desk of mine. There's nothing in it that I want. Here's the key. Thank goodness there's nothing wrong with the lock.'

'Quite a lively evening,' said Saunders. 'Now let's hear more about your uncle.'

They sat up together until early morning. Saunders had no desire for sleep. Eustace was trying to explain and forget; to conceal from himself a fear that he had never felt before – the fear of walking alone down the long corridor to his bedroom.

Whatever it was,' said Eustace to Saunders on the following morning, 'I propose that we drop the subject. There's nothing to keep us here for the next ten days. We'll motor up to the Lakes and get some climbing.'

'And see nobody all day, and sit bored to death with each other every night. Not for me, thanks. Why not run up to town? Run's the exact word in this case, isn't it? We're both in such a blessed funk. Pull yourself together, Eustace, and let's have another look at the hand.'

'As you like,' said Eustace; 'there's the key.'

They went into the library and opened the desk. The box was as they had left it on the previous night.

'What are you waiting for?' asked Eustace.

'I am waiting for you to volunteer to open the lid. However, since you seem to funk it, allow me. There doesn't seem to be the likelihood of any rumpus this morning at all events.' He opened the lid and picked out the hand.

'Cold?' asked Eustace.

'Tepid. A bit below blood heat by the feel. Soft and supple too. If it's the embalming, it's a sort of embalming I've never seen before. Is it your uncle's hand?'

'Oh, yes, it's his all right,' said Eustace. 'I should know those long thin fingers anywhere. Put it back in the box, Saunders. Never mind about the screws. I'll lock the desk, so that there'll be no chance of its getting out. We'll compromise by motoring up to town for a week. If we can get off soon after lunch, we ought to be at Grantham or Stamford by night.'

'Right,' said Saunders, 'and to-morrow – oh, well, by tomorrow we shall have forgotten all about this beastly thing.'

If, when the morrow came, they had not forgotten, it was certainly true that at the end of the week they were able to tell a very vivid ghost-story at the little supper Eustace gave on Hallowe'en.

'You don't want us to believe that it's true, Mr Borlsover? How perfectly awful!'

'I'll take my oath on it, and so would Saunders here; wouldn't you, old chap?'

'Any number of oaths,' said Saunders. 'It was a long, thin hand, you know, and it gripped me just like that.'

'Don't, Mr Saunders! Don't! How perfectly horrid! Now tell us another one, do! Only a really creepy one, please.'

'Here's a pretty mess!' said Eustace on the following day, as he threw a letter across the table to Saunders. 'It's your affair, though. Mrs Merritt, if I understand it, gives a month's notice.'

'Oh, that's quite absurd on Mrs Merritt's part,' replied Saunders. 'She doesn't know what she's talking about. Let's see what she says.'

Dear Sir [he read]: This is to let you know that I must give you a month's notice as from Tuesday, the 13th. For a long time I've felt the place too big for me; but when Jane Parfit and Emma Laidlaw go off with scarcely as much as an 'If you please,' after frightening the wits out of the other girls, so that they can't turn out a room by themselves or walk alone down the stairs for fear of treading on half-frozen toads or hearing it run along the passages at night, all I can say is that it's no place for me. So I must ask you, Mr Borlsover, sir, to find a new housekeeper, that has no objection to large and lonely houses, which some people do say, not that I believe them for a minute, my poor mother always having been a Wesleyan, are haunted.

Yours faithfully,
ELIZABETH MERRITT

PS. – I should be obliged if you would give my respects to Mr Saunders. I hope that he won't run any risks with his cold.

'Saunders,' said Eustace, 'you've always had a wonderful way with you in dealing with servants. You mustn't let poor old Merritt go.'

'Of course she shan't go,' said Saunders. 'She's probably only angling for a rise in salary. I'll write to her this morning.'

'No. There's nothing like a personal interview. We've had enough of town. We'll go back to-morrow, and you must work your cold for all it's worth. Don't forget that it's got on to the chest, and will require weeks of feeding up and nursing.'

'All right; I think I can manage Mrs Merritt.'

But Mrs Merritt was more obstinate than he had thought. She was very sorry to hear of Mr Saunders's cold, and how he lay awake all night in London coughing; very sorry indeed. She'd change his room for him gladly and get the south room aired, and wouldn't he have a hot basin of bread and milk last thing at night? But she was afraid that she would have to leave at the end of the month.

'Try her with an increase of salary,' was the advice of Eustace.

It was no use. Mrs Merritt was obdurate, though she knew of a Mrs Goddard, who had been housekeeper to Lord Gargrave, who might be glad to come at the salary mentioned.

'What's the matter with the servants, Morton?' asked Eustace that evening, when he brought the coffee into the library. 'What's all this about Mrs Merritt wanting to leave?'

'If you please, sir, I was going to mention it myself. I have a confession to make, sir. When I found your note, asking me to open that desk and take out the box with the rat, I broke the lock, as you told me, and was glad to do it, because I could hear the animal in the box making a great noise, and I thought it wanted food. So I took out the box, sir, and got a cage, and was going to transfer it, when the animal got away.'

'What in the world are you talking about? I never wrote any such note.'

'Excuse me, sir; it was the note I picked up here on the floor the day you and Mr Saunders left. I have it in my pocket now.'

It certainly seemed to be in Eustace's handwriting. It was written in pencil, and began somewhat abruptly.

'Get a hammer, Morton,' he read, 'or some tool and break open the lock in the old desk in the library. Take out the box that is inside. You need not do anything else. The lid is already open. Eustace Borlsover.'

'And you opened the desk?'

'Yes, sir; and, as I was getting the cage ready, the animal hopped out.'

'What animal?'

'The animal inside the box, sir.'

'What did it look like?'

'Well, sir, I couldn't tell you,' said Morton, nervously. 'My back was turned, and it was half way down the room when I looked up.'

'What was its colour?' asked Saunders. 'Black?'

'Oh, no, sir; a greyish white. It crept along in a very funny way, sir. I don't think it had a tail.'

'What did you do then?'

'I tried to catch it; but it was no use. So I set the rat-traps and kept the library shut. Then that girl, Emma Laidlaw, left the door open when she was cleaning, and I think it must have escaped.'

'And you think it is the animal that's been frightening the maids?'

'Well, no, sir, not quite. They said it was – you'll excuse me, sir – a hand that they saw. Emma trod on it once at the bottom of the stairs. She thought then it was a half-frozen toad, only white. And then Parfit was washing up the dishes in the scullery. She wasn't thinking about anything in particular. It was close on dusk. She took her hands out of the water and was drying them absent-minded like on the roller towel, when she found she was drying someone else's hand as well, only colder than hers.'

'What nonsense!' exclaimed Saunders.

'Exactly, sir; that's what I told her; but we couldn't get her to stop.'

'You don't believe all this?' said Eustace, turning suddenly towards the butler.

'Me, sir? Oh, no, sir! I've not seen anything.'

'Nor heard anything?'

'Well, sir, if you must know, the bells do ring at odd times, and there's nobody there when we go; and when we go round to draw the blinds of a night, as often as not somebody's been there before us. But, as I says to Mrs Merritt, a young monkey might do wonderful things, and we all know that Mr Borlsover has had some strange animals about the place.'

'Very well, Morton, that will do.'

'What do you make of it?' asked Saunders, when they were alone. 'I mean of the letter he said you wrote.'

'Oh, that's simple enough,' said Eustace. 'See the paper it's written on? I stopped using that paper years ago, but there were a few odd sheets and envelopes left in the old desk. We never fastened up the lid of the box before locking it in. The hand got out, found a pencil, wrote this note, and shoved it through the crack on to the floor, where Morton found it. That's plain as daylight.'

'But the hand couldn't write!'

'Couldn't it? You've not seen it do the things I've seen.' And he told Saunders more of what had happened at Eastbourne.

'Well,' said Saunders, 'in that case we have at least an explanation of the legacy. It was the hand which wrote, unknown to your uncle, that letter to your solicitor bequeathing itself to you. Your uncle had no more to do with that request than I. In fact, it would seem that he had some idea of this automatic writing and feared it.'

'Then if it's not my uncle, what is it?'

'I suppose some people might say that a disembodied spirit had got your uncle to educate and prepare a little body for it. Now it's got into that little body and is off on its own.'

'Well, what are we to do?'

'We'll keep our eyes open,' said Saunders, 'and try to catch it. If we can't do that, we shall have to wait till the bally clockwork runs down. After all, if it's flesh and blood, it can't live for ever.'

For two days nothing happened. Then Saunders saw it sliding down the banister in the hall. He was taken unawares and lost a full second before he started in pursuit, only to find that the thing had escaped him. Three days later, Eustace, writing alone in the library at night, saw it sitting on an open book at the other end of the room. The fingers crept over the page, as if it were reading; but before he had time to get up from his seat, it had taken the alarm, and was pulling itself up the curtains. Eustace watched it grimly, as it hung on to the cornice with three fingers and flicked thumb and forefinger at him in an expression of scornful derision.

'I know what I'll do,' he said. 'If I only get it into the open, I'll set the dogs on to it.'

He spoke to Saunders of the suggestion.

'It's a jolly good idea,' he said; 'only we won't wait till we find it out of doors. We'll get the dogs. There are the two terriers and the under-keeper's Irish mongrel, that's on to rats like a flash. Your spaniel has not got spirit enough for this sort of game.'

They brought the dogs into the house, and the keeper's Irish mongrel chewed up the slippers, and the terriers tripped up Morton, as he waited at table; but all three were welcome. Even false security is better than no security at all.

For a fortnight nothing happened. Then the hand was caught, not by the dogs, but by Mrs Merritt's grey parrot. The bird was in the habit of periodically removing the pins that kept its seed- and water-tins in place, and of escaping through the holes in the side of his cage. When once at liberty, Peter would show no inclination to return, and would often be about the house for days. Now, after six consecutive weeks of captivity, Peter had again discovered a new way of unloosing his bolts and was at large, exploring the tapestried forests of the curtains and singing songs in praise of liberty from cornice and picture-rail.

'It's no use your trying to catch him,' said Eustace to Mrs Merritt, as she came into the study one afternoon towards dusk with a step-ladder. 'You'd much better leave Peter alone. Starve him into surrender, Mrs Merritt; and don't leave bananas and seed about for him to peck at when he fancies he's hungry. You're far too soft-hearted.'

'Well, sir, I see he's right out of reach now on that picture-rail;

so, if you wouldn't mind closing the door, sir, when you leave the room, I'll bring his cage in to-night and put some meat inside it. He's that fond of meat, though it does make him pull out his feathers to suck the quills. They say that if you cook – '

'Never mind, Mrs Merritt,' said Eustace, who was busy writing; 'that will do; I'll keep an eye on the bird.'

For a short time there was silence in the room.

'Scratch poor Peter,' said the bird. 'Scratch poor old Peter!'

'Be quiet, you beastly bird!'

'Poor old Peter! Scratch poor Peter; do!'

'I'm more likely to wring your neck, if I get hold of you.' He looked up at the picture-rail, and there was the hand, holding on to a hook with three fingers, and slowly scratching the head of the parrot with the fourth. Eustace ran to the bell and pressed it hard; then across to the window, which he closed with a bang. Frightened by the noise, the parrot shook its wings preparatory to flight, and, as it did so, the fingers of the hand got hold of it by the throat. There was a shrill scream from Peter, as he fluttered across the room, wheeling round in circles that ever descended, borne down under the weight that clung to him. The bird dropped at last quite suddenly, and Eustace saw fingers and feathers rolled into an inextricable mass on the floor. The struggle abruptly ceased, as finger and thumb squeezed the neck; the bird's eyes rolled up to show the whites, and there was a faint, half-choked gurgle. But, before the fingers had time to lose their hold, Eustace had them in his own.

'Send Mr Saunders here at once,' he said to the maid who came in answer to the bell. 'Tell him I want him immediately.'

Then he went with the hand to the fire. There was a ragged gash across the back, where the bird's beak had torn it, but no blood oozed from the wound. He noted with disgust that the nails had grown long and discoloured.

'I'll burn the beastly thing,' he said. But he could not burn it. He tried to throw it into the flames, but his own hands, as if impelled by some old primitive feeling, would not let him. And so Saunders found him, pale and irresolute, with the hand still clasped tightly in his fingers.

'I've got it at last,' he said, in a tone of triumph.

'Good, let's have a look at it.'

'Not when it's loose. Get me some nails and a hammer and a board of some sort.'

'Can you hold it all right?'

'Yes, the thing's quite limp; tired out with throttling poor old Peter, I should say.'

'And now,' said Saunders, when he returned with the things, 'what are we going to do?'

'Drive a nail through it first, so that it can't get away. Then we can take our time over examining it.'

'Do it yourself,' said Saunders. 'I don't mind helping you with guinea-pigs occasionally, when there's something to be learned, partly because I don't fear a guinea-pig's revenge. This thing's different.'

'Oh, my aunt!' he giggled hysterically, 'look at it now.' For the hand was writhing in agonized contortions, squirming and wriggling upon the nail like a worm upon the hook.

'Well,' said Saunders, 'you've done it now. I'll leave you to examine it.'

'Don't go, in heaven's name! Cover it up, man; cover it up! Shove a cloth over it! Here!' and he pulled off the antimacassar from the back of a chair and wrapped the board in it. 'Now get the keys from my pocket and open the safe. Chuck the other things out. Oh, Lord, it's getting itself into frightful knots! Open it quick!' He threw the thing in and banged the door.

'We'll keep it there till it dies,' he said. 'May I burn in hell, if I ever open the door of that safe again.'

Mrs Merritt departed at the end of the month. Her successor, Mrs Handyside, certainly was more successful in the management of the servants. Early in her rule she declared that she would stand no nonsense, and gossip soon withered and died.

'I shouldn't be surprised if Eustace married one of these days,' said Saunders. 'Well, I'm in no hurry for such an event. I know him far too well for the future Mrs Borlsover to like me. It will be the same old story again; a long friendship slowly made – marriage – and a long friendship quickly forgotten.'

But Eustace did not follow the advice of his uncle and marry. Old habits crept over and covered his new experience. He was, if anything, less morose, and showed a greater inclination to take his natural part in country society.

Then came the burglary. The men, it was said, broke into the house by way of the conservatory. It was really little more than an attempt, for they only succeeded in carrying away a few pieces of plate from the pantry. The safe in the study was certainly found open and empty, but, as Mr Borlsover informed the police inspector, he had kept nothing of value in it during the last six months.

'Then you're lucky in getting off so easily, sir,' the man replied. 'By the way they have gone about their business, I should say they were experienced cracksmen. They must have caught the alarm when they were just beginning their evening's work.'

'Yes,' said Eustace, 'I suppose I am lucky.'

'I've no doubt,' said the inspector, 'that we shall be able to trace the men. I've said that they must have been old hands at the game. The way they got in and opened the safe shows that. But there's one little thing that puzzles me. One of them was careless enough not to wear gloves, and I'm bothered if I know what he was trying to do. I've traced his finger-marks on the new varnish on the window-sashes in every one of the downstairs rooms. They are very distinctive ones too.'

'Right or left hand, or both?' asked Eustace.

'Oh, right every time. That's the funny thing. He must have been a foolhardy fellow, and I rather think it was him that wrote that.' He took out a slip of paper from his pocket. 'That's what he wrote, sir: "I've got out, Eustace Borlsover, but I'll be back before long." Some jailbird just escaped, I suppose. It will make it all the easier for us to trace him. Do you know the writing, sir?'

'No,' said Eustace. 'It's not the writing of anyone I know.'

'I'm not going to stay here any longer,' said Eustace to Saunders at luncheon. 'I've got on far better during the last six months than I expected, but I'm not going to run the risk of seeing that thing again. I shall go up to town this afternoon. Get Morton to put my things together, and join me with the car at Brighton on the day after to-morrow. And bring the proofs of those two papers with you. We'll run over them together.'

'How long are you going to be away?'

'I can't say for certain, but be prepared to stay for some time.

We've stuck to work pretty closely through the summer, and I for one need a holiday. I'll engage the rooms at Brighton. You'll find it best to break the journey at Hitchin. I'll wire to you there at the "Crown" to tell you the Brighton address.'

The house he chose at Brighton was in a terrace. He had been there before. It was kept by his old college gyp, a man of discreet silence, who was admirably partnered by an excellent cook. The rooms were on the first floor. The two bedrooms were at the back, and opened out of each other. 'Mr Saunders can have the smaller one, though it is the only one with a fireplace,' he said. 'I'll stick to the larger of the two, since it's got a bathroom adjoining. I wonder what time he'll arrive with the car.'

Saunders came about seven, cold and cross and dirty. 'We'll light the fire in the dining-room,' said Eustace, 'and get Prince to unpack some of the things while we are at dinner. What were the roads like?'

'Rotten. Swimming with mud, and a beastly cold wind against us all day. And this is July. Dear old England!'

'Yes,' said Eustace, 'I think we might do worse than leave old England for a few months.'

They turned in soon after twelve.

'You oughtn't to feel cold, Saunders,' said Eustace, 'when you can afford to sport a great fur-lined coat like this. You do yourself very well, all things considered. Look at those gloves, for instance. Who could possibly feel cold when wearing them?'

'They are far too clumsy, though, for driving. Try them on and see'; and he tossed them through the door on to Eustace's bed and went on with his unpacking. A minute later he heard a shrill cry of terror. 'Oh, Lord,' he heard, 'it's in the glove! Quick, Saunders, quick!' Then came a smacking thud. Eustace had thrown it from him. 'I've chucked it into the bathroom,' he gasped; 'it's hit the wall and fallen into the bath. Come now, if you want to help.' Saunders, with a lighted candle in his hand, looked over the edge of the bath. There it was, old and maimed, dumb and blind, with a ragged hole in the middle, crawling, staggering, trying to creep up the slippery sides, only to fall back helpless.

'Stay there,' said Saunders. 'I'll empty a collar-box or something, and we'll jam it in. It can't get out while I'm away.'

'Yes, it can,' shouted Eustace. 'It's getting out now; it's climbing up the plug-chain. No, you brute, you filthy brute, you don't! Come back, Saunders; it's getting away from me. I can't hold it; it's all slippery. Curse its claws! Shut the window, you idiot! It's got out.' There was the sound of something dropping on to the hard flagstones below, and Eustace fell back fainting.

For a fortnight he was ill.

'I don't know what to make of it,' the doctor said to Saunders. 'I can only suppose that Mr Borlsover has suffered some great emotional shock. You had better let me send someone to help you nurse him. And by all means indulge that whim of his never to be left alone in the dark. I would keep a light burning all night, if I were you. But he *must* have more fresh air. It's perfectly absurd, this hatred of open windows.'

Eustace would have no one with him but Saunders.

'I don't want the other man,' he said. 'They'd smuggle it in somehow. I know they would.'

'Don't worry about it, old chap. This sort of thing can't go on indefinitely. You know I saw it this time as well as you. It wasn't half so active. It won't go on living much longer, especially after that fall. I heard it hit the flags myself. As soon as you're a bit stronger, we'll leave this place, not bag and baggage, but with only the clothes on our backs, so that it won't be able to hide anywhere. We'll escape it that way. We won't give any address, and we won't have any parcels sent after us. Cheer up, Eustace! You'll be well enough to leave in a day or two. The doctor says I can take you out in a chair to-morrow.'

'What have I done?' asked Eustace. 'Why does it come after me? I'm no worse than other men. I'm no worse than you, Saunders; you know I'm not. It was you who was at the bottom of that dirty business in San Diego, and that was fifteen years ago.'

'It's not that, of course,' said Saunders. 'We are in the twentieth century, and even the parsons have dropped the idea of your old sins finding you out. Before you caught the hand in the library, it was filled with pure malevolence – to you and all mankind. After you spiked it through with that nail, it naturally forgot about other people and concentrated its attention on you. It was shut up in that safe, you know, for nearly six months. That gives plenty of time for thinking of revenge.'

Eustace Borlsover would not leave his room, but he thought there might be something in Saunders's suggestion of a sudden departure from Brighton. He began rapidly to regain his strength.

'We'll go on the first of September,' he said.

The evening of the thirty-first of August was oppressively warm. Though at midday the windows had been wide open, they had been shut an hour or so before dusk. Mrs Prince had long since ceased to wonder at the strange habits of the gentlemen on the first floor. Soon after their arrival she had been told to take down the heavy window curtains in the two bedrooms, and day by day the rooms had seemed to grow more bare. Nothing was left lying about.

'Mr Borlsover doesn't like to have any place where dirt can collect,' Saunders had said as an excuse. 'He likes to see into all the corners of the room.'

'Couldn't I open the window just a little?' he said to Eustace that evening. 'We're simply roasting in here, you know.'

'No, leave well alone. We're not a couple of boarding-school misses fresh from a course of hygiene lectures. Get the chess-board out.'

They sat down and played. At ten o'clock Mrs Prince came to the door with a note. 'I am sorry I didn't bring it before,' she said, 'but it was left in the letter-box.'

'Open it, Saunders, and see if it wants answering.'

It was very brief. There was neither address nor signature.

'Will eleven o'clock to-night be suitable for our last appointment?'

'Who is it from?' asked Borlsover.

'It was meant for me,' said Saunders. 'There's no answer, Mrs Prince,' and he put the paper into his pocket.

'A dunning letter from a tailor; I suppose he must have got wind of our leaving.'

It was a clever lie, and Eustace asked no more questions. They went on with their game.

On the landing outside Saunders could hear the grandfather's clock whispering the seconds, blurting out the quarter-hours.

'Check,' said Eustace. The clock struck eleven. At the same time there was a gentle knocking on the door; it seemed to come from the bottom panel.

'Who's there?' asked Eustace.

There was no answer.

'Mrs Prince, is that you?'

'She is up above,' said Saunders; 'I can hear her walking about the room.'

'Then lock the door; bolt it too. Your move, Saunders.'

While Saunders sat with his eyes on the chess-board, Eustace walked over to the window and examined the fastenings. He did the same in Saunders's room, and the bathroom. There were no doors between the three rooms, or he would have shut and locked them too.

'Now, Saunders,' he said, 'don't stay all night over your move. I've had time to smoke one cigarette already. It's bad to keep an invalid waiting. There's only one possible thing for you to do. What was that?'

'The ivy blowing against the window. There, it's your move now, Eustace.'

'It wasn't the ivy, you idiot! It was someone tapping at the window'; and he pulled up the blind. On the outer side of the window, clinging to the sash, was the hand.

'What is that it's holding?'

'It's a pocket-knife. It's going to try to open the window by pushing back the fastener with the blade.'

'Well, let it try,' said Eustace. 'Those fasteners screw down; they can't be opened that way. Anyhow, we'll close the shutters. It's your move, Saunders. I've played.' But Saunders found it impossible to fix his attention on the game. He could not understand Eustace, who seemed all at once to have lost his fear. 'What do you say to some wine?' he asked. 'You seem to be taking things coolly, but I don't mind confessing that I'm in a blessed funk.'

'You've no need to be. There's nothing supernatural about that hand, Saunders. I mean, it seems to be governed by the laws of time and space. It's not the sort of thing that vanishes into thin air or slides through oaken doors. And since that's so, I defy it to get in here. We'll leave the place in the morning. I for one have bottomed the depths of fear. Fill your glass, man! The windows are all shuttered; the door is locked and bolted. Pledge me my Uncle Adrian! Drink, man! What are you waiting for?'

Saunders was standing with his glass half raised. 'It can get in,' he said hoarsely; 'it can get in! We've forgotten. There's a fireplace in my bedroom. It will come down the chimney.'

'Quick!' said Eustace, as he rushed into the other room; 'we haven't a minute to lose. What can we do? Light the fire, Saunders. Give me a match, quick!'

'They must be all in the other room. I'll get them.'

'Hurry, man, for goodness' sake! Look in the bookcase! Look in the bathroom! Here, come and stand here; I'll look.'

'Be quick!' shouted Saunders. 'I can hear something!'

'Then plug a sheet from your bed up the chimney. No, here's a match!' He had found one at last, that had slipped into a crack in the floor.

'Is the fire laid? Good, but it may not burn. I know – the oil from that old reading-lamp and this cotton-wool. Now the match, quick! Pull the sheet away, you fool! We don't want it now.'

There was a great roar from the grate, as the flames shot up. Saunders had been a fraction of a second too late with the sheet. The oil had fallen on to it. It, too, was burning.

'The whole place will be on fire!' cried Eustace, as he tried to beat out the flames with a blanket. 'It's no good! I can't manage it. You must open the door, Saunders, and get help.'

Saunders ran to the door and fumbled with the bolts. The key was stiff in the lock. 'Hurry,' shouted Eustace, 'or the heat will be too much for me.' The key turned in the lock at last. For half a second Saunders stopped to look back. Afterwards he could never be quite sure as to what he had seen, but at the time he thought that something black and charred was creeping slowly, very slowly, from the mass of flames towards Eustace Borlsover. For a moment he thought of returning to his friend; but the noise and the smell of the burning sent him running down the passage, crying; 'Fire! Fire!' He rushed to the telephone to summon help, and then back to the bathroom – he should have thought of that before – for water. As he burst into the bedroom there came a scream of terror which ended suddenly, and then the sound of a heavy fall.

This is the story which I heard on successive Saturday evenings from the senior mathematical master at a second-rate suburban school. For Saunders has had to earn a living in a way which other men might reckon less congenial than his old manner of life. I had mentioned by chance the name of Adrian Borlsover, and wondered at the time why he changed the conversation with such unusual abruptness. A week later Saunders began to tell me something of his own history; sordid enough, though shielded with a reserve I could well understand, for it had to cover not only his failings, but those of a dead friend. Of the final tragedy he was at first especially loath to speak; and it was only gradually that I was able to piece together the narrative of the preceding pages. Saunders was reluctant to draw any conclusions. At one time he thought that the fingered beast had been animated by the spirit of Sigismund Borlsover, a sinister eighteenth-century ancestor, who, according to legend, built and worshipped in the ugly pagan temple that overlooked the lake. At another time Saunders believed the spirit to belong to a man whom Eustace had once employed as a laboratory assistant, 'a black-haired, spiteful little brute,' he said, 'who died cursing his doctor because the fellow couldn't help him to live to settle some paltry score with Borlsover.'

From the point of view of direct contemporary evidence, Saunders story is practically uncorroborated. All the letters mentioned in the narrative were destroyed, with the exception of the last note which Eustace received, or rather, which he would have received, had not Saunders intercepted it. That I have seen myself. The handwriting was thin and shaky, the handwriting of an old man. I remember the Greek 'e' was used in 'appointment.' A little thing that amused me at the time was that Saunders seemed to keep the note pressed between the pages of his Bible.

I had seen Adrian Borlsover once. Saunders I learnt to know well. It was by chance, however, and not by design, that I met a third person of the story, Morton, the butler. Saunders and I were walking in the Zoological Gardens one Sunday afternoon, when he called my attention to an old man who was standing before the door of the Reptile House.

'Why, Morton,' he said, clapping him on the back, 'how is the world treating you?'

'Poorly, Mr Saunders,' said the old fellow, though his face lighted up at the greeting. 'The winters drag terribly nowadays. There don't seem no summers or springs.'

'You haven't found what you were looking for, I suppose?'

'No, sir, not yet; but I shall someday. I always told them that Mr Borlsover kept some queer animals.'

'And what is he looking for?' I asked, when we had parted from him.

'A beast with five fingers,' said Saunders. 'This afternoon, since he has been in the Reptile House, I suppose it will be a reptile with a hand. Next week it will be a monkey with practically no body. The poor old chap is a born materialist.'

THE AUTHOR
Angela Carter
THE STORY
The Company of Wolves
THE MOVIE
The Company of Wolves
THE DIRECTOR
Neil Jordan

One beast and only one howls in the woods by night.

The wolf is carnivore incarnate and he's as cunning as he is ferocious; once he's had a taste of flesh then nothing else will do.

At night, the eyes of wolves shine like candle flames, yellowish, reddish, but that is because the pupils of their eyes fatten on darkness and catch the light from your lantern to flash it back to you – red for danger; if a wolf's eyes reflect only moonlight, then they gleam a cold and unnatural green, a mineral, a piercing colour. If the benighted traveller spies those luminous, terrible sequins stitched suddenly on the black thickets, then he knows he must run, if fear has not struck him stock-still.

But those eyes are all you will be able to glimpse of the forest assassins as they cluster invisibly round your smell of meat as you go through the wood unwisely late. They will be like shadows, they will be like wraiths, grey members of a congregation of nightmare; hark! his long, wavering howl . . . an aria of fear made audible.

The wolfsong is the sound of the rending you will suffer, in itself a murdering.

It is winter and cold weather. In this region of mountain and forest, there is now nothing for the wolves to eat. Goats and sheep are locked up in the byre, the deer departed for the remaining pasturage on the southern slopes – wolves grow lean and famished. There is so little flesh on them that you could count the starveling ribs through their pelts, if they gave you time before they pounced. Those slavering jaws; the lolling tongue; the rime of saliva on the grizzled chops – of all the teeming perils of the night and the forest, ghosts, hobgoblins, ogres that grill babies upon gridirons, witches that fatten their captives in cages for cannibal tables, the wolf is worst for he cannot listen to reason.

You are always in danger in the forest, where no people are. Step between the portals of the great pines where the shaggy branches tangle about you, trapping the unwary traveller in nets as if the vegetation itself were in a plot with the wolves who live there, as though the wicked trees go fishing on behalf of their friends – step between the gateposts of the forest with the greatest trepidation and infinite precautions, for if you stray from the path for one instant, the wolves will eat you. They are grey as famine, they are as unkind as plague.

The grave-eyed children of the sparse villages always carry knives with them when they go out to tend the little flocks of goats that provide the homesteads with acrid milk and rank, maggoty cheeses. Their knives are half as big as they are, the blades are sharpened daily.

But the wolves have ways of arriving at your own hearthside. We try and try but sometimes we cannot keep them out. There is no winter's night the cottager does not fear to see a lean, grey, famished snout questing under the door, and there was a woman once bitten in her own kitchen as she was straining the macaroni.

Fear and flee the wolf; for, worst of all, the wolf may be more than he seems.

There was a hunter once, near here, that trapped a wolf in a pit. This wolf had massacred the sheep and goats; eaten up a mad old man who used to live by himself in a hut halfway up the mountain and sing to Jesus all day; pounced on a girl looking after the sheep, but she made such a commotion that men came with rifles and scared him away and tried to track him into the forest but he was cunning and easily gave them the slip. So this hunter dug a pit and put a duck in it, for bait, all alive-oh; and he covered the pit with straw smeared with wolfdung. Quack, quack! went the duck and a wolf came slinking out of the forest, a big one, a heavy one, he weighed as much as a grown man and the straw gave way beneath him – into the pit he tumbled. The hunter jumped down after him, slit his throat, cut off all his paws for a trophy.

And then no wolf at all lay in front of the hunter but the bloody trunk of a man, headless, footless, dying, dead.

A witch from up the valley once turned an entire wedding party into wolves because the groom had settled on another girl. She used to order them to visit her, at night, from spite, and they would sit and howl around her cottage for her, serenading her with their misery.

Not so very long ago, a young woman in our village married a man who vanished clean away on her wedding night. The bed was made with new sheets and the bride lay down in it; the groom said he was going out to relieve himself, insisted on it, for the sake of decency, and she drew the coverlet up to her chin and she lay there. And she waited and she waited and then she waited again – surely he's been gone a long time? Until she jumps up in bed and shrieks to hear a howling, coming on the wind from the forest.

That long-drawn, wavering howl has, for all its fearful resonance, some inherent sadness in it, as if the beasts would love to be less beastly if only they knew how and never cease to mourn their own condition. There is a vast melancholy in the canticles of the wolves, melancholy infinite as the forest, endless as these long nights of winter and yet that ghastly sadness, that mourning for their own, irremediable appetites, can never move the heart for not one phrase in it hints at the possibility of redemption; grace could not come to the wolf from its own despair, only through some external mediator, so that, sometimes, the beast will look as if he half welcomes the knife that despatches him.

The young woman's brothers searched the outhouses and the haystacks but never found any remains so the sensible girl dried her eyes and found herself another husband not too shy to piss into a pot who spent the nights indoors. She gave him a pair of bonny babies and all went right as a trivet until, one freezing night, the night of the solstice, the hinge of the year when things do not fit together as well as they should, the longest night, her first good man came home again.

A great thump on the door announced him as she was stirring the soup for the father of her children and she knew him the moment she lifted the latch to him although it was years since she'd worn black for him and now he was in rags and his hair hung down his back and never saw a comb, alive with lice.

'Here I am again, missus,' he said. 'Get me a bowl of cabbage and be quick about it.'

Then her second husband came in with wood for the fire and when the first one saw she'd slept with another man and, worse, clapped his red eyes on her little children who'd crept into the kitchen to see what all the din was about, he shouted: 'I wish I were a wolf again, to teach this whore a lesson!' So a wolf he instantly became and tore off the eldest boy's left foot before he was chopped up with the hatchet they used for chopping logs. But when the wolf lay bleeding and gasping its last, the pelt peeled off again and he was just as he had been, years ago, when he ran away from his marriage bed, so that she wept and her second husband beat her.

They say there's an ointment the Devil gives you that turns you into a wolf the minute you rub it on. Or, that he was born feet first and had a wolf for his father and his torso is a man's but his legs and genitals are a wolf's. And he has a wolf's heart.

Seven years is a werewolf's natural span but if you burn his human clothing you condemn him to wolfishness for the rest of his life, so old wives hereabouts think it some protection to throw a hat or an apron at the werewolf, as if clothes made the man. Yet by the eyes, those phosphorescent eyes, you know him in all his shapes; the eyes alone unchanged by metamorphosis.

Before he can become a wolf, the lycanthrope strips stark naked. If you spy a naked man among the pines, you must run as if the Devil were after you.

It is midwinter and the robin, the friend of man, sits on the handle of the gardener's spade and sings. It is the worst time in all the year for wolves but this strong-minded child insists she will go off through the wood. She is quite sure the wild beasts cannot harm her although, well-warned, she lays a carving knife in the basket her mother has packed with cheeses. There is a bottle of harsh liquor distilled from brambles; a batch of flat oatcakes baked on the hearthstone; a pot or two of jam. The flaxen-haired girl will take these delicious gifts to a reclusive grandmother so old the burden of her years is crushing her to death. Granny lives two hours' trudge through the winter woods; the child wraps herself up in her thick shawl, draws it over her head. She steps into her stout wooden shoes; she is dressed and ready and it is Christmas Eve. The malign door of the solstice still swings upon its hinges but she has been too much loved ever to feel scared.

Children do not stay young for long in this savage country. There are no toys for them to play with so they work hard and grow wise but this one, so pretty and the youngest of her family, a little late-comer, had been indulged by her mother and the grandmother who'd knitted her the red shawl that, today, has the ominous if brilliant look of blood on snow. Her breasts have just begun to swell; her hair is like lint, so fair it hardly makes a shadow on her pale forehead; her cheeks are an emblematic scarlet and white and she has just started her woman's bleeding, the clock inside her that will strike, henceforward, once a month.

She stands and moves within the invisible pentacle of her own virginity. She is an unbroken egg; she is a sealed vessel; she has inside her a magic space the entrance to which is shut tight with a plug of membrane; she is a closed system; she does not know how to shiver. She has her knife and she is afraid of nothing.

Her father might forbid her, if he were home, but he is away in the forest, gathering wood, and her mother cannot deny her.

The forest closed upon her like a pair of jaws.

There is always something to look at in the forest, even in the middle of winter – the huddled mounds of birds, succumbed to the lethargy of the season, heaped on the creaking boughs and too forlorn to sing; the bright frills of the winter fungi on the blotched trunks of the trees; the cuneiform slots of rabbits and deer, the herringbone tracks of the birds, a hare as lean as a rasher of bacon streaking across the path where the thin sunlight dapples the russet brakes of last year's bracken.

When she heard the freezing howl of a distant wolf, her practised hand sprang to the handle of her knife, but she saw no sign of a wolf at all, nor of a naked man, neither, but then she heard a clattering among the brushwood and there sprang on to the path a fully clothed one, a very handsome young one, in the green coat and wideawake hat of a hunter, laden with carcasses of game birds. She had her hand on her knife at the first rustle of twigs but he laughed with a flash of white teeth when he saw her and made her a comic yet flattering little bow; she'd never seen such a fine fellow before, not among the rustic clowns of her native village. So on they went together, through the thickening light of the afternoon.

Soon they were laughing and joking like old friends. When he offered to carry her basket, she gave it to him although her knife was in it because he told her his rifle would protect them. As the day darkened, it began to snow again; she felt the first flakes settle on her eyelashes but now there was only half a mile to go and there would be a fire, and hot tea, and a welcome, a warm one, surely, for the dashing huntsman as well as for herself.

This young man had a remarkable object in his pocket. It was a compass. She looked at the little round glass face in the palm of his hand and watched the wavering needle with a vague wonder. He assured her this compass had taken him safely through the wood on his hunting trip because the needle always told him with perfect accuracy where the north was. She did not believe it; she knew she should never leave the path on the way through the wood or else she would be lost instantly. He laughed at her again; gleaming trails of spittle clung to his teeth. He said, if he plunged off the path into the forest that surrounded them, he could guarantee to arrive at her grandmother's house a good quarter of an hour before she did, plotting his way through the undergrowth with his compass, while she trudged the long way, along the winding path.

I don't believe you. Besides, aren't you afraid of the wolves?

He only tapped the gleaming butt of his rifle and grinned.

Is it a bet? he asked her. Shall we make a game of it? What will you give me if I get to your grandmother's house before you?

What would you like? she asked disingenuously.

A kiss.

Commonplace of a rustic seduction; she lowered her eyes and blushed.

He went through the undergrowth and took her basket with him but she forgot to be afraid of the beasts, although now the moon was rising, for she wanted to dawdle on her way to make sure the handsome gentleman would win his wager.

Grandmother's house stood by itself a little way out of the village. The freshly falling snow blew in eddies about the kitchen garden and the young man stepped delicately up the snowy path to the door as if he were reluctant to get his feet wet, swinging his bundle of game and the girl's basket and humming a little tune to himself.

There is a faint trace of blood on his chin; he has been snacking on his catch.

He rapped upon the panels with his knuckles.

Aged and frail, granny is three-quarters succumbed to the mortality the ache in her bones promises her and almost ready to give in entirely. A boy came out from the village to build up her hearth for the night an hour ago and the kitchen crackles with busy firelight. She has her Bible for company, she is a pious old woman. She is propped up on several pillows in the bed set into the wall peasant-fashion, wrapped up in the patchwork quilt she made before she was married, more years ago than she cares to remember. Two china spaniels with liver coloured blotches on their coats and black noses sit on either side of the fireplace. There is a bright run of woven rags on the pantiles. The grandfather clock ticks away her eroding time.

We keep the wolves outside by living well.

He rapped upon the panels with his hairy knuckles.

It is your granddaughter, he mimicked in a high soprano.

Lift up the latch and walk in, my darling.

You can tell them by their eyes, eyes of a beast of prey, nocturnal, devastating eyes as red as a wound; you can hurl your Bible at him and your apron after, granny, you thought that was a sure prophylactic against these infernal vermin . . . now call on Christ and his mother and all the angels in heaven to protect you but it won't do you any good.

His feral muzzle is sharp as a knife; he drops his golden burden of gnawed pheasant on the table and puts down your dear girl's basket, too. Oh, my God, what have you done with her?

Off with his disguise, that coat of forest-coloured cloth, the hat with the feather tucked into the ribbon; his matted hair streams down his white shirt and she can see the lice moving in it. The sticks in the hearth shift and hiss; night and the forest has come into the kitchen with darkness tangled in its hair.

He strips off his shirt. His skin is the colour and texture of vellum. A crisp stripe of hair runs down his belly, his nipples are ripe and dark as poison fruit but he's so thin you could count the ribs under his skin if only he gave you the time. He strips off his trousers and she can see how hairy his legs are. His genitals, huge. Ah! huge.

The last thing the old lady saw in all this world was a young man, eyes like cinders, naked as a stone, approaching her bed.

The wolf is carnivore incarnate.

When he had finished with her, he licked his chops and quickly dressed himself again, until he was just as he had been when he came through her door. He burned the inedible hair in the fireplace and wrapped the bones up in a napkin that he hid away under the bed in the wooden chest in which he found a clean pair of sheets. These he carefully put on the bed instead of the tell-tale stained ones he stowed away in the laundry basket. He plumped up the pillows and shook out the patchwork quilt, he picked up the Bible from the floor, closed it and laid it on the table. All was as it had been before except that grandmother was gone. The sticks twitched in the grate, the clock ticked and the young man sat patiently, deceitfully beside the bed in granny's nightcap.

Rat-a-tap-tap.

Who's there, he quavers in granny's antique falsetto.

Only your granddaughter.

So she came in, bringing with her a flurry of snow that melted in tears on the tiles, and perhaps she was a little disappointed to see only her grandmother sitting beside the fire. But then he flung off the blanket and sprang to the door, pressing his back against it so that she could not get out again.

The girl looked round the room and saw there was not even the indentation of a head on the smooth cheek of the pillow and how, for the first time she'd seen it so, the Bible lay closed on the table. The tick of the clock cracked like a whip. She wanted her knife from her basket but she did not dare reach for it because his eyes were fixed upon her – huge eyes that now seemed to shine with a unique, interior light, eyes the size of saucers, saucers full of Greek fire, diabolic phosphorescence.

What big eyes you have.

All the better to see you with.

No trace at all of the old woman except for a tuft of white hair that had caught in the bark of an unburned log. When the girl saw that, she knew she was in danger of death.

Where is my grandmother?

There's nobody here but we two, my darling.

Now a great howling rose up all around them, near, very near, as close as the kitchen garden, the howling of a multitude of wolves; she knew the worst wolves are hairy on the inside and she shivered, in spite of the scarlet shawl she pulled more closely round herself as if it could protect her although it was as red as the blood she must spill.

Who has come to sing us carols, she said.

Those are the voices of my brothers, darling; I love the company of wolves. Look out of the window and you'll see them.

Snow half-caked the lattice and she opened it to look into the garden. It was a white night of moon and snow; the blizzard whirled round the gaunt, grey beasts who squatted on their haunches among the rows of winter cabbage, pointing their sharp snouts to the moon and howling as if their hearts would break. Ten wolves; twenty wolves – so many wolves she could not count them, howling in concert as if demented or deranged. Their eyes reflected the light from the kitchen and shone like a hundred candles.

It is very cold, poor things, she said; no wonder they howl so.

She closed the window on the wolves' threnody and took off her scarlet shawl, the colour of poppies, the colour of sacrifices, the colour of her menses, and, since her fear did her no good, she ceased to be afraid.

What shall I do with my shawl?

Throw it on the fire, dear one. You won't need it again.

She bundled up her shawl and threw it on the blaze, which instantly consumed it. Then she drew her blouse over her head; her small breasts gleamed as if the snow had invaded the room.

What shall I do with my blouse?

Into the fire with it, too, my pet.

The thin muslin went flaring up the chimney like a magic bird and now off came her skirt, her woollen stockings, her shoes, and on to the fire they went, too, and were gone for good. The firelight shone through the edges of her skin; now she was clothed only in her untouched integument of flesh. This dazzling, naked she combed out her hair with her fingers; her hair looked white as the snow outside. Then went directly to the man with red eyes in whose unkempt mane the lice moved; she stood up on tiptoe and unbuttoned the collar of his shirt.

What big arms you have.

All the better to hug you with.

Every wolf in the world now howled a prothalamion outside the window as she freely gave the kiss she owed him.

What big teeth you have!

She saw how his jaw began to slaver and the room was full of clamour of the forest's Liebestod but the wise child never flinched, even when he answered:

All the better to eat you with.

The girl burst out laughing; she knew she was nobody's meat. She laughed at him full in the face, she ripped off his shirt for him and flung it into the fire, in the fiery wake of her own discarded clothing.

The flames danced like dead souls on Walpurgisnacht and the old bones under the bed set up a terrible clattering but she did not pay them any heed.

Carnivore incarnate, only immaculate flesh appeases him.

She will lay his fearful head on her lap and she will pick out the lice from his pelt and perhaps she will put the lice into her mouth and eat them, as he will bid her, as she would do in a savage marriage ceremony.

The blizzard will die down.

The blizzard died down, leaving the mountains as randomly covered with snow as if a blind woman had thrown a sheet over them, the upper branches of the forest pines limed, creaking, swollen with the fall.

Snowlight, moonlight, a confusion of paw-prints.

All silent, all still.

Midnight; and the clock strikes. It is Christmas Day, the were-wolves' birthday, the door of the solstice stands wide open; let them all sink through.

See! sweet and sound she sleeps in granny's bed, between the paws of the tender wolf.

THE AUTHOR
I.L. Peretz
THE STORY
The Golem
THE MOVIE
The Golem
THE DIRECTORS
Paul Wegener & Carl Boese

G reat men were once capable of great miracles.
When the ghetto of Prague was being attacked, and they were about to rape the women, roast the children, and slaughter the rest; when it seemed that the end had finally come, the great Rabbi Loeb put aside his *Gemarah*, went into the street, stopped before a heap of clay in front of the teacher's house, and molded a clay image. He blew into the nose of the *golem* – and it began to stir; then he whispered the Name into its ear, and our *golem* left the ghetto. The rabbi returned to the House of Prayer, and the *golem* fell upon our enemies, threshing them as with flails. Men fell on all sides.

Prague was filled with corpses. It lasted, so they say, through Wednesday and Thursday. Now it is already Friday, the clock strikes twelve, and the *golem* is still busy at its work.

'Rabbi,' cries the head of the ghetto, 'the *golem* is slaughtering all of Prague! There will not be a gentile left to light the Sabbath fires or take down the Sabbath lamps.'

Once again the rabbi left his study. He went to the altar and began singing the psalm 'A song of the Sabbath.'

The *golem* ceased its slaughter. It returned to the ghetto, entered the House of Prayer, and waited before the rabbi. And again the rabbi whispered into its ear. The eyes of the *golem* closed, the soul that had dwelt in it flew out, and it was once more a *golem* of clay.

To this day the *golem* lies hidden in the attic of the Prague synagogue, covered with cobwebs that extend from wall to wall. No living creature may look at it, particularly women in pregnancy. No one may touch the cobwebs, for whoever touches them dies. Even the oldest people no longer remember the *golem*, though the wise man Zvi, the grandson of the great Rabbi Loeb, ponders the problem: may such a *golem* be included in a congregation of worshippers or not?

The *golem*, you see, has not been forgotten. It is still here! But the Name by which it could be called to life in a day of need, the Name has disappeared. And the cobwebs grow and grow, and no one may touch them.

What are we to do?

THE AUTHOR
Robert Bloch

THE STORY
Lucy Comes To Stay

THE MOVIE
Asylum

THE DIRECTOR
Roy Ward Baker

'You can't go on this way.'

Lucy kept her voice down low, because she knew the nurse had her room just down the hall from mine, and I wasn't supposed to see any visitors.

'But George is doing everything he can – poor dear, I hate to think of what all those doctors and specialists are costing him, and the sanatorium bill, too. And now that nurse, that Miss Higgins, staying here every day.'

'It won't do any good. You know it won't.' Lucy didn't sound like she was arguing with me. She knew. That's because Lucy is smarter than I am. Lucy wouldn't have started the drinking and gotten into such a mess in the first place. So it was about time I listened to what she said.

'Look, Vi,' she murmured. 'I hate to tell you this. You aren't well, you know. But you're going to find out one of these days anyway, and you might as well hear it from me.'

'What is it, Lucy?'

'About George, and the doctors. They don't think you're going to get well.' She paused. 'They don't want you to.'

'Oh, Lucy!'

'Listen to me, you little fool. Why do you suppose they sent you to that sanatorium in the first place? They said it was to take the cure. So you took it. All right, you're cured, then. But you'll notice that you still have the doctor coming every day, and George makes you stay here in your room, and that Miss Higgins who's supposed to be a special nurse – you know what she is, don't you? She's a guard.'

I couldn't say anything. I just sat there and blinked. I wanted to cry, but I couldn't, because deep down inside I knew that Lucy was right.

'Just try to get out of here,' Lucy said. 'You'll see how fast she locks the door on you. All that talk about special diets and rest doesn't fool me. Look at yourself – you're as well as I am! You ought to be getting out, seeing people, visiting your friends.'

'But I have no friends,' I reminded her. 'Not after that party, not after what I did – '

'That's a lie,' Lucy nodded. 'That's what George wants you to think. Why, you have hundreds of friends, Vi. They still love you. They tried to see you at the hospital and George wouldn't let them in. They sent flowers to the sanatorium and George told the nurses to burn them.'

'He did? He told the nurses to burn the flowers?'

'Of course. Look, Vi, it's about time you faced the truth. George wants them to think you're sick. George wants you to think you're sick. Why? Because then he can put you away for good. Not in a private sanatorium, but in the – '

'No!' I began to shake. I couldn't stop shaking. It was ghastly. But it proved something. They told me at the sanatorium, the doctors told me, that if I took the cure I wouldn't get the shakes any more. Or the dreams, or any of the other things. Yet here it was – I was shaking again.

'Shall I tell you some more?' Lucy whispered. 'Shall I tell you what they're putting in your food? Shall I tell you about George and Miss Higgins?'

'But she's older than he is, and besides he'd never – ' Lucy laughed.

'Stop it!' I yelled.

'All right. But don't yell, you little fool. Do you want Miss Higgins to come in?'

'She thinks I'm taking a nap. She gave me a sedative.'

'Lucky I dumped it out.' Lucy frowned. 'Vi, I've got to get you away from here. And there isn't much time.'

She was right. There wasn't much time. Seconds, hours, days, weeks – how long had it been since I'd had a drink?

'We'll sneak off,' Lucy said. 'We could take a room together where they wouldn't find us. I'll nurse you until you're well.'

'But rooms cost money.'

'You have that fifty dollars George gave you for a party dress.'

'Why, Lucy,' I said. 'How did you know that?'

'You told me ages ago, dear. Poor thing, you don't remember things very well, do you? All the more reason for trusting me.'

I nodded. I could trust Lucy. Even though she was responsible, in a way, for me starting to drink. She just had thought it would cheer me up when George brought all his high-class friends to the house and we went out to impressed his clients. Lucy had tried to help. I could trust her. I must trust her –

'We can leave as soon as Miss Higgins goes tonight,' Lucy was saying. 'We'll wait until George is asleep, eh? Why not get dressed now, and I'll come back for you.'

I got dressed. It isn't easy to dress when you have the shakes, but I did it. I even put on some makeup and trimmed my hair a little with the big scissors. Then I looked at myself in the mirror and said out loud, 'Why, you can't tell, can you?'

'Of course not,' said Lucy. 'You look radiant. Positively radiant.'

I stood there smiling, and the sun was going down, just shining through the window on the scissors in a way that hurt my eyes, and all at once I was so sleepy.

'George will be here soon, and Miss Higgins will leave,' Lucy said. 'I'd better go now. Why don't you rest until I come for you?'

'Yes,' I said. 'You'll be very careful, won't you?'

'Very careful,' Lucy whispered, as she tiptoed out quietly.

I lay down on the bed and then I was sleeping, really sleeping for the first time in weeks, sleeping so the scissors wouldn't hurt my eyes, the way George hurt me inside when he wanted to shut me up in the asylum so he and Miss Higgins could make love on my bed and laugh at me the way they all laughed except Lucy and she would take care of me she knew what to do now I could trust her when George came and I must sleep and sleep and nobody can blame you for what you think in your sleep or do in your sleep . . .

It was all right until I had the dreams, and even then I didn't really worry about them because a dream is only a dream, and when I was drunk I had a lot of dreams.

When I woke up I had the shakes again, but it was Lucy shaking me, standing there in the dark shaking me, I looked around and saw that the door to my room was open, but Lucy didn't bother to whisper.

She stood there with the scissors in her hand and called to me.

'Come on, let's hurry.'

'What are you doing with the scissors?' I asked.

'Cutting the telephone wires, silly! I got into the kitchen after Miss Higgins left and dumped some of that sedative into George's coffee. Remember, I told you the plan.'

I couldn't remember now, but I knew it was all right. Lucy and I went out through the hall, past George's room, and he never stirred. Then we went downstairs and out the front door and the streetlights hurt my eyes. Lucy made me hurry right along, though.

We took a bus around the corner. This was the difficult part, getting away. Once we were out of the neighborhood there'd be no worry. The wires were cut.

The lady at the rooming house on the South Side didn't know about the wires being cut. She didn't know about me, either, because Lucy got the room.

Lucy marched in bold as brass and laid my fifty dollars down on the desk. The rent was $12.50 a week in advance, and Lucy didn't even ask to see the room. I guess that's why the landlady wasn't worried about baggage.

We got upstairs and locked the door, and then I had the shakes again.

Lucy said, 'Vi – cut it out?'

'But I can't help it. What'll I do now, Lucy? Oh, what'll I do? Why did I ever – '

'Shut up! Lucy opened my purse and pulled something out. I had been wondering why my purse felt so heavy but I never dreamed about the secret.

She held the secret up. It glittered under the light, like the scissors, only this was a nice glittering. A golden glittering

'A whole pint!' I gasped. 'Where did you get it?'

'From the cupboard downstairs, naturally. You knew George still keeps the stuff around. I slipped it into your purse, just in case.'

I had the shakes, but I got that bottle open in ten seconds. One of my fingernails broke, and then the stuff was burning and warming and softening –

'Pig!' said Lucy.

'You know I had to have it,' I whispered. 'That's why you brought it.'

'I don't like to see you drink,' Lucy answered. 'I never drink and I don't like to see you hang one on, either.'

'Please, Lucy. Just this once.'

'Why can't you take a shot and then leave it alone? That's all I ask.'

'Just this once, Lucy, I have to.'

'I won't sit here and watch you make a spectacle of yourself. You know what always happens – another mess.'

I took another gulp. The bottle was half-empty.

'I did all I could for you, Vi. But if you don't stop now, I'm going.'

That made me pause. 'You couldn't do that to me. I need you, Lucy. Until I'm straightened out, anyway.'

Lucy laughed, the way I didn't like. 'Straightened out! That's a hot one! Talking about straightening out with a bottle in your hand. It's no use, Vi. Here I do everything I can for you, stop at nothing to get you away, and you're off on another.'

'Please. You know I can't help it.'

'Oh, yes, you can help it, Vi. But you don't want to. You've always had to make a choice, you know. George or the bottle. Me or the bottle. And the bottle always wins. I think deep down inside you hate George. You hate me.'

'You're my best friend.'

'Nuts!' Lucy talked vulgar sometimes, when she got really mad. And she was mad, now. It made me so nervous I had another drink.

'Oh, I'm good enough for you when you're in trouble, or have nobody else around to talk to. I'm good enough to lie for you, pull you out of your messes. But I've never been good enough for your friends, for George. And I can't even win over a bottle of rotgut whiskey. It's no use, Vi. What I've done for you today you'll never know. And it isn't enough. Keep your lousy whiskey. I'm going.'

I know I started to cry. I tried to get up, but the room was turning round and round. Then Lucy was walking out the door and I dropped the bottle and the light kept shining the way it did on the scissors and I closed my eyes and dropped after the bottle to the floor. . . .

When I woke up they were all pestering me, the landlady and the doctor and Miss Higgins and the man who said he was a policeman.

I wondered if Lucy had gone to them and betrayed me, but when I asked the doctor said no, they just discovered me through a routine checkup on hotels and rooming houses after they found George's body in his bed with my scissors in his throat.

All at once I knew what Lucy had done, and why she ran out on me that way. She knew they'd find me and call it murder.

So I told them about her and how it must have happened. I even figured out how Lucy managed to get my fingerprints on the scissors.

But Miss Higgins said she'd never seen Lucy in my house, and the landlady told a lie and said I had registered for the room alone, and the man from the police just laughed when I kept begging him to find Lucy and make her tell the truth.

Only the doctor seemed to understand, and when we were alone together in the little room he asked me all about her and what she looked like, and I told him.

Then he brought over the mirror and held it up and asked me if I could see her. And sure enough –

She was standing right behind me, laughing. I could see her in the mirror and I told the doctor so, and he said yes, he thought he understood now.

So it was all right after all. Even when I got the shakes just then and dropped the mirror, so that the little jagged pieces hurt my eyes to look at, it was all right.

Lucy was back with me now, and she wouldn't ever go away any more. She'd stay with me forever. I knew that. I knew it, because even though the light hurt my eyes, Lucy began to laugh.

After a minute, I began to laugh, too. And then the two of us were laughing together, we couldn't stop even when the doctor went away. We just stood there against the bars, Lucy and I, laughing like crazy.

THE AUTHOR
H.P. Lovecraft
THE STORY
The Color Out of Space
THE MOVIE
Die, Monster, Die
THE DIRECTOR
Daniel Haller

West of the Arkham hills rise wild, and there are valleys with deep woods that no axe has ever cut. There are dark narrow glens where the trees slope fantastically, and where thin brooklets trickle without ever having caught the glint of sunlight. On the gentler slopes there are farms, ancient and rocky, with squat, moss-coated cottages brooding eternally over old New England secrets in the lee of great ledges; but these are all vacant now, the wide chimneys crumbling and the shingled sides bulging perilously beneath low gambrel roofs.

The old folk have gone away, and foreigners do not like to live there. French-Canadians have tried it, Italians have tried it, and the Poles have come and departed. It is not because of anything that can be seen or heard or handled, but because of something that is imagined. The place is not good for imagination, and does not bring restful dreams at night. It must be this which keeps the foreigners away, for old Ammi Pierce has never told them of anything he recalls from the strange days. Ammi, whose head has been a little queer for years, is the only one who still remains, or who ever talks of the strange days; and he dares to do this because his house is so near the open fields and the travelled roads around Arkham.

There was once a road over the hills and through the valleys, that ran straight where the blasted heath is now; but people ceased to use it and a new road was laid curving far toward the south. Traces of the old one can still be found amidst the weeds of a returning wilderness, and some of them will doubtless linger even when half the hollows are flooded for the new reservoir. Then the dark woods will be cut down and the blasted heath will slumber far below blue waters whose surface will mirror the sky and ripple in the sun. And the secrets of the strange days will be one with the deep's secrets; one with the hidden lore of old ocean, and all the mystery of primal earth.

When I went into the hills and vales to survey for the new reservoir they told me the place was evil. They told me this in Arkham, and because that is a very old town full of witch legends I thought the evil must be something which grandams had whispered to children through centuries. The name 'blasted heath' seemed to me very odd and theatrical, and I wondered how it had come into the folklore of a Puritan people. Then I saw that dark westward tangle of glens and slopes for myself, and ceased to wonder at anything beside its own elder mystery. It was morning when I saw it, but shadow lurked always there. The trees grew too thickly, and their trunks were too big for any healthy New England wood. There was too much silence in the dim alleys between them, and the floor was too soft with the dank moss and mattings of infinite years of decay.

In the open spaces, mostly along the line of the old road, there were little hillside farms; sometimes with all the buildings standing, sometimes with only one or two, and sometimes with only a lone chimney or fast-filling cellar. Weeds and briers reigned, and furtive wild things rustled in the undergrowth. Upon everything was a haze of restlessness and oppression; a touch of the unreal and the grotesque, as if some vital element of perspective or chiaroscuro were awry. I did not wonder that the foreigners would not stay, for this was no region to sleep in. It was too much like a landscape of Salvator Rosa; too much like some forbidden woodcut in a tale of terror.

But even all this was not so bad as the blasted heath. I knew it the moment I came upon it at the bottom of a spacious valley; for no other name could fit such a thing, or any other thing fit such a name. It was as if the poet had coined the phrase from having seen this one particular region. It must, I thought as I viewed it, be the outcome of a fire; but why had nothing new ever grown over those five acres of grey desolation that sprawled open to the sky like a great spot eaten by acid in the woods and fields? It lay largely to the north of the ancient road line, but encroached a little on the other side. I felt an odd reluctance about approaching, and did so at last only because my business took me through and past it. There was no vegetation of any kind on that broad expanse, but only a fine grey dust or ash which no wind seemed ever to blow about. The trees near it were sickly and stunted, and many dead trunks stood or lay rotting at the rim. As I walked hurriedly by I saw the tumbled bricks and stones of an old chimney and cellar on my right, and the yawning black maw of an abandoned well whose stagnant vapours played strange tricks with the hues of the sunlight. Even the long, dark woodland climb beyond seemed welcome in contrast, and I marvelled no more at the frightened whispers of Arkham people. There had been no house or ruin near; even in the old days the place must have been lonely and remote. And at twilight, dreading to repass that ominous spot, I walked circuitously back to the town by the curving road on the south. I vaguely wished some clouds would gather, for an odd timidity about the deep skyey voids above had crept into my soul.

In the evening I asked old people in Arkham about the blasted heath, and what was meant by that phrase 'strange days' which so many evasively muttered. I could not, however, get any good answers, except that all the mystery was much more recent than I had dreamed. It was not a matter of old legendry at all, but something within the lifetime of those who spoke. It had happened in the 'eighties, and a family had disappeared or was killed. Speakers would not be exact; and because they all told me to pay no attention to old Ammi Pierce's crazy tales, I sought him out the next morning, having heard that he lived alone in the ancient tottering cottage where the trees first begin to get very thick. It was a fearsomely ancient place, and had begun to exude the faint miasmal odour which clings about houses that have stood too long. Only with persistent knocking could I rouse the aged man, and when he shuffled timidly to the door I could tell he was not glad to see me. He was not so feeble as I had expected; but his eyes drooped in a curious way, and his unkempt clothing and white beard made him seem very worn and dismal.

Not knowing just how he could best be launched on his tales, I feigned a matter of business; told him of my surveying, and asked vague questions about the district. He was far brighter and more educated than I had been led to think, and before I knew it had grasped quite as much of the subject as any man I had talked with in Arkham. He was not like other rustics I had known in the sections where reservoirs were to be. From him there were no protests at the miles of old wood and farmland to be blotted out, though perhaps there would have been had not his home lain outside the bounds of the future lake. Relief was all that he showed; relief at the doom of the dark ancient valleys through which he had roamed all his life. They were better under water now – better under water since the strange days. And with this opening his husky voice sank low, while his body leaned forward and his right forefinger began to point shakily and impressively.

It was then that I heard the story, and as the rambling voice scraped and whispered on I shivered again and again despite the summer day. Often I had to recall the speaker from ramblings, piece out scientific points which he knew only by a fading parrot memory of professors' talk, or bridge over gaps where his sense of logic and continuity broke down. When he was done I did not wonder that his mind had snapped a trifle, or that the folk of Arkham would not speak much of the blasted heath. I hurried back before sunset to my hotel, unwilling to have the stars come out above me in the open; and the next day returned to Boston to give up my position. I could not go into that dim chaos of old forest and slope again, or face another time that grey blasted heath where the black well yawned deep beside the tumbled bricks and stones. The reservoir will soon be built now, and all those elder secrets will be safe forever under watery fathoms. But even then I do not believe I would like to visit that country by night – at least not when the sinister stars are out; and nothing could bribe me to drink the new city water of Arkham.

It all began, old Ammi said, with the meteorite. Before that time there had been no wild legends at all since the witch trials, and even then these western woods were not feared half so much as the small island in the Miskatonic where the devil held court beside a curious stone altar older than the Indians. These were not haunted woods, and their fantastic dusk was never terrible till the strange days. Then there had come that white noontide cloud, that string of explosions in the air, and that pillar of smoke from the valley far in the wood. And by night all Arkham had heard of the great rock that fell out of the sky and bedded itself in the ground beside the well at the Nahum Gardner place. That was the house which had stood where the blasted heath was to come – the trim white Nahum Gardner house amidst its fertile gardens and orchards.

Nahum had come to town to tell people about the stone, and dropped in at Ammi Pierce's on the way. Ammi was forty then, and all the queer things were fixed very strongly in his mind. He and his wife had gone with the three professors from Miskatonic University who hastened out the next morning to see the weird visitor from unknown stellar space, and had wondered why Nahum had called it so large the day before. It had shrunk, Nahum said, as he pointed out the big brownish mound above the ripped earth and charred grass near the archaic well-sweep in his front yard; but the wise men answered that stones do not shrink. Its heat lingered persistently, and Nahum declared it had glowed faintly in the night. The professors tried it with a geologist's hammer and found it was oddly soft. It was, in truth, so soft as to be almost plastic; and they gouged rather than chipped a specimen to take back to the college for testing. They took it in an old pail borrowed from Nahum's kitchen, for even the small piece refused to grow cool. On the trip back they stopped at Ammi's to rest, and seemed thoughtful when Mrs Pierce remarked that the fragment was growing smaller and burning the bottom of the pail. Truly, it was not large, but perhaps they had taken less than they thought.

The day after that – all this was in June of '82 – the professors had trooped out again in a great excitement. As they passed Ammi's they told him what queer things the specimen had done, and how it had faded wholly away when they put it in a glass beaker. The beaker had gone, too, and the wise men talked of the strange stone's affinity for silicon. It had acted quite unbelievably in that well-ordered laboratory; doing nothing at all and showing no occluded gases when heated on charcoal, being wholly negative in the borax bead, and soon proving itself absolutely non-volatile at any producible temperature, including that of the oxy-hydrogen blowpipe. On an anvil it appeared highly malleable, and in the dark its luminosity was very marked. Stubbornly refusing to grow cool, it soon had the college in a state of real excitement; and when upon heating before the spectroscope it displayed shining bands unlike any known colours of the normal spectrum there was much breathless talk of new elements, bizarre optical properties, and other things which puzzled men of science are wont to say when faced by the unknown.

Hot as it was, they tested it in a crucible with all the proper reagents. Water did nothing. Hydrochloric acid was the same. Nitric acid and even aqua regia merely hissed and spattered against its torrid invulnerability. Ammi had difficulty in recalling all these things, but recognized some solvents as I mentioned them in the usual order of use. There were ammonia and caustic soda, alcohol and ether, nauseous carbon disulphide and a dozen others; but although the weight grew steadily less as time passed, and the fragment seemed to be slightly cooling, there was no change in the solvents to show that they had attacked the substance at all. It was a metal, though, beyond a doubt. It was magnetic, for one thing; and after its immersion in the acid solvents there seemed to be faint traces of the Widmänstätten figures found on meteoric iron. When the cooling had grown very considerable, the testing was carried on in glass; and it was in a glass beaker that they left all the chips made of the original fragment during the work. The next morning both chips and beaker were gone without trace, and only a charred spot marked the place on the wooden shelf where they had been.

All this the professors told Ammi as they paused at his door, and once more he went with them to see the stony messenger from the stars, though this time his wife did not accompany him. It had now most certainly shrunk, and even the sober professors could not doubt the truth of what they saw. All around the dwindling brown lump near the well was a vacant space, except where the earth had caved in; and whereas it had been a good seven feet across the day before, it was now scarcely five. It was still hot, and the sages studied its surface curiously as they detached another and larger piece with hammer and chisel. They gouged deeply this time, and as they pried away the smaller mass they saw that the core of the thing was not quite homogeneous.

They had uncovered what seemed to be the side of a large coloured globule embedded in the substance. The colour, which resembled some of the bands in the meteor's strange spectrum, was almost impossible to describe; and it was only by analogy that they called it colour at all. Its texture was glossy, and upon tapping it appeared to promise both brittleness and hollowness. One of the professors gave it a smart blow with a hammer, and it burst with a nervous little pop. Nothing was emitted, and all trace of the thing vanished with the puncturing. It left behind a hollow spherical space about three inches across, and all thought it probable that others would be discovered as the enclosing substance wasted away.

Conjecture was vain; so after a futile attempt to find additional globules by drilling, the seekers left again with their new specimen – which proved, however, as baffling in the laboratory as its pre-decessor. Aside from being almost plastic, having heat, magnetism, and slight luminosity, cooling slightly in powerful acids, possessing an unknown spectrum, wasting away in air, and attacking silicon compounds with mutual destruction as a result, it presented no identifying features whatsoever; and at the end of the tests the college scientists were forced to own that they could not place it. It was nothing of this earth, but a piece of the great outside; and as such dowered with outside properties and obedient to outside laws.

That night there was a thunderstorm, and when the professors went out to Nahum's the next day they met with a bitter disappointment. The stone, magnetic as it had been, must have had some peculiar electrical property; for it had 'drawn the lightning,' as Nahum said, with a singular persistence. Six times within an hour the farmer saw the lightning strike the furrow in the front yard, and when the storm was over nothing remained but a ragged pit by the ancient well-sweep, half-choked with a caved-in earth. Digging had borne no fruit, and the scientists verified the fact of the utter vanishment. The failure was total; so that nothing was left to do but go back to the laboratory and test again the disappearing fragment left carefully cased in lead. That fragment lasted a week, at the end of which nothing of value had been learned of it. When it had gone, no residue was left behind, and in time the professors felt scarcely sure they had indeed seen with waking eyes that cryptic vestige of the fathomless gulfs outside; that lone, weird message from other universes and other realms of matter, force, and entity.

As was natural, the Arkham papers made much of the incident with its collegiate sponsoring, and sent reporters to talk with Nahum Gardner and his family. At least one Boston daily also sent a scribe, and Nahum quickly became a kind of local celebrity. He was a lean, genial person of about fifty, living with his wife and three sons on the pleasant farmstead in the valley. He and Ammi exchanged visits frequently, as did their wives; and Ammi had nothing but praise for him after all these years. He seemed slightly proud of the notice his place had attracted, and talked often of the meteorite in the succeeding weeks. That July and August were hot; and Nahum worked hard at his haying in the ten-acre pasture across Chapman's Brook; his rattling wain wearing deep ruts in the shadowy lanes between. The labour tired him more than it had in other years, and he felt that age was beginning to tell on him.

Then fell the time of fruit and harvest. The pears and apples slowly ripened, and Nahum vowed that his orchards were prospering as never before. The fruit was growing to phenomenal size and unwonted gloss, and in such abundance that extra barrels were ordered to handle the future crop. But with the ripening came sore disappointment, for of all that gorgeous array of specious lusciousness not one single jot was fit to eat. Into the fine flavour of the pears and apples had crept a stealthy bitterness and sickishness, so that even the smallest bites induced a lasting disgust. It was the same with the melons and tomatoes, and Nahum sadly saw that his entire crop was lost. Quick to connect events, he declared that the meteorite had poisoned the soil, and thanked Heaven that most of the other crops were in the upland lot along the road.

Winter came early, and was very cold. Ammi saw Nahum less often than usual, and observed that he had begun to look worried. The rest of his family too, seemed to have grown taciturn; and were far from steady in their church-going or their attendance at the various social events of the countryside. For this reserve or melancholy no cause could be found, though all the household confessed now and then to poorer health and a feeling of vague disquiet. Nahum himself gave the most definite statement of anyone when he said he was disturbed about certain footprints in the snow. They were the usual winter prints of red squirrels, white rabbits, and foxes, but the brooding farmer professed to see something not quite right about their nature and arrangement. He was never specific, but appeared to think that they were not as characteristic of the anatomy and habits of squirrels and rabbits and foxes as they ought to be. Ammi listened without interest to this talk until one night when he drove past Nahum's house in his sleigh on the way back from Clark's Corners. There had been a moon, and a rabbit had run across the road, and the leaps of that rabbit were longer than either Ammi or his horse liked. The latter, indeed, had almost run away when brought up by a firm rein. Thereafter Ammi gave Nahum's tales more respect, and wondered why the Gardner dogs seemed so cowed and quivering every morning. They had, it developed, nearly lost the spirit to bark.

In February the McGregor boys from Meadow Hill were out shooting woodchucks, and not far from the Gardner place bagged a very peculiar specimen. The proportions of its body seemed slightly altered in a queer way impossible to describe, while its face had taken on an expression which no one ever saw in a woodchuck before. The boys were genuinely frightened, and threw the thing away at once, so that only their grotesque tales of it ever reached the people of the countryside. But the shying of horses near Nahum's house had now become an acknowledged thing, and all the basis for a cycle of whispered legend was fast taking form.

People vowed that the snow melted faster around Nahum's than it did anywhere else, and early in March there was an awed discussion in Potter's general store at Clark's Corners. Stephen Rice had driven past Gardner's in the morning, and had noticed the skunk-cabbages coming up through the mud by the woods across the road. Never were things of such size seen before, and they held strange colours that could not be put into any words. Their shapes were monstrous, and the horse had snorted at an odour which struck Stephen as wholly unprecedented. That afternoon several persons drove past to see the abnormal growth, and all agreed that plants of that kind ought never to sprout in a healthy world. The bad fruit of the fall before was freely mentioned, and it went from mouth to mouth that there was poison in Nahum's ground. Of course it was the meteorite; and remembering how strange the men from the college had found that stone to be, several farmers spoke about the matter to them.

One day they paid Nahum a visit; but having no love of wild tales and folklore were very conservative in what they inferred. The plants were certainly odd, but all skunk-cabbages are more or less odd in shape and hue. Perhaps some mineral element from the stone had entered the soil, but it would soon be washed away. And as for the footprints and frightened horses – of course this was mere country talk which such a phenomenon as the aerolite would be certain to start. There was really nothing for serious men to do in cases of wild gossip, for superstitious rustics will say and believe anything. And so all through the strange days the professors stayed away in contempt. Only one of them, when given two phials of dust for analysis in a police job over a year and a half later, recalled that the queer colour of that skunk-cabbage had been very like one of the anomalous bands of light shown by the meteor fragment in the college spectroscope, and like the brittle globule found imbedded in the stone from the abyss. The samples in this analysis case gave the same odd bands at first, though later they lost the property.

The trees budded prematurely around Nahum's, and at night they swayed ominously in the wind. Nahum's second son Thaddeus, a lad of fifteen, swore that they swayed also when there was no wind; but even the gossips would not credit this. Certainly, however, restlessness was in the air. The entire Gardner family developed the habit of stealthy listening, though not for any sound which they could consciously name. The listening was, indeed, rather a product of moments when consciousness seemed half to slip away. Unfortunately such moments increased week by week, till it became common speech that 'something was wrong with all Nahum's folks'. When the early saxifrage came out it had another strange colour; not quite that of the skunk-cabbage, but plainly related and equally unknown to anyone who saw it. Nahum took some blossoms to Arkham and showed them to the editor of the *Gazette*, but that dignitary did no more than write a humorous article about them, in which the dark fears of rustics were held up to polite ridicule. It was a mistake of Nahum's to tell a stolid city man about the way the great, overgrown mourning-cloak butterflies behaved in connection with these saxifrages.

April brought a kind of madness to the country folk, and began that disuse of the road past Nahum's which led to its ultimate abandonment. It was the vegetation. All the orchard trees blossomed forth in strange colours, and through the stony soil of the yard and adjacent pasturage there sprang up a bizarre growth which only a botanist could connect with the proper flora of the region. No sane wholesome colours were anywhere to be seen except in the green grass and leafage; but everywhere were those hectic and prismatic variants of some diseased, underlying primary tone without a place among the known tints of earth. The 'Dutchman's breeches' became a thing of sinister menace, and the bloodroots grew insolent in their chromatic perversion. Ammi and the Gardners thought that most of the colours had a sort of haunting familiarity, and decided that they reminded one of the brittle globule in the meteor. Nahum ploughed and sowed the ten-acre pasture and the upland lot, but did nothing with the land around the house. He knew it would be of no use, and hoped that the summer's strange growths would draw all the poison from the soil. He was prepared for almost anything now, and had grown used to the sense of something near him waiting to be heard. The shunning of his house by neighbours told on him, of course; but it told on his wife more. The boys were better off, being at school each day; but they could not help being frightened by the gossip. Thaddeus, an especially sensitive youth, suffered the most.

In May the insects came, and Nahum's place became a nightmare of buzzing and crawling. Most of the creatures seemed not quite usual in their aspects and motions, and their nocturnal habits contradicted all former experience. The Gardners took to watching at night – watching in all directions at random for something – they could not tell what. It was then that they all owned that Thaddeus had been right about the trees. Mrs Gardner was the next to see it from the window as she watched the swollen boughs of a maple against a moonlit sky. The boughs surely moved, and there was no wind. It must be the sap. Strangeness had come into everything growing now. Yet it was none of Nahum's family at all who made the next discovery. Familiarity had dulled them, and what they could not see was glimpsed by a timid windmill salesman from Bolton who drove by one night in ignorance of the country legends. What he told in Arkham was given a short paragraph in the *Gazette*; and it was there that all the farmers, Nahum included, saw it first. The night had been dark and the buggy-lamps faint, but around a farm in the valley which everyone knew from the account must be Nahum's, the darkness had been less thick. A dim though distinct luminosity seemed to inhere in all the vegetation, grass, leaves, and blossoms alike, while at one moment a detached piece of the phosphorescence appeared to stir furtively in the yard near the barn.

The grass had so far seemed untouched, and the cows were freely pastured in the lot near the house, but towards the end of May the milk began to be bad. Then Nahum had the cows driven to the uplands, after which this trouble ceased. Not long after this the change in grass and leaves became apparent to the eye. All the verdure was going grey, and was developing a highly singular quality of brittleness. Ammi was now the only person who ever visited the place, and his visits were becoming fewer and fewer. When school closed the Gardners were virtually cut off from the world, and sometimes let Ammi do their errands in town. They were failing curiously both physically and mentally, and no one was surprised when the news of Mrs Gardner's madness stole around.

It happened in June, about the anniversary of the meteor's fall, and the poor woman screamed about things in the air which she could not describe. In her raving there was not a single specific noun, but only verbs and pronouns. Things moved and changed and fluttered, and ears tingled to impulses which were not wholly sounds. Something was taken away – she was being drained of something – something was fastening itself on her that ought not to be – someone must make it keep off – nothing was ever still in the night – the walls and windows shifted. Nahum did not send her to the county asylum, but let her wander about the house as long as she was harmless to herself and others. Even when her expression changed he did nothing. But when the boys grew afraid of her, and Thaddeus nearly fainted at the way she made faces at him, he decided to keep her locked in the attic. By July she had ceased to speak and crawled on all fours, and before that month was over Nahum got the mad notion that she was slightly luminous in the dark, as he now clearly saw was the case with the nearby vegetation.

It was a little before this that the horses had stampeded. Something had aroused them in the night, and their neighing and kicking in their stalls had been terrible. There seemed virtually nothing to do to calm them, and when Nahum opened the stable door they all bolted out like frightened woodland deer. It took a week to track all four, and when found they were seen to be quite useless and unmanageable. Something had snapped in their brains, and each one had to be shot for its own good. Nahum borrowed a horse from Ammi for his haying, but found it would not approach the barn. It shied, balked, and whinnied, and in the end he could do nothing but drive it into the yard while the men used their own strength to get the heavy wagon near enough the hayloft for convenient pitching. And all the while the vegetation was turning grey and brittle. Even the flowers whose hues had been so strange were greying now, and the fruit was coming out grey and dwarfed and tasteless. The asters and golden-rod bloomed grey and distorted, and the roses and zinnias and hollyhocks in the front yard were such blasphemous-looking things that Nahum's oldest boy Zenas cut them down. The strangely puffed insects died about that time, even the bees that had left their hives and taken to the woods.

By September all the vegetation was fast crumbling to a greyish powder, and Nahum feared that the trees would die before the poison was out of the soil. His wife now had spells of terrific screaming, and he and the boys were in a constant state of nervous tension. They shunned people now, and when school opened the boys did not go. But it was Ammi, on one of his rare visits, who first realised that the well water was no longer good. It had an evil taste that was not exactly fetid nor exactly salty, and Ammi advised his friend to dig another well on higher ground to use till the soil was good again. Nahum, however, ignored the warning, for he had by that time become calloused to strange and unpleasant things. He and the boys continued to use the tainted supply, drinking it as listlessly and mechanically as they ate their meagre and ill-cooked meals and did their thankless and monotonous chores through the aimless days. There was something of stolid resignation about them all, as if they walked half in another world between lines of nameless guards to a certain and familiar doom.

Thaddeus went mad in September after a visit to the well. He had gone with a pail and had come back empty-handed, shrieking and waving his arms, and sometimes lapsing into an inane titter or a whisper about 'the moving colours down there'. Two in one family was pretty bad, but Nahum was very brave about it. He let the boy run about for a week until he began stumbling and hurting himself, and then he shut him in an attic room across the hall from his mother's. The way they screamed at each other from behind their locked doors was very terrible, especially to little Merwin, who fancied they talked in some terrible language that was not of earth. Merwin was getting frightfully imaginative, and his restlessness was worse after the shutting away of the brother who had been his greatest playmate.

Almost at the same time the mortality among the livestock commenced. Poultry turned greyish and died very quickly, their meat being found dry and noisome upon cutting. Hogs grew inordinately fat, then suddenly began to undergo loathsome changes which no one could explain. Their meat was of course useless, and Nahum was at his wits' end. No rural veterinary would approach his place, and the city veterinary from Arkham was openly baffled. The swine began growing grey and brittle and falling to pieces before they died, and their eyes and muzzles developed singular alterations. It was very inexplicable, for they had never been fed from the tainted vegetation. Then something struck the cows. Certain areas or sometimes the whole body would be uncannily shrivelled or compressed, and atrocious collapses or disintegrations were common. In the last stages – and death was always the result – there would be a greying and turning brittle like that which beset the hogs. There could be no question of poison, for all the cases occurred in a locked and undisturbed barn. No bites of prowling things could have brought the virus, for what live beast of earth can pass through solid obstacles? It must be only natural disease – yet what disease could wreak such results was beyond any mind's guessing. When the harvest came there was not an animal surviving on the place, for the stock and poultry were dead and the dogs had run away. These dogs, three in number, had all vanished one night and were never heard of again. The five cats had left some time before, but their going was scarcely noticed since there now seemed to be no mice, and only Mrs Gardner had made pets of the graceful felines.

On the nineteenth of October Nahum staggered into Ammi's house with hideous news. The death had come to poor Thaddeus in his attic room, and it had come in a way which could not be told. Nahum had dug a grave in the railed family plot behind the farm, and had put therein what he found. There could have been nothing from outside, for the small barred window and locked door were intact; but it was much as it had been in the barn. Ammi and his wife consoled the stricken man as best as they could, but shuddered as they did so. Stark terror seemed to cling round the Gardners and all they touched, and the very presence of one in the house was a breath from regions unnamed and unnameable. Ammi accompanied Nahum home with the greatest reluctance, and did what he might to calm the hysterical sobbing of little Merwin. Zenas needed no calming. He had come of late to do nothing but stare into space and obey what his father told him; and Ammi thought that his fate was very merciful. Now and then Merwin's screams were answered faintly from the attic, and in response to an inquiring look Nahum said that his wife was getting very feeble. When night approached,

Ammi managed to get away; for not even friendship could make him stay in that spot when the faint glow of the vegetation began and the trees may or may not have swayed without wind. It was really lucky for Ammi that he was not more imaginative. Even as things were, his mind was bent ever so slightly; but had he been able to connect and reflect upon all the portents around him he must inevitably have turned a total maniac. In the twilight he hastened home, the screams of the mad woman and the nervous child ringing horribly in his ears.

Three days later Nahum burst into Ammi's kitchen in the early morning, and in the absence of his host stammered out a desperate tale once more, while Mrs Pierce listened in a clutching fright. It was little Merwin this time. He was gone. He had gone out late at night with a lantern and pail for water, and had never come back. He'd been going to pieces for days, and hardly knew what he was about. Screamed at everything. There had been a frantic shriek from the yard then, but before the father could get to the door the boy was gone. There was no glow from the lantern he had taken, and of the child himself no trace. At the time Nahum thought the lantern and pail were gone too; but when dawn came, and the man had plodded back from his all-night search of the woods and fields, he had found some very curious things near the well.

There was a crushed and apparently somewhat melted mass of iron which had certainly been the lantern; while a bent handle and twisted iron hoops beside it, both half-fused, seemed to hint at the remnants of the pail. That was all. Nahum was past imagining, Mrs Pierce was blank, and Ammi, when he had reached home and heard the tale, could give no guess. Merwin was gone, and there would be no use in telling the people around, who shunned all Gardners now. No use, either, in telling the city people at Arkham who laughed at everything. Thad was gone, and now Merwin was gone. Something was creeping and creeping and waiting to be seen and heard. Nahum would go soon, and he wanted Ammi to look after his wife and Zenas if they survived him. It must all be a judgment of some sort; though he could not fancy what for, since he had always walked uprightly in the Lord's ways so far as he knew.

For over two weeks Ammi saw nothing of Nahum; and then, worried about what might have happened, he overcame his fears

and paid the Gardner place a visit. There was no smoke from the
great chimney, and for a moment the visitor was apprehensive of the
worst. The aspect of the whole farm was shocking – greyish withered
grass and leaves on the ground, vines falling in brittle wreckage from
archaic walls and gables, and great bare trees clawing up at the grey
November sky with a studied malevolence which Ammi could not
but feel had come from some subtle change in the tilt of the branches.
But Nahum was alive, after all. He was weak, and lying on a couch
in the low-ceiled kitchen, but perfectly conscious and able to give
simple orders to Zenas. The room was deadly cold; and as Ammi
visibly shivered, the host shouted huskily to Zenas for more wood.
Wood, indeed, was sorely needed; since the cavernous fireplace was
unlit and empty, with a cloud of soot blowing about in the chill
wind that came down the chimney. Presently Nahum asked him
if the extra wood had made him any more comfortable, and then
Ammi saw what had happened. the stoutest cord had broken at last,
and the hapless farmer's mind was proof against more sorrow.

Questioning tactfully, Ammi could get no clear data at all about
the missing Zenas. 'In the well – he lives in the well – ' was all that
the clouded father would say. Then there flashed across the visitor's
mind a sudden thought of the mad wife, and he changed his line of
inquiry. 'Nabby? Why, here she is!' was the surprised response of
poor Nahum, and Ammi soon saw that he must search for himself.
Leaving the harmless babbler on the couch, he took the keys from
their nail beside the door and climbed the creaking stairs to the attic.
It was very close and noisome up there, and no sound could be heard
from any direction. Of the four doors in sight, only one was locked,
and on this he tried various keys of the ring he had taken. The third
key proved the right one, and after some fumbling Ammi threw open
the low white door.

It was quite dark inside, for the window was small and half-
obscured by the crude wooden bars; and Ammi could see nothing
at all on the wide-planked floor. The stench was beyond enduring,
and before proceeding further he had to retreat to another room
and return with his lungs filled with breathable air. When he did
enter he saw something dark in the corner, and upon seeing it
more clearly he screamed outright. While he screamed he thought
a momentary cloud eclipsed the window, and a second later he felt

himself brushed as if by some hateful current of vapour. Strange colours danced before his eyes; and had not a present horror numbed him he would have thought of the globule in the meteor that the geologist's hammer had shattered, and of the morbid vegetation that had sprouted in the spring. As it was he thought only of the blasphemous monstrosity which confronted him, and which all too clearly had shared the nameless fate of young Thaddeus and the live-stock. But the terrible thing about the horror was that it very slowly and perceptibly moved as it continued to crumble.

Ammi would give me no added particulars of this scene, but the shape in the corner does not reappear in his tale as a moving object. There are things which cannot be mentioned, and what is done in common humanity is sometimes cruelly judged by the law. I gathered that no moving thing was left in that attic room, and that to leave anything capable of motion there would have been a deed so monstrous as to damn any accountable being to eternal torment. Anyone but a stolid farmer would have fainted or gone mad, but Ammi walked conscious through that low doorway and locked the accursed secret behind him. There would be Nahum to deal with now; he must be fed and tended, and removed to some place where he could be cared for.

Commencing his descent of the dark stairs, Ammi heard a thud below him. He even thought a scream had been suddenly choked off, and recalled nervously the clammy vapour which had brushed by him in that frightful room above. What presence had his cry and entry started up? Halted by some vague fear, he heard still further sounds below. Indubitably there was a sort of heavy dragging, and a most detestably sticky noise as of some fiendish and unclean species of suction. With an associative sense goaded to feverish heights, he thought unaccountably of what he had seen upstairs. Good God! What eldritch dream-world was this into which he had blundered? He dared move neither backward nor forward, but stood there trembling at the black curve of the boxed-in staircase. Every trifle of the scene burned itself into his brain. The sounds, the sense of dread expectancy, the darkness, the steepness of the narrow steps – and merciful Heaven! – the faint but unmistakable luminosity of all the woodwork in sight; steps, sides, exposed laths, and beams alike.

Then there burst forth a frantic whinny from Ammi's horse

outside, followed at once by a clatter which told of a frenzied runaway. In another moment horse and buggy had gone beyond earshot, leaving the frightened man on the dark stairs to guess what had sent them. But that was not all. There had been another sound out there. A sort of liquid splash – water – it must have been the well. He had left Hero untied near it, and a buggywheel must have brushed the coping and knocked in a stone. And still the pale phosphorescence glowed in that detestably ancient woodwork. God! how old the house was! Most of it built before 1670, and the gambrel roof no later than 1730.

A feeble scratching on the floor downstairs now sounded distinctly, and Ammi's grip tightened on a heavy stick he had picked up in the attic for some purpose. Slowly nerving himself, he finished his descent and walked boldly toward the kitchen. But he did not complete the walk, because what he sought was no longer there. It had come to meet him, and it was still alive after a fashion. Whether it had crawled or whether it had been dragged by any external forces, Ammi could not say; but the death had been at it. Everything had happened in the last half-hour, but collapse, greying, and disintegration were already far advanced. There was a horrible brittleness, and dry fragments were scaling off. Ammi could not touch it, but looked horrifiedly into the distorted parody that had been a face. 'What was it, Nahum – what was it?' he whispered, and the cleft, bulging lips were just able to crackle out a final answer.

'Nothin' . . . nothin' . . . the colour . . . it burns . . . cold an' wet, but it burns . . . it lived in the well . . . I seen it . . . a kind of smoke . . . jest like the flowers last spring . . . the well shone at night . . . Thad an' Merwin an' Zenas . . . everything alive . . . suckin' the life out of everything . . . in that stone . . . it must a' come in that stone . . . pizened the whole place . . . dun't know what it wants . . . that round thing them men from the college dug outen the stone . . . they smashed it . . . it was that same colour . . . jest the same, like the flowers an' plants . . . must a' ben more of 'em . . . seeds . . . seeds . . . they growed . . . I seen it the fust time this week . . . must a' got strong on Zenas . . . he was a big boy, full o' life . . . it beats down your mind an' then gets ye . . . burns ye up . . . in the well water . . . you was right about that . . . evil water . . . Zenas never come back from the well . . . can't git away . . . draws ye

. . . ye know summ'at's comin' but tain't no use . . . I seen it time an' agin sence Zenas was took . . . whar's Nabby, Ammi? . . . my head's no good . . . dun't know how long sence I fed her . . . it'll git her ef we ain't keerful . . . jest a colour . . . her face is gittin' to hev that colour sometimes towards night . . . an' it burns an' sucks . . . it come from some place whar things ain't as they is here . . . one o' them professors said so . . . he was right . . . look out, Ammi, it'll do suthin' more . . . sucks the life out . . .'

But that was all. That which spoke could speak no more because it had completely caved in. Ammi laid a red checked tablecloth over what was left and reeled out the back door into the fields. He climbed the slope to the ten-acre pasture and stumbled home by the north road and the woods. He could not pass that well from which his horses had run away. He had looked at it through the window, and had seen that no stone was missing from the rim. Then the lurching buggy had not dislodged anything after all – the splash had been something else – something which went into the well after it had done with poor Nahum. . . .

When Ammi reached his house the horses and buggy had arrived before him and thrown his wife into fits of anxiety. Reassuring her without explanations, he set out at once for Arkham and notified the authorities that the Gardner family was no more. He indulged in no details, but merely told of the deaths of Nahum and Nabby, that of Thaddeus being already known, and mentioned that the cause seemed to be the same strange ailment which had killed the live-stock. He also stated that Merwin and Zenas had disappeared. There was considerable questioning at the police station, and in the end Ammi was compelled to take three officers to take three officers to the Gardner farm, together with the coroner, the medical examiner, and the veterinary who had treated the diseased animals. He went much against his will, for the afternoon was advancing and he feared the fall of night over that accursed place, but it was some comfort to have so many people with him.

The six men drove out in a democrat-wagon, following Ammi's buggy, and arrived at the pest-ridden farmhouse about four o'clock. Used as the officers were to gruesome experiences, not one remained unmoved at what was found in the attic and under the red checked tablecloth on the floor below. The whole aspect of the farm with its grey desolation was terrible enough, but those two crumbling objects were beyond all bounds. No one could look long at them, and even the medical examiner admitted that there was very little to examine. Specimens could be analysed, of course, so he busied himself in obtaining them – and here it develops that a very puzzling aftermath occurred at the college laboratory where the two phials of dust were finally taken. Under the spectroscope both samples gave off an unknown spectrum, in which many of the baffling bands were precisely like those which the strange meteor had yielded in the previous year. The property of emitting this spectrum vanished in a month, the dust thereafter consisting mainly of alkaline phosphates and carbonates.

Ammi would not have told the men about the well if he had thought they meant to do anything then and there. It was getting toward sunset, and he was anxious to be away. But he could not help glancing nervously at the stony kerb by the great sweep, and when a detective questioned him he admitted that Nahum had feared something down there – so much so that he had never even thought of searching it for Merwin or Zenas. After that nothing would do but that they empty and explore the well immediately, so Ammi had to wait trembling while pail after pail of rank water was hauled up and splashed on the soaking ground outside. The men sniffed in disgust at the fluid, and toward the last held their noses against the foetor they were uncovering. It was not so long a job as they had feared it would be, since the water was phenomenally low. There is no need to speak too exactly of what they found. Merwin and Zenas were both there, in part, though the vestiges were mainly skeletal. There were also a small deer and a large dog in about the same state, and a number of bones of small animals. The ooze and slime at the bottom seemed inexplicably porous and bubbling, and a man who descended on hand-holds with a long pole found that he could sink the wooden shaft to any depth in the mud of the floor without meeting any solid obstruction.

Twilight had now fallen, and lanterns were brought from the house. Then, when it was seen that nothing further could be gained from the well, everyone went indoors and conferred in the ancient sitting-room while the intermittent light of a spectral half-moon played wanly on the grey desolation outside. The men were frankly nonplussed by the entire case, and could find no convincing common element to link the strange vegetable conditions, the unknown disease of live-stock and humans, and the unaccountable deaths of Merwin and Zenas in the tainted well. They had heard the common country talk, it is true; but could not believe that anything contrary to natural law had occurred. No doubt the meteor had poisoned the soil, but the illness of persons and animals who had eaten nothing grown in that soil was another matter. Was it the well water? Very possibly. It might be a good idea to analyse it. But what peculiar madness could have made both boys jump into the well? Their deeds were so similar – and the fragments showed that they had both suffered from the grey brittle death. Why was everything so grey and brittle?

It was the coroner, seated near a window overlooking the yard, who first noticed the glow about the well. Night had fully set in, and all the abhorrent grounds seemed faintly luminous with more than the fitful moonbeams; but this new glow was something definite and distinct, and appeared to shoot up from the black pit like a softened ray from a searchlight, giving dull reflections in the little ground pools where the water had been emptied. It had a very queer colour, and as all the men clustered round the window Ammi gave a violent start. For this strange beam of ghastly miasma was to him of no unfamiliar hue. He had seen that colour before, and feared to think what it might mean. He had seen it in the nasty brittle globule in that aerolite two summers ago, had seen it in the crazy vegetation of the springtime, and had thought he had seen it for an instant that very morning against the small barred window of that terrible attic room where nameless things had happened. It had flashed there a second, and a clammy and hateful current of vapour had brushed past him – and then poor Nahum had been taken by something of that colour. He had said so at the last – said it was like the globule and the plants. After that had come the runaway in the yard and the splash in the well – and now that well was belching forth to the night a pale insidious beam of the same demoniac tint.

It does credit to the alertness of Ammi's mind that he puzzled even at that tense moment over a point which was essentially scientific. He could not but wonder at his gleaning of the same impression from a vapour glimpsed in the daytime, against a window opening on the morning sky, and from a nocturnal exhalation seen as a phosphorescent mist against the black and blasted landscape. It wasn't right – it was against Nature – and he thought of those terrible last words of his stricken friend, 'It come from some place whar things ain't as they is here . . . one o' them professors said so. . . .'

All three horses outside, tied to a pair of shrivelled saplings by the road, were now neighing and pawing frantically. The wagon driver started for the door to do something, but Ammi laid a shaky hand on his shoulder. 'Dun't go out thar,' he whispered. 'They's more to this nor what we know. Nahum said somethin' lived in the well that sucks your life out. He said it must be some'at growed from a round ball like one we all seen in the meteor stone that fell a year ago June. Sucks an' burns, he said, an' is jest a cloud of colour like that light out thar now, that ye can hardly see an' can't tell what it is. Nahum thought it feeds on everything livin' an' gits stronger all the time. He said he seen it this last week. It must be somethin' from away off in the sky like the men from the college last year says the meteor stone was. The way it's made an' the way it works ain't like no way o' God's world. It's summ'at from beyond.'

So the men paused indecisively as the light from the well grew stronger and the hitched horses pawed and whinnied in increasing frenzy. It was truly an awful moment; with terror in that ancient and accursed house itself, four monstrous sets of fragments – two from the house and two from the well – in the woodshed behind, and that shaft of unknown and unholy iridescence from the slimy depths in front. Ammi had restrained the driver on impulse, forgetting how uninjured he himself was after the clammy brushing of that coloured vapour in the attic room, but perhaps it is just as well that he acted as he did. No one will ever know what was abroad that night; and though the blasphemy from beyond had not so far hurt any human of unweakened mind, there is no telling what it might not have done at that last moment, with its seemingly increased strength and the special signs of purpose it was soon to display beneath the half-clouded moonlit sky.

All at once one of the detectives at the window gave a short, sharp gasp. The others looked at him, and then quickly followed his own gaze upward to the point at which its idle straying had been suddenly arrested. There was no need for words. What had been disputed in country gossip was disputable no longer, and it is because of the thing which every man of that party agreed in whispering later on, that the strange days are never talked about in Arkham. It is necessary to premise that there was no wind at that hour of the evening. One did arise not long afterward, but there was absolutely none then. Even the dry tips of the lingering hedge-mustard, grey and blighted, and the fringe on the roof of the standing democrat-wagon were unstirred. And yet amid that tense, godless calm the high bare boughs of all the trees in the yard were moving. They were twitching morbidly and spasmodically, clawing in convulsive and epileptic madness at the moonlit clouds; scratching impotently in the noxious air as if jerked by some allied and bodiless line of linkage with subterrene horrors writhing and struggling below the black roots.

Not a man breathed for several seconds. Then a cloud of darker depth passed over the moon, and the silhouette of clutching branches faded out momentarily. At this there was a general cry; muffled with awe, but husky and almost identical from every throat. For the terror had not faded with the silhouette, and in a fearsome instant of deeper darkness the watchers saw wriggling at that tree-top height a thousand tiny points of faint and unhallowed radiance, tipping each bough like the fire of St Elmo or the flames that come down on the apostles' heads at Pentecost. It was a monstrous constellation of unnatural light, like a glutted swarm of corpse-fed fireflies dancing hellish sarabands over an accursed marsh; and its colour was that same nameless intrusion which Ammi had come to recognize and dread. All the while the shaft of phosphorescence from the well was getting brighter and brighter, bringing, to the minds of the huddled men, a sense of doom and abnormality which far outraced any image their conscious minds could form. It was no longer *shining* out; it was *pouring* out; and as the shapeless stream of unplaceable colour left the well it seemed to flow directly into the sky.

The veterinary shivered, and walked to the front door to drop the heavy extra bar across it. Ammi shook no less, and had to tug and point for lack of controllable voice when he wished to draw notice to the growing luminosity of the trees. The neighing and stamping of the horses had become utterly frightful, but not a soul of that group in the old house would have ventured forth for any earthly reward. With the moments the shining of the trees increased, while their restless branches seemed to strain more and more toward verticality. The wood of the well-sweep was shining now, and presently a policeman dumbly pointed to some wooden sheds and bee-hives near the stone wall on the west. They were commencing to shine, too, though the tethered vehicles of the visitors seemed so far unaffected. Then there was a wild commotion and clopping in the road, and as Ammi quenched the lamp for better seeing they realized that the span of frantic greys had broken their sapling and run off with the democrat-wagon.

The shock served to loosen several tongues, and embarrassed whispers were exchanged. 'It spreads on everything organic that's been around here,' muttered the medical examiner. No one replied, but the man who had been in the well gave a hint that his long pole must have stirred up something intangible. 'It was awful,' he added. 'There was no bottom at all, just ooze and bubbles and the feeling of something lurking under there.' Ammi's horse still pawed and screamed deafeningly in the road outside, and nearly drowned its owner's faint quaver as he mumbled his formless reflections. 'It come from that stone – it growed down thar – it got everything livin' – it fed itself on 'em, mind and body – Thad an' Merwin, Zenas an' Nabby – Nahum was the last – they all drunk the water – it got strong on 'em – it come from beyond, whar things ain't like they be here – now it's goin' home – '

At this point, as the column of unknown colour flared suddenly stronger and began to weave itself into fantastic suggestions of shape which each spectator later described differently, there came from poor tethered Hero such a sound as no man before or since ever heard from a horse. Every person in that low-pitched sitting room stopped his ears, and Ammi turned away from the window in horror and nausea. Words could not convey it – when Ammi looked out again the hapless beast lay huddled inert on the moonlit ground between the splintered shafts of the buggy. That was the last of Hero till they buried him next day. But the present was no time to mourn, for almost at this instant a detective silently called attention to something terrible in the very room with them. In the absence of the lamplight it was clear that a faint phosphorescence had begun to pervade the entire apartment. It glowed on the broad-planked floor and the fragment of rag carpet, and shimmered over the sashes of the small-paned windows. It ran up and down the exposed corner-posts, coruscated about the shelf and mantel, and infected the very doors and furniture. Each minute saw it strengthen, and at last it was very plain that healthy living things must leave that house.

Ammi showed them the back door and the path up through the fields to the ten-acre pasture. They walked and stumbled as in a dream, and did not dare look back till they were far away on the high ground. They were glad of the path, for they could not have gone the front way, by that well. It was bad enough passing the glowing barn and sheds, and those shining orchard trees with their gnarled, fiendish contours; but thank Heaven the branches did their worst twisting high up. The moon went under some very black clouds as they crossed the rustic bridge over Chapman's Brook, and it was blind groping from there to the open meadows.

When they looked back toward the valley and the distant Gardner place at the bottom they saw a fearsome sight. All the farm was shining with the hideous unknown blend of colour: trees, buildings, and even such grass and herbage as had not been wholly changed to lethal grey brittleness. The boughs were all straining skyward, tipped with tongues of foul flame, and lambent tricklings of the same monstrous fire were creeping about the ridgepoles of the house, barn and sheds. It was a scene from a vision of Fuseli, and over all the rest reigned that riot of luminous amorphousness, that alien and undimensioned rainbow of cryptic poison from the well – seething, feeling, lapping, reaching, scintillating, straining, and malignly bubbling in its cosmic and unrecognizable chromaticism.

Then without warning the hideous thing shot vertically up toward the sky like a rocket or meteor, leaving behind no trail and disappearing through a round and curiously regular hole in the clouds before any man could gasp or cry out. No watcher can ever forget that sight, and Ammi stared blankly at the stars of Cygnus, Deneb twinkling above the others, where the unknown colour had melted into the Milky Way. But his gaze was the next moment called swiftly to earth by the crackling in the valley. It was just that. Only a wooden ripping and crackling, and not an explosion, as so many others of the party vowed. Yet the outcome was the same, for in one feverish kaleidoscopic instant there burst up from that doomed and accursed farm a gleamingly eruptive cataclysm of unnatural sparks and substance; blurring the glance of the few who saw it, and sending forth to the zenith a bombarding cloudburst of such coloured and fantastic fragments as our universe must needs disown. Through quickly re-closing vapours they followed the great morbidity that had vanished, and in another second they had vanished too. Behind and below was only a darkness to which the men dared not return, and all about was a mounting wind which seemed to sweep down in black, frore gusts from interstellar space. It shrieked and howled, and lashed the fields and distorted woods in a mad cosmic frenzy, till soon the trembling party realized it would be no use waiting for the moon to show what was left down there at Nahum's.

Too awed even to hint theories, the seven shaking men trudged back toward Arkham by the north road. Ammi was worse than his fellows, and begged them to see him inside his own kitchen, instead of keeping straight on to town. He did not wish to cross the blighted, wind-whipped woods alone to his home on the main road. For he had had an added shock that the others were spared, and was crushed forever with a brooding fear he dared not even mention for many years to come. As the rest of the watchers on that tempestuous hill had stolidly set their faces toward the road, Ammi had looked back an instant at the shadowed valley of desolation so lately sheltering his ill-starred friend. And from that stricken, faraway spot he had seen something feebly rise, only to sink down again upon the place from which the great shapeless horror had shot into the sky. It was just a colour – but not any colour of our earth or heavens. And because Ammi recognized that colour, and knew that this last faint remnant must still lurk down there in the well, he has never been quite right since.

Ammi would never go near the place again. It is forty-four years now since the horror happened, but he has never been there, and will be glad when the new reservoir blots it out. I shall be glad, too, for I do not like the way the sunlight changed colour around the mouth of that abandoned well I passed. I hope the water will always be very deep – but even so, I shall never drink it. I do not think I shall visit the Arkham country hereafter. Three of the men who had been with Ammi returned the next morning to see the ruins by daylight, but there were not any real ruins. Only the bricks of the chimney, the stones of the cellar, some mineral and metallic litter here and there, and the rim of that nefandous well. Save for Ammi's dead horse, which they towed away and buried, and the buggy which they shortly returned to him, everything that had ever been living had gone. Five eldritch acres of dusty grey desert remained, nor has anything ever grown there since. To this day it sprawls open to the sky like a great spot eaten by acid in the woods and fields, and the few who have ever dared glimpse it in spite of the rural tales have named it 'the blasted heath'.

The rural tales are queer. They might be even queerer if city men and college chemists could be interested enough to analyse the water from that disused well, or the grey dust that no wind seems to disperse. Botanists, too, ought to study the stunted flora on the borders of that spot, for they might shed light on the country notion that the blight is spreading – little by little, perhaps an inch a year. People say the colour of the neighbouring herbage is not quite right in the spring, and that wild things leave queer prints in the light winter snow. Snow never seems quite so heavy on the blasted heath as it is elsewhere. Horses – the few that are left in this motor age – grow skittish in the silent valley; and hunters cannot depend on their dogs too near the splotch of greyish dust.

They say the mental influences are very bad, too; numbers went queer in the years after Nahum's taking, and always they lacked the power to get away. Then the stronger-minded folk all left the region, and only the foreigners tried to live in the crumbling old homesteads. They could not stay, though; and one sometimes wonders what insight beyond ours their wild, weird stories of whispered magic have given them. Their dreams at night, they protest, are very horrible in that grotesque country; and surely the very look of the dark realm is enough to stir a morbid fancy. No traveller has ever escaped a sense of strangeness in those deep ravines, and artists shiver as they paint thick woods whose mystery is as much of the spirit as of the eye. I myself am curious about the sensation I derived from my one lone walk before Ammi told me his tale. When twilight came I had vaguely wished some clouds would gather, for an odd timidity about the deep skyey voids above had crept into my soul.

Do not ask me for my opinion. I do not know – that is all.

There was no one but Ammi to question; for Arkham people will not talk about the strange days, and all three professors who saw the aerolite and its coloured globule are dead. There were other globules – depend upon that. One must have fed itself and escaped, and probably there was another which was too late. No doubt it is still down the well – I know there was something wrong with the sunlight I saw above the miasmal brink. The rustics say the blight creeps an inch a year, so perhaps there is a kind of growth or nourishment even now. But whatever daemon hatching is there, it must be tethered to something or else it would quickly spread. Is it fastened to the roots of those trees that claw the air? One of the current Arkham tales is about fat oaks that shine and move as they ought not to do at night.

What it is, only God knows. In terms of matter I suppose the things Ammi described would be called a gas, but this gas obeyed the laws that are not of our cosmos. This was no fruit of such worlds and suns as shine on the telescopes and photographic plates of our observatories. This was no breath from the skies whose motions and dimensions our astronomers measure or deem too vast to measure. It was just a colour out of space – a frightful messenger from unformed realms of infinity beyond all Nature as we know it; from realms whose mere existence stuns the brain and numbs us with the black extra-cosmic gulfs it throws open before our frenzied eyes.

I doubt very much if Ammi consciously lied to me, and I do not think his tale was all a freak of madness as the townsfolk had forewarned. Something terrible came to the hills and valleys on that meteor, and something terrible – though I know not in what proportion – still remains. I shall be glad to see the water come. Meanwhile I hope nothing will happen to Ammi. He saw so much of the thing – and its influence was so insidious. Why has he never been able to move away? How clearly he recalled those dying words of Nahum's – 'can't git away – draws ye – ye know summ'at's comin' but tain't no use – ' Ammi is such a good old man – when the reservoir gang gets to work I must write the chief engineer to keep a sharp watch on him. I would hate to think of him as the grey, twisted, brittle monstrosity which persists more and more in troubling my sleep.

THE AUTHOR
Jerome Bixby
THE STORY
It's A Good Life
THE MOVIE
Twilight Zone, The Movie
THE DIRECTOR
Joe Dante

Aunt Amy was out on the front porch, rocking back and forth in the highbacked chair and fanning herself, when Bill Soames rode his bicycle up the road and stopped in front of the house.

Perspiring under the afternoon 'sun,' Bill lifted the box of groceries out of the big basket over the front wheel of the bike, and came up the front walk.

Little Anthony was sitting on the lawn, playing with a rat. He had caught the rat down in the basement – he had made it think that it smelled cheese, the most rich-smelling and crumbly-delicious cheese a rat had ever thought it smelled, and it had come out of its hole, and now Anthony had hold of it with his mind and was making it do tricks.

When the rat saw Bill Soames coming, it tried to run, but Anthony thought at it, and it turned a flip-flop on the grass, and lay trembling, its eyes gleaming in small black terror.

Bill Soames hurried past Anthony and reached the front steps, mumbling. He always mumbled when he came to the Fremont house, or passed by it, or even thought of it. Everybody did. They thought about silly things, things that didn't mean very much, like two-and-two-is-four-and-twice-is-eight and so on; they tried to jumble up their thoughts and keep them skipping back and forth, so Anthony couldn't read their minds. The mumbling helped. Because if Anthony got anything strong out of your thoughts, he might take a notion to do something about it – like curing your wife's sick headaches or your kid's mumps, or getting your old milk cow back on schedule, or fixing the privy. And while Anthony mightn't actually mean any harm, he couldn't be expected to have much notion of what was the right thing to do in such cases.

That was if he liked you. He might try to help you, in his way. And that could be pretty horrible.

If he didn't like you . . . well, that could be worse.

Bill Soames set the box of groceries on the porch railing, and stopped his mumbling long enough to say, 'Everythin' you wanted, Miss Amy.'

'Oh, fine, William,' Amy Fremont said lightly. 'My, ain't it terrible hot today?'

Bill Soames almost cringed. His eyes pleaded with her. He shook his head violently *no*, and then interrupted his mumbling again, though obviously he didn't want to: 'Oh, don't say that, Miss Amy . . . it's fine, just fine. A real *good* day!'

Amy Fremont got up from the rocking chair, and came across the porch. She was a tall woman, thin, a smiling vacancy in her eyes. About a year ago, Anthony had gotten mad at her, because she'd told him he shouldn't have turned the cat into a cat-rug, and although he had always obeyed her more than anyone else, which was hardly at all, this time he'd snapped at her. With his mind. And that had been the end of Amy Fremont's bright eyes, and the end of Amy Fremont as everyone had known her. And that was when word got around in Peaksville (population: 46) that even the members of Anthony's own family weren't safe. After that, everyone was twice as careful.

Someday Anthony might undo what he'd done to Aunt Amy. Anthony's Mom and Pop hoped he would. When he was older, and maybe sorry. If it was possible, that is. Because Aunt Amy had changed a lot, and besides, now Anthony wouldn't obey anyone.

'Land alive, William,' Aunt Amy said, 'you don't have to mumble like that. Anthony wouldn't hurt you. My goodness, Anthony likes you!' She raised her voice and called to Anthony, who had tired of the rat and was making it eat itself. 'Don't you, dear? Don't you like Mr Soames?'

Anthony looked across the lawn at the grocery man – a bright, wet, purple gaze. He didn't say anything. Bill Soames tried to smile at him. After a second Anthony returned his attention to the rat. It had already devoured its tail, or at least chewed it off – for Anthony had made it bite faster than it could swallow, and little pink and red furry pieces lay around it on the green grass. Now the rat was having trouble reaching its hindquarters.

Mumbling silently, thinking of nothing in particular as hard as he could, Bill Soames went stiff-legged down the walk, mounted his bicycle and pedaled off.

'We'll see you tonight, William,' Aunt Amy called after him.

As Bill Soames pumped the pedals, he was wishing deep down that he could pump twice as fast, to get away from Anthony all the faster, and away from Aunt Amy, who sometimes just forgot how *careful* you had to be. And he shouldn't have thought that. Because Anthony caught it. He caught the desire to get away from the Fremont house as if it was something *bad*, and his purple gaze blinked, and he snapped a small, sulky thought after Bill Soames – just a small one, because he was in a good mood today, and besides, he liked Bill Soames, or at least didn't dislike him, at least today. Bill Soames wanted to go away – so, petulantly, Anthony helped him.

Pedaling with superhuman speed – or rather, appearing to, because in reality the bicycle was pedaling *him* – Bill Soames vanished down the road in a cloud of dust, his thin, terrified wail drifting back across the summerlike heat.

Anthony looked at the rat. It had devoured half its belly, and had died from pain. He thought it into a grave out deep in the cornfield – his father had once said, smiling, that he might do that with the things he killed – and went around the house, casting his odd shadow in the hot, brassy light from above.

In the kitchen, Aunt Amy was unpacking the groceries. She put the Mason-jarred goods on the shelves, and the meat and milk in the icebox, and the beet sugar and coarse flour in big cans under the sink. She put the cardboard box in the corner, by the door, for Mr Soames to pick up next time he came. It was stained and battered and torn and worn fuzzy, but it was one of the few left in Peaksville. In faded red letters it said *Campbell's Soup*. The last cans of soup, or of anything else, had been eaten long ago, except for a small communal hoard which the villagers dipped into for special occasions – but the box lingered on, like a coffin, and when it and the other boxes were gone, the men would have to make some out of wood.

Aunt Amy went out the back, where Anthony's Mom – Aunt Amy's sister – sat in the shade of the house, shelling peas. The peas, every time Mom ran a finger along a pod, went *lollop-lollop-lollop* into the pan on her lap.

'William brought the groceries,' Aunt Amy said. She sat down wearily in the straightbacked chair beside Mom, and began fanning herself again. She wasn't really old; but ever since Anthony had snapped at her with his mind, something had seemed to be wrong with her body as well as her mind, and she was tired all the time.

'Oh, good,' said Mom. *Lollop* went the fat peas into the pan.

Everybody in Peaksville always said 'Oh, fine,' or 'Good,' or 'Say, that's swell!' when almost anything happened or was mentioned – even unhappy things like accidents or even deaths. They'd always say 'Good,' because if they didn't try to cover up how they really felt, Anthony might overhear with his mind, and then nobody knew what might happen. Like the time Mrs Kent's husband, Sam, had come walking back from the graveyard, because Anthony liked Mrs Kent and had heard her mourning.

Lollop.

'Tonight's television night,' said Aunt Amy. 'I'm glad. I look forward to it so much every week. I wonder what we'll see tonight?'

'Did Bill bring the meat?' asked Mom.

'Yes.' Aunt Amy fanned herself, looking up at the featureless brassy glare of the sky. 'Goodness, it's so hot. I wish Anthony would make it just a little cooler – '

'*Amy!*'

'Oh!' Mom's sharp tone had penetrated, where Bill Soames' agonized expression had failed. Aunt Amy put one thin hand to her mouth in exaggerated alarm. 'Oh . . . I'm sorry, dear.' Her pale blue eyes shuttled around, right and left, to see if Anthony was in sight. Not that it would make any difference if he was or wasn't – he didn't have to be near you to know what you were thinking. Usually, though, unless he had his attention on somebody, he would be occupied with thoughts of his own.

But some things attracted his attention – you could never be sure just what.

'This weather's just *fine*,' Mom said.

Lollop.

'Oh, yes,' Aunt Amy said. 'It's a wonderful day. I wouldn't want it changed for the world!'

Lollop.

Lollop.

'What time is it?' Mom asked.

Aunt Amy was sitting where she could see through the kitchen window to the alarm clock on the shelf above the stove. 'Four-thirty,' she said.

Lollop.

'I want tonight to be something special,' Mom said. 'Did Bill bring a good lean roast?'

'Good and lean, dear. They butchered just today, you know, and sent us over the best piece.'

'Dan Hollis will be *so* surprised when he finds out that tonight's television party is a birthday party for him too!'

'Oh *I* think he will! Are you sure nobody's told him?'

'Everybody swore they wouldn't.'

'That'll be real nice,' Aunt Amy nodded, looking off across the cornfield. 'A birthday party.'

'Well – ' Mom put the pan of peas down beside her, stood up and brushed her apron. 'I'd better get the roast on. Then we can set the table.' She picked up the peas.

Anthony came around the corner of the house. He didn't look at them, but continued on down through the carefully kept garden – the gardens in Peaksville were carefully kept, very carefully kept – and went past the rusting, useless hulk that had been the Fremont family car, and went smoothly over the fence and out into the cornfield.

'Isn't this a lovely day!' said Mom, a little loudly, as they went toward the back door.

Aunt Amy fanned herself. 'A beautiful day, dear. Just *fine*!'

Out in the cornfield, Anthony walked between the tall, rustling rows of green stalks. He liked to smell the corn. The alive corn overhead, and the old dead corn underfoot. Rich Ohio earth, thick with weeds and brown, dry-rotting ears of corn, pressed between his bare toes with every step – he had made it rain last night so everything would smell and feel nice today.

He walked clear to the edge of the cornfield, and over to where a grove of shadowy green trees covered cool, moist, dark ground, and lots of leafy undergrowth, and jumbled moss-covered rocks, and a small spring that made a clear, clean pool. Here Anthony liked to rest and watch the birds and insects and small animals that rustled and scampered and chirped about. He liked to lie on the cool ground and look up through the moving greenness overhead, and watch the insects flit in the hazy soft sunbeams that stood like slanting, glowing bars between ground and treetops. Somehow, he liked the thoughts of the little creatures in this place better than the thoughts outside; and while the thoughts he picked up here weren't very strong or very clear, he could get enough out of them to know what the little creatures liked and wanted, and he spent a lot of time making the grove more like what they wanted it to be. The spring hadn't always been here; but one time he had found thirst in one small furry mind, and had brought subterranean water to the surface in a clear cold flow, and had watched blinking as the creature drank, feeling its pleasure. Later he had made the pool, when he found a small urge to swim.

He had made rocks and trees and bushes and caves, and sunlight here and shadows there, because he had felt in all the tiny minds around him the desire – or the instinctive want – for this kind of resting place, and that kind of mating place, and this kind of place to play, and that kind of home.

And somehow the creatures from all the fields and pastures around the grove had seemed to know that this was a good place, for there were always more of them coming in – every time Anthony came out here there were more creatures than the last time, and more desires and needs to be tended to. Every time there would be some kind of creature he had never seen before, and he would find its mind, and see what it wanted, and then give it to it.

He liked to help them. He liked to feel their simple gratification.

Today, he rested beneath a thick elm, and lifted his purple gaze to a red and black bird that had just come to the grove. It twittered on a branch over his head, and hopped back and forth, and thought its tiny thoughts, and Anthony made a big, soft nest for it, and pretty soon it hopped in.

A long, brown, sleek-furred animal was drinking at the pool. Anthony found its mind next. The animal was thinking about a smaller creature that was scurrying along the ground on the other side of the pool, grubbing for insects. The little creature didn't know that it was in danger. The long, brown animal finished drinking and tensed its legs to leap, and Anthony thought it into a grave in the cornfield.

He didn't like those kinds of thoughts. They reminded him of the thoughts outside the grove. A long time ago some of the people outside had thought that way about *him*, and one night they'd hidden and waited for him to come back from the grove – and he'd just thought them all into the cornfield. Since then, the rest of the people hadn't thought that way – at least, very clearly. Now their thoughts were all mixed up and confusing whenever they thought about him or near him, so he didn't pay much attention.

He liked to help them too, sometimes – but it wasn't simple, or very gratifying either. They never thought happy thoughts when he did – just the jumble. So he spent more time out here.

He watched all the birds and insects and furry creatures for a while, and played with a bird, making it soar and dip and streak madly around tree trunks until, accidentally, when another bird caught his attention for a moment, he ran it into a rock. Petulantly, he thought the rock into a grave in the cornfield; but he couldn't do anything more with the bird. Not because it was dead, though it was; but because it had a broken wing. So he went back to the house. He didn't feel like walking back through the cornfield, so he just *went* to the house, right down into the basement.

It was nice down here. Nice and dark and damp and sort of fragrant, because once Mom had been making preserves in a rack along the far wall, and then she'd stopped coming down ever since Anthony had started spending time here, and the preserves had spoiled and leaked down and spread over the dirt floor, and Anthony liked the smell.

He caught another rat, making it smell cheese, and after he played with it, he thought it into a grave right beside the long animal he'd killed in the grove. Aunt Amy hated rats, and so he killed a lot of them, because he liked Aunt Amy most of all and sometimes did things that Aunt Amy wanted. Her mind was more like the little furry minds out in the grove. She hadn't thought anything bad at all about him for a long time.

After the rat, he played with a big black spider in the corner under the stairs, making it run back and forth until its web shook and shimmered in the light from the cellar window like a reflection in silvery water. Then he drove fruit flies into the web until the spider was frantic trying to wind them all up. The spider liked flies, and its thoughts were stronger than theirs, so he did it. There was something bad in the way it liked flies, but it wasn't clear – and besides, Aunt Amy hated flies too.

He heard footsteps overhead – Mom moving around in the kitchen. He blinked his purple gaze, and almost decided to make her hold still – but instead he *went* up to the attic, and, after looking out the circular window at the front end of the long V-roofed room for a while at the front lawn and the dusty road and Henderson's tip-waving wheatfield beyond, he curled into an unlikely shape and went partly to sleep.

Soon people would be coming for television, he heard Mom think.

He went more to sleep. He liked television night. Aunt Amy had always liked television a lot, so one time he had thought some for her, and a few other people had been there at the time, and Aunt Amy had felt disappointed when they wanted to leave. He'd done something to them for that – and now everybody came to television.

He liked all the attention he got when they did.

Anthony's father came home around six-thirty, looking tired and dirty and bloody. He'd been over in Dun's pasture with the other men, helping pick out the cow to be slaughtered this month and doing the job, and then butchering the meat and salting it away in Soames's icehouse. Not a job he cared for, but every man had his turn. Yesterday, he had helped scythe down old McIntyre's wheat. Tomorrow, they would start threshing. By hand. Everything in Peaksville had to be done by hand.

He kissed his wife on the cheek and sat down at the kitchen table. He smiled and said, 'Where's Anthony?'

'Around someplace,' Mom said.

Aunt Amy was over at the wood-burning stove, stirring the big pot of peas. Mom went back to the oven and opened it and basted the roast.

'Well, it's been a *good* day,' Dad said. By rote. Then he looked at the mixing bowl and breadboard on the table. He sniffed at the dough. 'M'm,' he said. 'I could eat a loaf all by myself, I'm so hungry.'

'No one told Dan Hollis about its being a birthday party, did they?' his wife asked.

'Nope. We kept as quiet as mummies.'

'We've fixed up such a lovely surprise!'

'Um? What?'

'Well . . . you know how much Dan likes music. Well, last week Thelma Dunn found a *record* in her attic!'

'No!'

'Yes! And we had Ethel sort of ask – you know, without really *asking* – if he had that one. And he said no. Isn't that a wonderful surprise?'

'Well, now, it sure is. A record, imagine! That's a real nice thing to find! What record is it?'

'Perry Como, singing *You Are My Sunshine*.'

'Well, I'll be darned. I always liked that tune.' Some raw carrots were lying on the table. Dad picked up a small one, scrubbed it on his chest, and took a bite. 'How did Thelma happen to find it?'

'Oh, you know – just looking around for new things.'

'M'm.' Dad chewed the carrot. 'Say, who has that picture we found a while back? I kind of liked it – that old clipper sailing along – '

'The Smiths. Next week the Sipichs get it, and they give the Smiths old McIntyre's music-box, and we give the Sipichs – ' and she went down the tentative order of things that would exchange hands among the women at church this Sunday.

He nodded. 'Looks like we can't have the picture for a while, I guess. Look, honey, you might try to get that detective book back from the Reillys. I was so busy the week we had it, I never got to finish all the stories – '

'I'll try,' his wife said doubtfully. 'But I hear the van Husens have a stereoscope they found in the cellar.' Her voice was just a little accusing. 'They had it two whole months before they told anybody about it – '

'Say,' Dad said, looking interested. 'That'd be nice, too. Lots of pictures?'

'I suppose so. I'll see on Sunday. I'd like to have it – but we still owe the van Husens for their canary. I don't know why that bird had to pick *our* house to die . . . it must have been sick when we got it. Now there's just no satisfying Betty van Husen – she even hinted she'd like our *piano* for a while!'

'Well, honey, you try for the stereoscope – or just anything you think we'll like.' At last he swallowed the carrot. It had been a little young and tough. Anthony's whims about the weather made it so that people never knew what crops would come up, or what shape they'd be in if they did. All they could do was plant a lot; and always enough of something came up any one season to live on. Just once there had been a grain surplus; tons of it had been hauled to the edge of Peaksville and dumped off into the nothingness. Otherwise, nobody could have breathed, when it started to spoil.

'You know,' Dad went on. 'It's nice to have the new things around. It's nice to think that there's probably still a lot of stuff nobody's found yet, in cellars and attics and barns and down behind things. They help, somehow. As much as anything can help – '

'Sh-h!' Mom glanced nervously around.

'Oh,' Dad said, smiling hastily. 'It's all right! The new things are *good*! It's *nice* to be able to have something around you've never seen before, and know that something you've given somebody else is making them happy . . . that's a real *good* thing.'

'A good thing,' his wife echoed.

'Pretty soon,' Aunt Amy said, from the stove, 'there won't be any more new things. We'll have found everything there is to find. Goodness, that'll be too bad – '

'*Amy!*'

'Well – ' her pale eyes were shallow and fixed, a sign of her recurrent vagueness. 'It will be kind of a shame – no new things – '

'Don't *talk* like that,' Mom said, trembling. 'Amy, be *quiet!*'

'It's *good*,' said Dad, in the loud, familiar, wanting-to-be-overheard tone of voice. 'Such talk is *good*. It's okay, honey – don't you see? It's good for Amy to talk any way she wants. It's good for her to feel bad. Everything's good. Everything *has* to be good . . .'

Anthony's mother was pale. And so was Aunt Amy – the peril of the moment had suddenly penetrated the clouds surrounding her mind. Sometimes it was difficult to handle words so that they might not prove disastrous. You just never *knew*. There were so many things it was wise not to say, or even think – but remonstration for saying or thinking them might be just as bad, if Anthony heard and decided to do anything about it. You could just never tell what Anthony was liable to do.

Everything had to be good. Had to be fine just as it was, even if it wasn't. Always. Because any change might be worse. So terribly much worse.

'Oh, my goodness, yes, of course it's good,' Mom said. 'You talk any way you want to, Amy, and it's just fine. Of course, you want to remember that some ways are *better* than others . . .'

Aunt Amy stirred the peas, fright in her pale eyes.

Oh, yes,' she said. 'But I don't feel like talking right now. It . . . it's *good* that I don't feel like talking.'

Dad said tiredly, smiling, 'I'm going out and wash up.'

They started arriving around eight o'clock. By that time, Mom and Aunt Amy had the big table in the dining room set, and two more tables off to the side. The candles were burning, and the chairs situated, and Dad had a big fire going in the fireplace.

The first to arrive were the Sipichs, John and Mary. John wore his best suit, and was well-scrubbed and pink-faced after his day in McIntyre's pasture. The suit was neatly pressed, but getting threadbare at elbows and cuffs. Old McIntyre was working on a loom, designing it out of schoolbooks, but so far it was slow going. McIntyre was a capable man with wood and tools, but a loom was a big order when you couldn't get metal parts. McIntyre had been one of the ones who, at first, had wanted to try to get Anthony to make things the villagers needed, like clothes and canned goods and medical supplies and gasoline. Since then, he felt that what had happened to the whole Terrance family and Joe Kinney was his fault, and he worked hard trying to make it up to the rest of them. And since then, no one had tried to get Anthony to do anything.

Mary Sipich was a small, cheerful woman in a simple dress. She immediately set about helping Mom and Aunt Amy put the finishing touches on the dinner.

The next arrivals were the Smiths and the Dunns, who lived right next to each other down the road, only a few yards from the nothingness. They drove up in the Smiths' wagon, drawn by their old horse.

Then the Reillys showed up, from across the darkened wheatfield, and the evening really began. Pat Reilly sat down at the big upright in the front room, and began to play from the popular sheet music on the rack. He played softly, as expressively as he could – and nobody sang. Anthony liked piano playing a whole lot, but not singing; often he would come up from the basement, or down from the attic, or just *come*, and sit on top of the piano, nodding his head as Pat played *Lover* or *Boulevard of Broken Dreams* or *Night and Day.* He seemed to prefer ballads, sweet-sounding songs – but the one time somebody had started to sing, Anthony had looked over from the top of the piano and done something that made everybody afraid of singing from then on. Later, they'd decided that the piano was what Anthony had heard first, before anybody had ever tried to sing, and now anything else added to it didn't sound right and distracted him from his pleasure.

So, every television night, Pat would play the piano, and that was the beginning of the evening. Wherever Anthony was, the music would make him happy, and put him in a good mood, and he would know that they were gathering for television and waiting for him.

By eight-thirty everybody had shown up, except for the seventeen children and Mrs Soames who was off watching them in the schoolhouse at the far end of town. The children of Peaksville were never, never allowed near the Fremont house – not since little Fred Smith had tried to play with Anthony on a dare. The younger children weren't even told about Anthony. The others had mostly forgotten about him, or were told that he was a nice, nice goblin but they must never go near him.

Dan and Ethel Hollis came late, and Dan walked in not suspecting a thing. Pat Reilly had played the piano until his hands ached – he'd worked pretty hard with them today – and now he got up, and everybody gathered around to wish Dan Hollis a happy birthday.

'Well, I'll be darned,' Dan grinned. 'This is swell. I wasn't expecting this at all . . . gosh, this is *swell!*'

They gave him his presents – mostly things they had made by hand, though some were things that people had possessed as their own and now gave him as his. John Sipich gave him a watch charm, hand-carved out of a piece of hickory wood. Dan's watch had broken down a year or so ago, and there was nobody in the village who knew how to fix it, but he still carried it around because it had been his grandfather's and was a fine old heavy thing of gold and silver. He attached the charm to the chain, while everybody laughed and said John had done a nice job of carving. Then Mary

Sipich gave him a knitted necktie, which he put on, removing the one he'd worn.

The Reillys gave him a little box they had made, to keep things in. They didn't say what things, but Dan said he'd keep his personal jewelry in it. The Reillys had made it out of a cigar box, carefully peeled of its paper and lined on the inside with velvet. The outside had been polished, and carefully if not expertly carved by Pat – but his carving got complimented too. Dan Hollis received many other gifts – a pipe, a pair of shoelaces, a tie pin, a knitted pair of socks, some fudge, a pair of garters made from old suspenders.

He unwrapped each gift with vast pleasure, and wore as many of them as he could right there, even the garters. He lit up the pipe, and said he'd never had a better smoke; which wasn't quite true, because the pipe wasn't broken in yet. Pete Manners had had it lying around ever since he'd received it as a gift four years ago from an out-of-town relative who hadn't known he'd stopped smoking.

Dan put the tobacco into the bowl very carefully. Tobacco was precious. It was only pure luck that Pat Reilly had decided to try to grow some in his backyard just before what had happened to Peaksville had happened. It didn't grow very well, and then they had to cure it and shred it and all, and it was just precious stuff. Everybody in town used wooden holders old McIntyre had made, to save on butts.

Last of all, Thelma Dunn gave Dan Hollis the record she had found.

Dan's eyes misted even before he opened the package. He knew it was a record.

'Gosh,' he said softly. 'What one is it? I'm almost afraid to look . . .'

'You haven't got it, darling,' Ethel Hollis smiled. 'Don't you remember, I asked about *You Are My Sunshine*?'

'Oh, gosh,' Dan said again. Carefully he removed the wrapping and stood there fondling the record, running his big hands over the worn grooves with their tiny, dulling crosswise scratches. He looked around the room, eyes shining, and they all smiled back, knowing how delighted he was.

'Happy birthday, darling!' Ethel said, throwing her arms around him and kissing him.

He clutched the record in both hands, holding it off to one side as she pressed against him. 'Hey,' he laughed, pulling back his head. 'Be careful . . . I'm holding a priceless object!' He looked around again, over his wife's arms, which were still around his neck. His eyes were hungry. 'Look . . . do you think we could play it? Lord, what I'd give to hear some new music . . . just the first part, the orchestra part, before Como sings?'

Faces sobered. After a minute, John Sipich said, 'I don't think we'd better, Dan. After all, we don't know just where the singer comes in – it'd be taking too much of a chance. Better wait till you get home.'

Dan Hollis reluctantly put the record on the buffet with all his other presents. 'It's *good*,' he said automatically, but disappointedly, 'that I can't play it here.'

'Oh, yes,' said Sipich. 'It's good.' To compensate for Dan's disappointed tone, he repeated, 'It's *good*.'

They ate dinner, the candles lighting their smiling faces, and ate it all right down to the last delicious drop of gravy. They complimented Mom and Aunt Amy on the roast beef, and the peas and carrots, and the tender corn on the cob. The corn hadn't come from the Fremont's cornfield, naturally – everybody knew what was out there; and the field was going to weeds.

Then they polished off the dessert – homemade ice cream and cookies. And then they sat back, in the flickering light of the candles, and chatted, waiting for television.

There never was a lot of mumbling on television night – everybody came and had a good dinner at the Fremonts', and that was nice, and afterwards there was television, and nobody really thought much about that – it just had to be put up with. So it was a pleasant enough get-together, aside from your having to watch what you said just as carefully as you always did everyplace. If a dangerous thought came into your mind, you just started mumbling, even right in the middle of a sentence. When you did that, the others just ignored you until you felt happier again and stopped.

Anthony liked television night. He had done only two or three awful things on television night in the whole past year.

Mom had put a bottle of brandy on the table, and they each had a tiny glass of it. Liquor was even more precious than tobacco. The villagers could make wine, but the grapes weren't right, and certainly the techniques weren't, and it wasn't very good wine. There were only a few bottles of real liquor left in the village – four rye, three Scotch, three brandy, nine real wine and half a bottle of Drambuie belonging to old McIntyre (only for marriages) – and when those were gone, that was it.

Afterward, everybody wished that the brandy hadn't been brought out. Because Dan Hollis drank more of it than he should have, and mixed it with a lot of the homemade wine. Nobody thought anything about it at first, because he didn't show it much outside, and it was his birthday party and a happy party, and Anthony liked these get-togethers and shouldn't see any reason to do anything even if he was listening.

But Dan Hollis got high, and did a fool thing. If they'd seen it coming, they'd have taken him outside and walked him around.

The first thing they knew, Dan stopped laughing right in the middle of the story about how Thelma Dunn had found the Perry Como record and dropped it and it hadn't broken because she'd moved faster than she ever had before in her life and caught it. He was fondling the record again, and looking longingly at the Fremonts' gramophone over in the corner, and suddenly he stopped laughing and his face got slack, and then it got ugly, and he said, 'Oh, *Christ!*'

Immediately the room was still. So still they could hear the whirring movement of the grandfather's clock out in the hall. Pat Reilly had been playing the piano, softly. He stopped, his hands poised over the yellowed keys.

The candles on the dining-room table flickered in a cool breeze that blew through the lace curtains over the bay window.

'Keep playing, Pat,' Anthony's father said softly.

Pat started again. He played *Night and Day*, but his eyes were sidewise on Dan Hollis, and he missed notes.

Dan stood in the middle of the room, holding the record. In his other hand he held a glass of brandy so hard his hand shook.

They were all looking at him.

'*Christ*,' he said again, and he made it sound like a dirty word.

Reverend Younger, who had been talking with Mom and Aunt Amy by the dining-room door, said 'Christ' too – but he was using it in a prayer. His hands were clasped, and his eyes were closed.

John Sipich moved forward. 'Now, Dan . . . it's *good* for you to talk that way. But you don't want to talk too much, you know.'

Dan shook off the hand Sipich put on his arm.

'Can't even play my record,' he said loudly. He looked down at the record, and then around at their faces. 'Oh, my *God* . . .'

He threw the glassful of brandy against the wall. It splattered and ran down the wallpaper in streaks.

Some of the women gasped.

'Dan,' Sipich said in a whisper. 'Dan, cut it out – '

Pat Reilly was playing *Night and Day* louder, to cover up the sounds of the talk. It wouldn't do any good, though, if Anthony was listening.

Dan Hollis went over to the piano and stood by Pat's shoulder, swaying a little.

'Pat,' he said. 'Don't play *that*. Play *this*.' And he began to sing. Softly, hoarsely, miserably: 'Happy birthday to me . . . Happy birthday to me . . .'

'*Dan!*' Ethel Hollis screamed. She tried to run across the room to him. Mary Sipich grabbed her arm and held her back. 'Dan,' Ethel screamed again. 'Stop – '

'My God, be quiet!' hissed Mary Sipich, and pushed her toward one of the men, who put his hand over her mouth and held her still.

'– Happy birthday, dear Danny,' Dan sang. 'Happy birthday to me!' He stopped and looked down at Pat Reilly. 'Play it, Pat. Play it, so I can sing right . . . you know I can't carry a tune unless somebody plays it!'

Pat Reilly put his hands on the keys and began *Lover* – in a slow waltz tempo, the way Anthony liked it. Pat's face was white. His hands fumbled.

Dan Hollis stared over at the dining-room door. At Anthony's mother, and at Anthony's father who had gone to join her.

'*You* had him,' he said. Tears gleamed on his cheeks as the candle-light caught them. '*You* had to go and *have* him . . .'

He closed his eyes, and the tears squeezed out. He sang loudly, 'You are my sunshine . . . my only sunshine . . . you make me happy . . . when I am blue . . .'

Anthony *came* into the room.

Pat stopped playing. He froze. Everybody froze. The breeze rippled the curtains. Ethel Hollis couldn't even try to scream – she had fainted.

'Please don't take my sunshine . . . away . . .' Dan's voice faltered into silence. His eyes widened. He put both hands out in front of him, the empty glass in one, the record in the other. He hiccupped, and said, '*No* – '

'Bad man,' Anthony said, and thought Dan Hollis into something like nothing anyone would have believed possible, and then he thought the thing into a grave deep, deep in the cornfield.

The glass and record thumped on the rug. Neither broke.

Anthony's purple gaze went around the room.

Some of the people began mumbling. They all tried to smile. The sound of mumbling filled the room like a far-off approval. Out of the murmuring came one or two clear voices:

'Oh, it's a very *good* thing,' said John Sipich.

'A good thing,' said Anthony's father, smiling. He'd had more practice in smiling than most of them. 'A wonderful thing.'

'It's swell . . . just swell,' said Pat Reilly, tears leaking from eyes and nose, and he began to play the piano again, softly, his trembling hands feeling for *Night and Day*.

Anthony climbed up on top of the piano, and Pat played for two hours.

Afterward, they watched television. They all went into the front room, and lit just a few candles, and pulled up chairs around the set. It was a small-screen set, and they couldn't all sit close enough to it to see, but that didn't matter. They didn't even turn the set on. It wouldn't have worked anyway, there being no electricity in Peaksville.

They just sat silently, and watched the twisting, writhing shapes on the screen, and listened to the sounds that came out of the speaker, and none of them had any idea of what it was all about. They never did. It was always the same.

'It's real nice,' Aunt Amy said once, her pale eyes on the meaningless flickers and shadows. 'But I liked it a little better when there were cities outside and we could get real – '

'Why, Amy!' said Mom. 'It's good for you to say such a thing. Very good. But how can you mean it? Why, this television is *much* better than anything we ever used to get!'

'Yes,' chimed in John Sipich. 'It's fine. It's the best show we've ever seen!'

He sat on the couch, with two other men, holding Ethel Hollis flat against the cushions, holding her arms and legs and putting their hands over her mouth, so she couldn't start screaming again.

'It's really *good!*' he said again.

Mom looked out of the front window, across the darkened road, across Henderson's darkened wheat field to the vast, endless, gray nothingness in which the little village of Peaksville floated like a soul – the huge nothingness that was most evident at night, when Anthony's brassy day had gone.

It did no good to wonder where they were . . . no good at all. Peaksville was just someplace. Someplace away from the world. It was wherever it had been since that day three years ago when Anthony had crept from her womb and old Doc Bates – God rest him – had screamed and dropped him and tried to kill him, and Anthony had whined and done the thing. Had taken the village someplace. Or had destroyed the world and left only the village, nobody knew which.

It did no good to wonder about it. Nothing at all did any good – except to live as they must live. Must always, always live, if Anthony would let them.

These thoughts were dangerous, she thought.

She began to mumble. The others started mumbling too. They had all been thinking, evidently.

The men on the couch whispered and whispered to Ethel Hollis, and when they took their hands away, she mumbled too.

While Anthony sat on top of the set and made television, they sat around and mumbled and watched the meaningless, flickering shapes far into the night.

Next day it snowed, and killed off half the crops – but it was a *good* day.

SOURCES AND ACKNOWLEDGEMENTS

'Duel' by Richard Matheson, first published in *Playboy*, reprinted by permission of Abner Stein Agency.

'Spurs' by Tod Robbins, copyright © 1932 by Clarence Robbins, reprinted by permission of the executors of the Author's Estate.

'While Zombies Walked' by Thorp McClusky, first published in *Weird Tales*, 1939.

'We Can Remember It For You Wholesale' by Philip K. Dick, first published in *The Magazine of Fantasy and Science Fiction*, 1966, collected in *The Preserving Machine* (Ace, 1966), copyright © 1966 by the Estate of Philip K. Dick, reprinted by permission of the Author's Estate and their Agents, Scott Meredith Literary Agency, Inc., 845 Third Avenue, New York, NY 10022.

'The Fly' by George Langelaan, from *Out of Time* (New English Library, 1964), reprinted by permission of the Author's Agent.

'The Swimmer' by John Cheever, from *The Stories of John Cheever* (Cape, 1979), copyright © 1965 by John Cheever, reprinted with the permission of Wylie, Aitken & Stone, Inc.

'The Beast With Five Fingers' by William Fryer Harvey, from *The Beast With Five Fingers, and Other Tales*, copyright © 1947 by E. P. Dutton & Co., Inc., reprinted by permission of the Publishers.

'The Company of Wolves' by Angela Carter, first published in *Bananas*, collected (in revised form) in *The Bloody Chamber, and Other Stories* by permission of Victor Gollancz Ltd and ICM, New York.

'The Golem' by I. L. Peretz, from *A Treasury of Yiddish Stories*, ed. Howe and Greenberg (Deutsch, 1955), reprinted by permission of the Publishers.

'Lucy Comes to Stay' by Robert Bloch, first published in *Weird Tales*, collected in *The Living Demons* (Belmont, 1967), copyright © 1952 by Robert Bloch, reprinted by permission of the Author.

'The Color Out Of Space' by H. P. Lovecraft, first published in *Amazing Stories*, 1927, collected in *The Haunter of the Dark, and Other Tales of Terror* (Victor Gollancz, 1951).

'It's a *Good* Life' by Jerome Bixby, from *The Science Fiction Hall of Fame*, ed. Robert Silverberg (1970), copyright © 1953 by Ballantine Books, Inc., reprinted by permission of the Author's Agent, Forrest J. Ackerman.

Every effort has been made to trace authors and copyright-holders. The Editor and Publishers would be glad to hear from any such parties in the event of the above details being incomplete or incorrect so that they can be corrected in future editions of the book.